United States District Court for the District of Columbia

The United States of America v. Donald J. Trump, Defendant

1. Conspiracy to Defraud the United States
2. Conspiracy to Obstruct an Official Proceeding
3. Obstruction of and Attempt to Obstruct an Official Proceeding
4. Conspiracy against Rights

Fulton Superior Court

The State of Georgia v. Donald J. Trump et al., Defendants

1. Violation of the Georgia RICO Act
2. Solicitation of Violation of Oath by Public Officer
3. Conspiracy to Commit Impersonating a Public Officer
4. Conspiracy to Commit Forgery in the First Degree
5. Conspiracy to Commit False Statements and Writings
6. Conspiracy to Commit Filing False Documents
7. Conspiracy to Commit Forgery in the First Degree
8. Conspiracy to Commit False Statements and Writings
9. Filing False Documents
10. Solicitation of Violation of Oath by Public Officer
11. False Statements and Writings
12. Solicitation of Violation of Oath by Public Officer
13. False Statements and Writings

United States District Court, Southern District of Florida

The United States of America v. Donald J. Trump et al., Defendants

1. Conspiracy to Obstruct Justice
2. Withholding a Document or Record
3. Corruptly Concealing a Document or Record

4. Concealing a Document in a Federal Inves
5. Sche
6. Fals   ntations
7. Alte   ting or Conc
8. Corru   ng, Mutilating or Concealing a Document, Record or Other Object
9. Willful Retention of National Defense Information
10. Willful Retention of National Defense Information
11. Willful Retention of National Defense Information
12. Willful Retention of National Defense Information
13. Willful Retention of National Defense Information
14. Willful Retention of National Defense Information
15. Willful Retention of National Defense Information
16. Willful Retention of National Defense Information
17. Willful Retention of National Defense Information
18. Willful Retention of National Defense Information
19. Willful Retention of National Defense Information
20. Willful Retention of National Defense Information
21. Willful Retention of National Defense Information
22. Willful Retention of National Defense Information
23. Willful Retention of National Defense Information
24. Willful Retention of National Defense Information
25. Willful Retention of National Defense Information
26. Willful Retention of National Defense Information
27. Willful Retention of National Defense Information
28. Willful Retention of National Defense Information

(Continued on back page)

DAY ONE DICTATOR

TRUMP
VALUE PAK!
• 2 Bibles
• 2 Shoes
UP TO
50%
OFF!
T
T
T
HOLY BIBLE
HOLY BIBLE

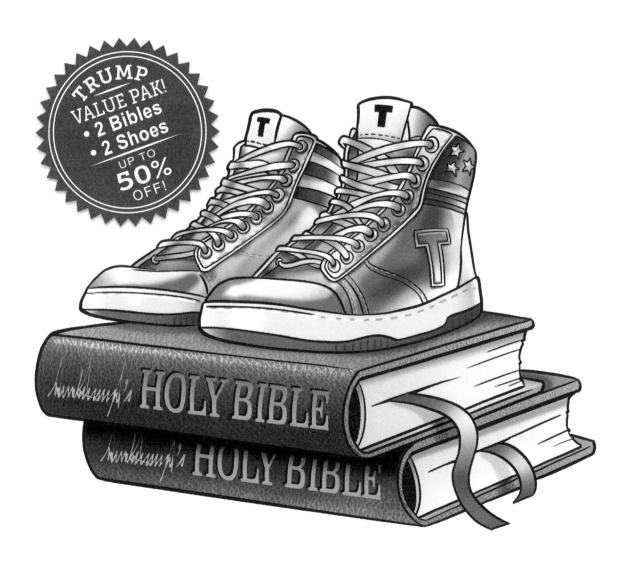

Recent Collections

Virtual Doonesbury
Planet Doonesbury
Buck Wild Doonesbury
Duke 2000: Whatever It Takes
The Revolt of the English Majors
Peace Out, Dawg!
Got War?
Talk to the Hand
Heckuva Job, Bushie!
Welcome to the Nerd Farm!
Tee Time in Berzerkistan
Red Rascal's War
Squared Away
The Weed Whisperer
YUGE!: 30 Years of Doonesbury on Trump
#SAD!: Doonesbury in the Time of Trump
LEWSER!: More Doonesbury in the Time of Trump
FORMER GUY: Doonesbury in the Time of Trumpism

Anthologies

The Doonesbury Chronicles
Doonesbury's Greatest Hits
The People's Doonesbury
Doonesbury Dossier: The Reagan Years
Doonesbury Deluxe: Selected Glances Askance
Recycled Doonesbury: Second Thoughts on a Gilded Age
The Portable Doonesbury
The Bundled Doonesbury
40: A Doonesbury Retrospective

Special Collections

Flashbacks: Twenty-Five Years of Doonesbury
Action Figure!: The Life and Times of Doonesbury's Uncle Duke
Dude: The Big Book of Zonker
The Sandbox: Dispatches from Troops in Iraq and Afghanistan
The War in Quotes
"My Shorts R Bunching. Thoughts?": The Tweets of Roland Hedley
Dbury@50: The Complete Digital Doonesbury

Wounded Warrior Series

The Long Road Home: One Step at a Time
The War Within: One More Step at a Time
Signature Wound: Rocking TBI
Mel's Story: Surviving Military Sexual Assault

DAY ONE DICTATOR

More Doonesbury in the Time of Trumpism

A DOONESBURY BOOK
by G. B. TRUDEAU

Andrews McMeel
PUBLISHING®

DOONESBURY is distributed internationally by Andrews McMeel Syndication.

DAY ONE DICTATOR: More Doonesbury in the Time of Trumpism copyright © 2024 by G.B. Trudeau. All rights reserved. Printed in the United States of America. No part of this book may be used or reproduced in any manner whatsoever without written permission, except in the case of reprints in the context of reviews.

Andrews McMeel Publishing
a division of Andrews McMeel Universal
1130 Walnut Street, Kansas City, Missouri 64106

www.andrewsmcmeel.com

24 25 26 27 28 VEP 10 9 8 7 6 5 4 3 2 1

ISBN: 978-1-5248-9434-4

Library of Congress Control Number: 2024937832

DOONESBURY may be viewed on the Internet at
www.doonesbury.com and www.GoComics.com.

ATTENTION: SCHOOLS AND BUSINESSES

Andrews McMeel books are available at quantity discounts with bulk purchase for educational, business, or sales promotional use. For information, please e-mail the Andrews McMeel Publishing Special Sales Department: sales@amuniversal.com.

PREFACE

"We'll re-ve-du. Ohhhh."
— Trump

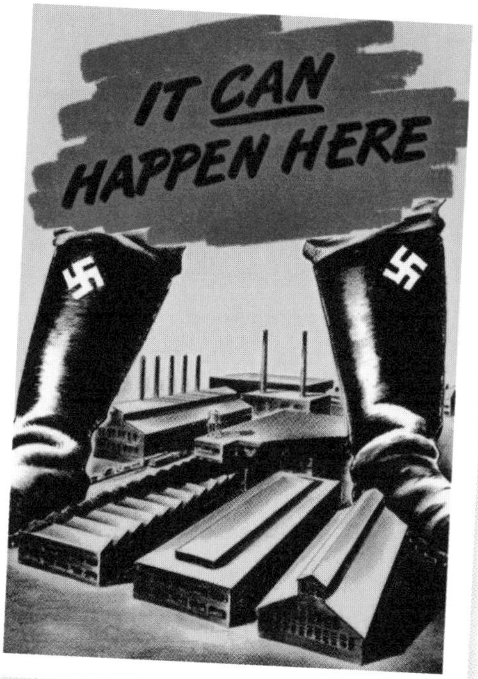
IT CAN
HAPPEN HERE

It's beautiful spring day, and I've just concluded a spirited discussion with myself over whether this latest volume should be titled *Day One Dictator* or *Day One Dementia*. I chose the former on the grounds that it's less terrifying.

Some readers may disagree. The stench of pending authoritarianism is so overpowering that it may distract from the gathering psychiatric consensus that Trump is rapidly slipping into senility—doubly alarming as this new deficit is eating away at the brainpan of a sociopath. Last weekend in Dayton, Trump said, "Joe Biden won against Barack Hussein Obama! Has anyone ever heard of him? Barack Hussein Obaba [*sic*]!" Rallygoers, primed to cheer, instead exchanged nervous glances.

As well they might. MAGA long ago embraced the crazy—Trump's loud, transgressive behavior is what endeared him to the mob in the first place. Humans, like apes, are wired to respect the bellowing of alphas, which, in Trump's case, his followers still mistake for strength, not the hypomania it actually is. Dementia, on the other hand, is scary. Most people have seen it in their own lives—a sad, silent aunt, a raging, profane grandfather—and regard it with abject horror. As they listen to Trump freestyling around the stems of common words, at least some of them are surely starting to think, "Uh-oh."

Or not. Cult members are, by definition, resistant to reality, and with the help of right-wing media, they have set up false equivalencies, likening Biden's occasional lapses to Trump's aphasic word salads. But you have to wonder if there might be some concern among campaign workers, those who see Trump with his guard down, exhausted, floundering, deeply frightened that he's sliding into the same dark realm that swallowed up his father. Do they worry, not for themselves but for the country? Are they truly comfortable about the prospect of installing a mad king in the White House? Reagan was in absentia for the last year of his presidency, but at least he had a good heart and was surrounded by institutionalists and career public servants who kept the ship steadied. Trump will have no such support—he's done with competence in his advisors. Only ideologues, sycophants, and ex-cons need apply.

 Let's be clear: It's no fun mocking someone falling apart before our eyes, but what are the alternatives, particularly given the country's current glide path to calamity? As you peruse the strips that follow, don't judge me harshly for doing exactly that to Trump.

Garry Trudeau
March 19, 2024

"Dee, boom! This is me! I here! Bing!"

— Trump

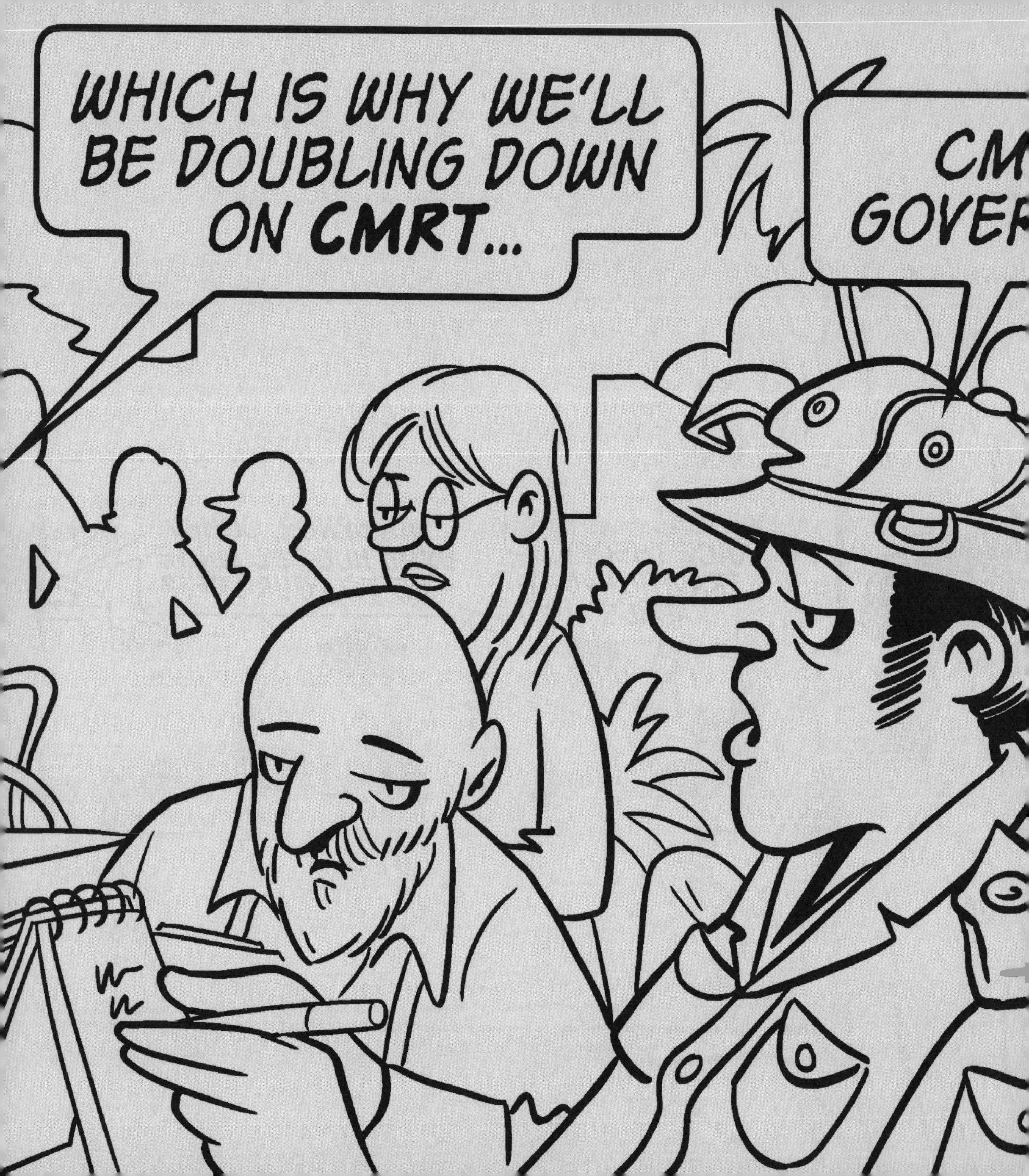
WHICH IS WHY WE'LL BE DOUBLING DOWN ON CMRT...

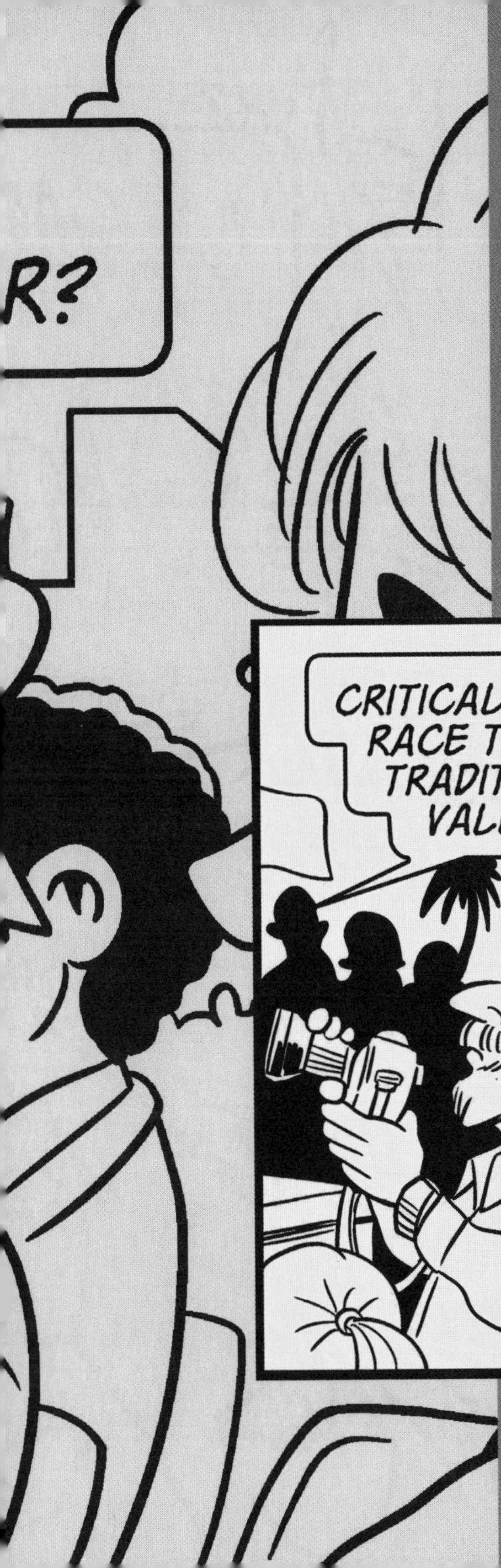

PART 1

Critical Master Race Theory

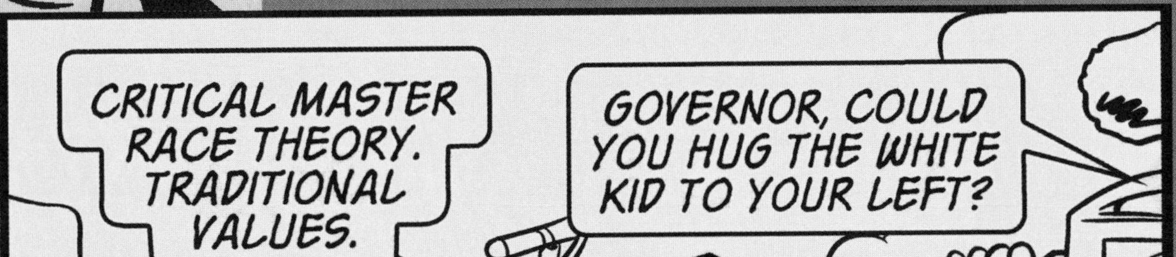
CRITICAL MASTER RACE THEORY. TRADITIONAL VALUES.
GOVERNOR, COULD YOU HUG THE WHITE KID TO YOUR LEFT?

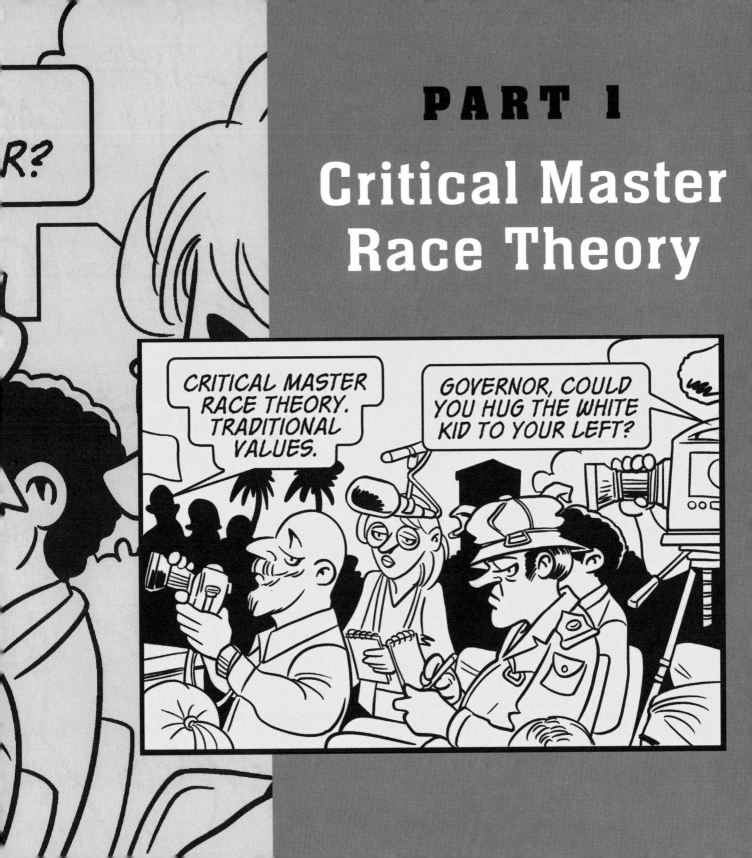

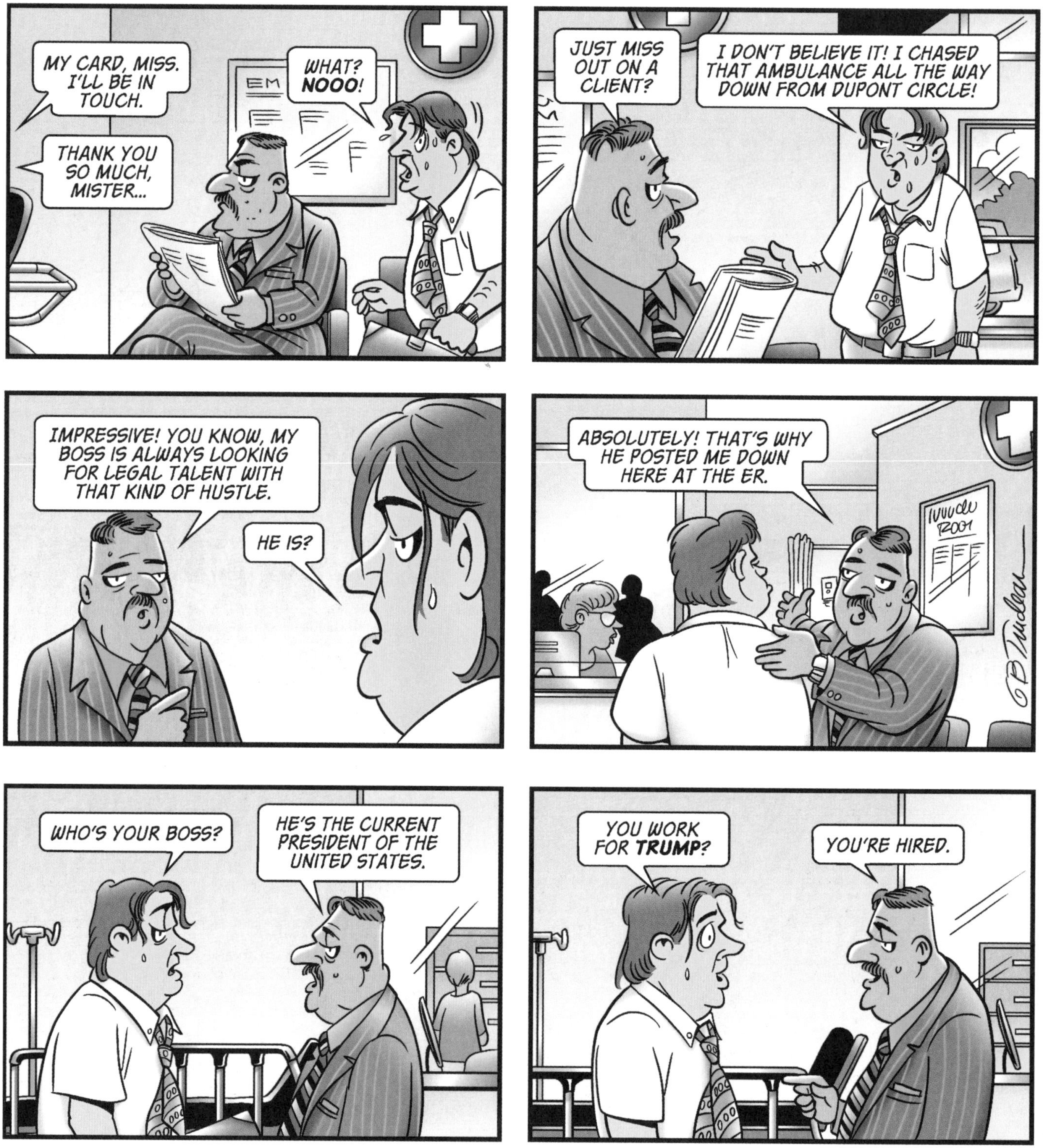
MY CARD, MISS. I'LL BE IN TOUCH.
THANK YOU SO MUCH, MISTER...
WHAT? **NOOO**!
EM
JUST MISS OUT ON A CLIENT?
I DON'T BELIEVE IT! I CHASED THAT AMBULANCE ALL THE WAY DOWN FROM DUPONT CIRCLE!
IMPRESSIVE! YOU KNOW, MY BOSS IS ALWAYS LOOKING FOR LEGAL TALENT WITH THAT KIND OF HUSTLE.
HE IS?
ABSOLUTELY! THAT'S WHY HE POSTED ME DOWN HERE AT THE ER.
WHO'S YOUR BOSS?
HE'S THE CURRENT PRESIDENT OF THE UNITED STATES.
YOU WORK FOR **TRUMP**?
YOU'RE HIRED.

June 26, 2022

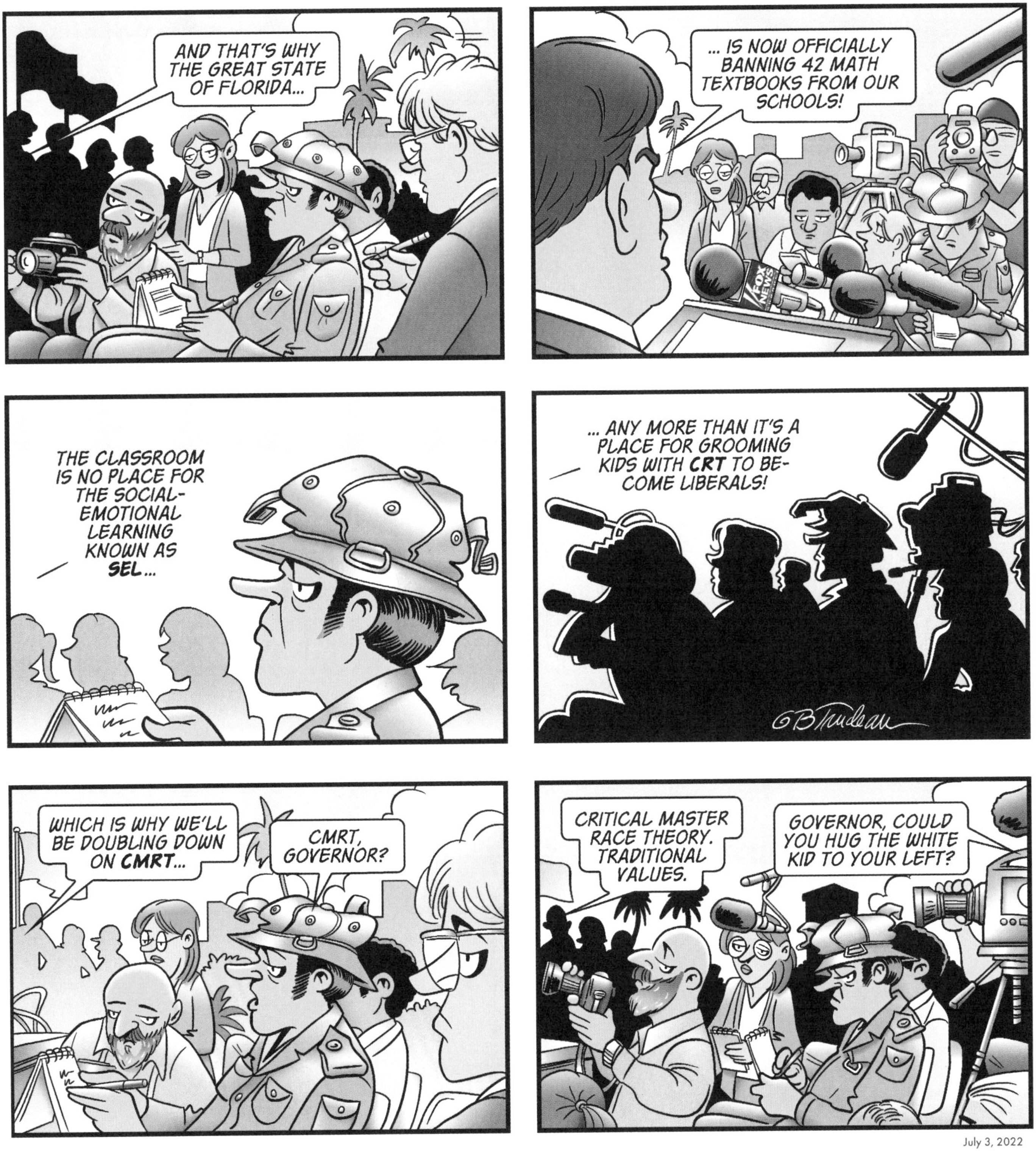
AND THAT'S WHY THE GREAT STATE OF FLORIDA...
... IS NOW OFFICIALLY BANNING 42 MATH TEXTBOOKS FROM OUR SCHOOLS!
FOX NEWS
THE CLASSROOM IS NO PLACE FOR THE SOCIAL-EMOTIONAL LEARNING KNOWN AS SEL...
... ANY MORE THAN IT'S A PLACE FOR GROOMING KIDS WITH CRT TO BE-COME LIBERALS!
GBTrudeau
WHICH IS WHY WE'LL BE DOUBLING DOWN ON CMRT...
CMRT, GOVERNOR?
CRITICAL MASTER RACE THEORY. TRADITIONAL VALUES.
GOVERNOR, COULD YOU HUG THE WHITE KID TO YOUR LEFT?

July 3, 2022

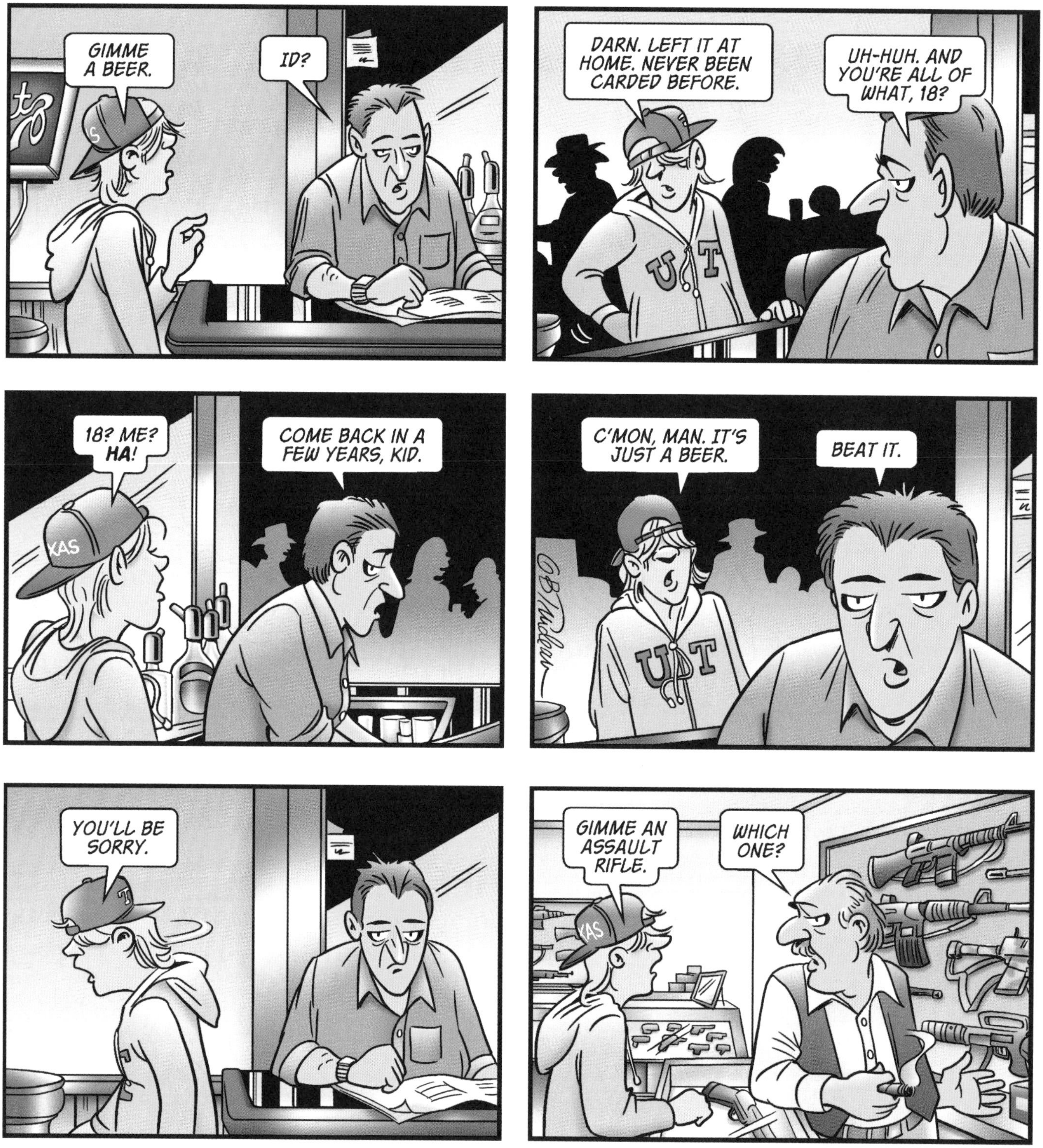
GIMME A BEER.
ID?
DARN. LEFT IT AT HOME. NEVER BEEN CARDED BEFORE.
UH-HUH. AND YOU'RE ALL OF WHAT, 18?
18? ME? **HA!**
COME BACK IN A FEW YEARS, KID.
C'MON, MAN. IT'S JUST A BEER.
BEAT IT.
YOU'LL BE SORRY.
GIMME AN ASSAULT RIFLE.
WHICH ONE?

July 10, 2022

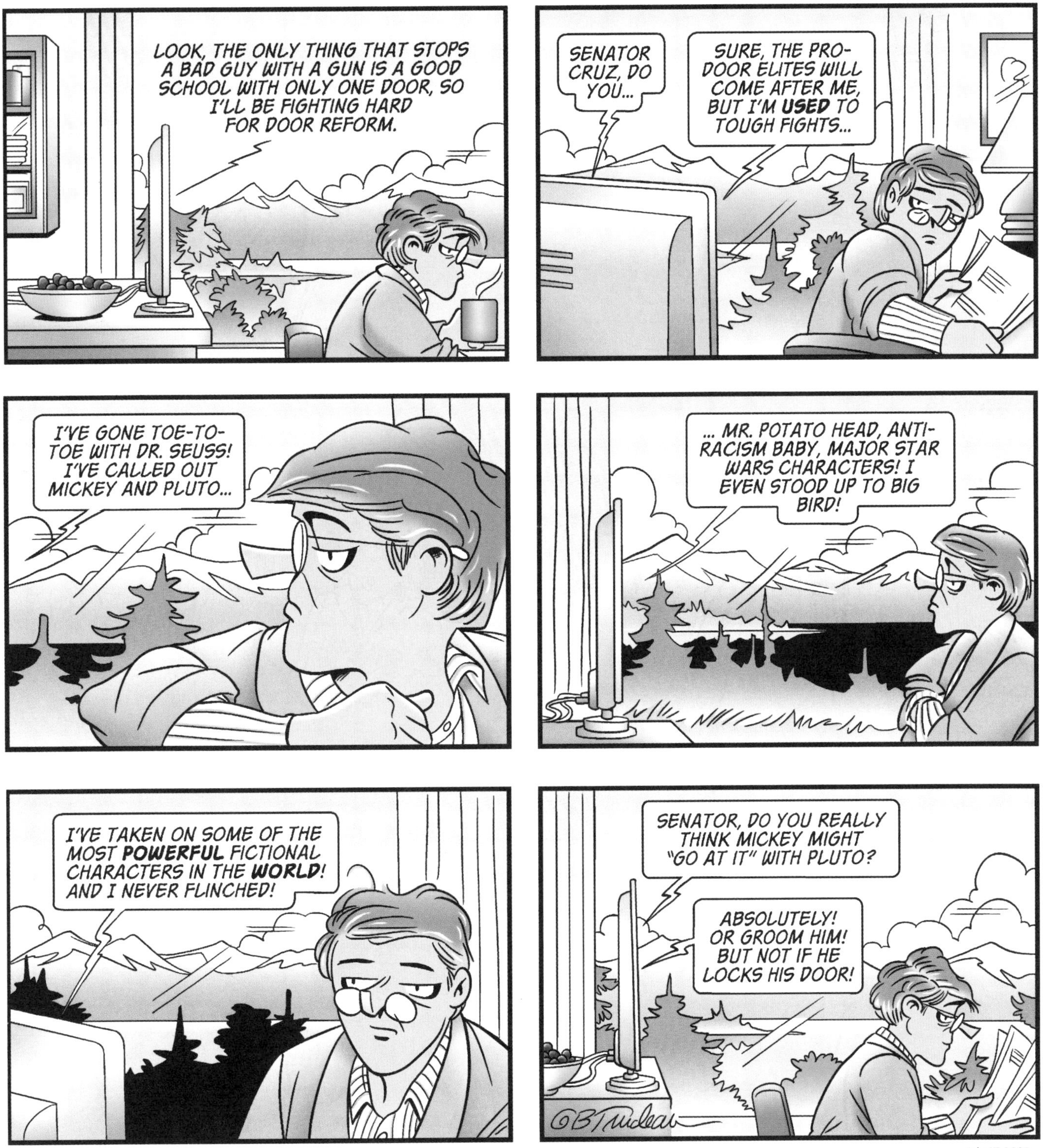
LOOK, THE ONLY THING THAT STOPS A BAD GUY WITH A GUN IS A GOOD SCHOOL WITH ONLY ONE DOOR, SO I'LL BE FIGHTING HARD FOR DOOR REFORM.
SENATOR CRUZ, DO YOU...
SURE, THE PRO-DOOR ELITES WILL COME AFTER ME, BUT I'M USED TO TOUGH FIGHTS...
I'VE GONE TOE-TO-TOE WITH DR. SEUSS! I'VE CALLED OUT MICKEY AND PLUTO...
... MR. POTATO HEAD, ANTI-RACISM BABY, MAJOR STAR WARS CHARACTERS! I EVEN STOOD UP TO BIG BIRD!
I'VE TAKEN ON SOME OF THE MOST POWERFUL FICTIONAL CHARACTERS IN THE WORLD! AND I NEVER FLINCHED!
SENATOR, DO YOU REALLY THINK MICKEY MIGHT "GO AT IT" WITH PLUTO?
ABSOLUTELY! OR GROOM HIM! BUT NOT IF HE LOCKS HIS DOOR!
©BTrudeau

July 17, 2022

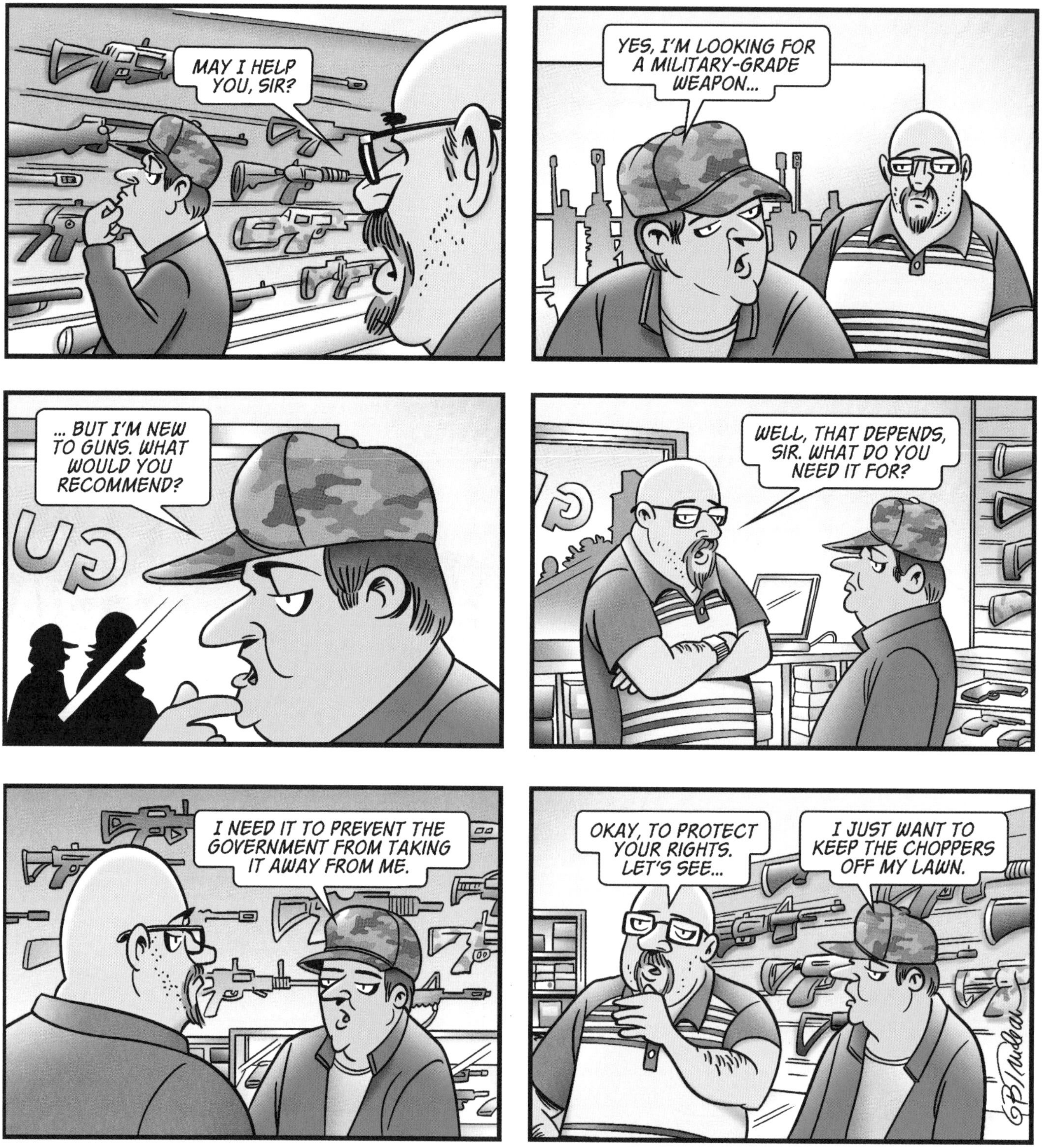
MAY I HELP YOU, SIR?
YES, I'M LOOKING FOR A MILITARY-GRADE WEAPON...
... BUT I'M NEW TO GUNS. WHAT WOULD YOU RECOMMEND?
WELL, THAT DEPENDS, SIR. WHAT DO YOU NEED IT FOR?
I NEED IT TO PREVENT THE GOVERNMENT FROM TAKING IT AWAY FROM ME.
OKAY, TO PROTECT YOUR RIGHTS. LET'S SEE...
I JUST WANT TO KEEP THE CHOPPERS OFF MY LAWN.
GBTrudeau

July 24, 2022

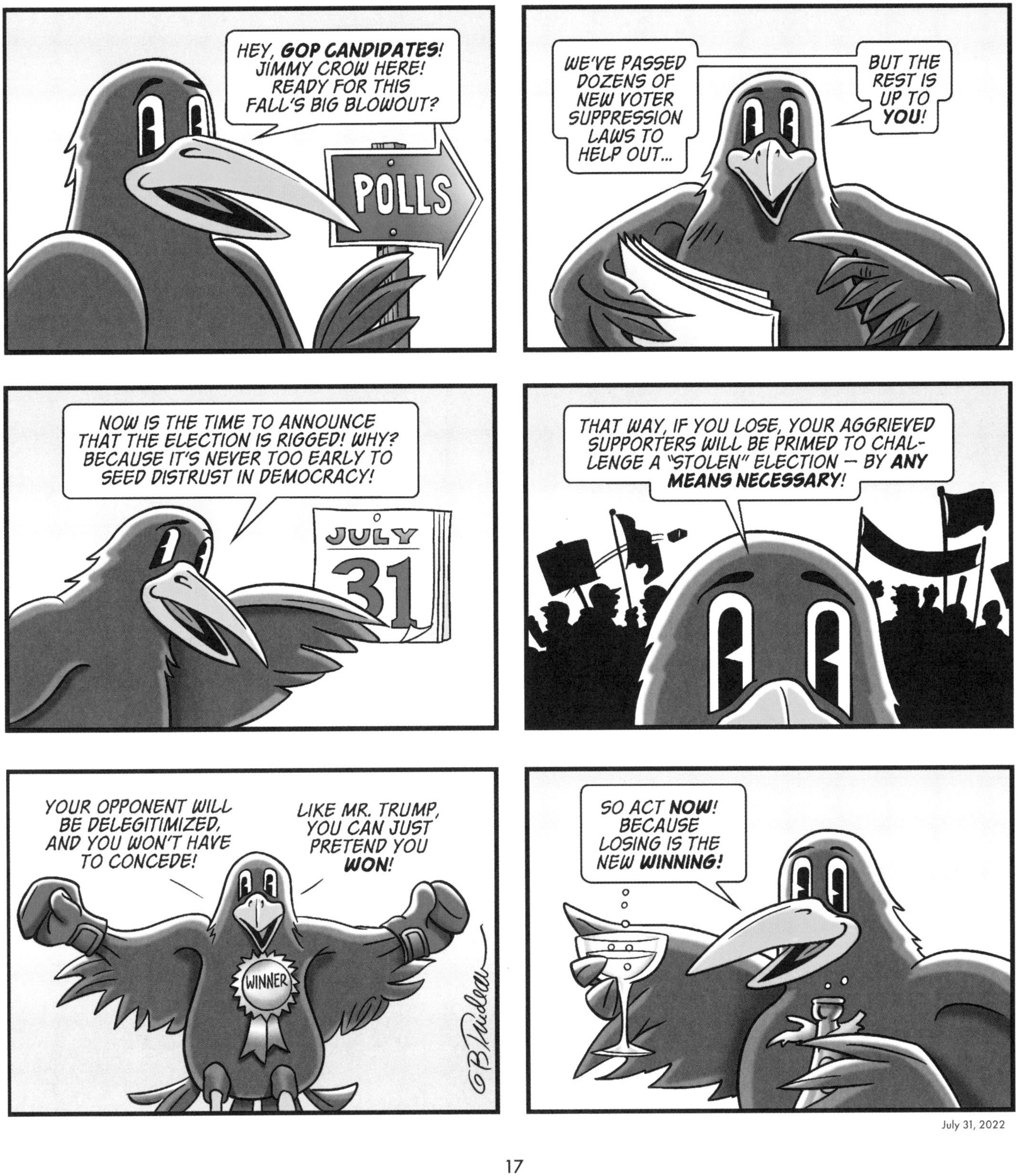

HEY, **GOP CANDIDATES**! JIMMY CROW HERE! READY FOR THIS FALL'S BIG BLOWOUT?
POLLS
WE'VE PASSED DOZENS OF NEW VOTER SUPPRESSION LAWS TO HELP OUT...
BUT THE REST IS UP TO **YOU**!
NOW IS THE TIME TO ANNOUNCE THAT THE ELECTION IS RIGGED! WHY? BECAUSE IT'S NEVER TOO EARLY TO SEED DISTRUST IN DEMOCRACY!
JULY 31
THAT WAY, IF YOU LOSE, YOUR AGGRIEVED SUPPORTERS WILL BE PRIMED TO CHAL-LENGE A "STOLEN" ELECTION — BY **ANY MEANS NECESSARY**!
YOUR OPPONENT WILL BE DELEGITIMIZED, AND YOU WON'T HAVE TO CONCEDE!
LIKE MR. TRUMP, YOU CAN JUST PRETEND YOU **WON**!
WINNER
©B Trudeau
SO ACT **NOW**! BECAUSE LOSING IS THE NEW **WINNING**!

July 31, 2022

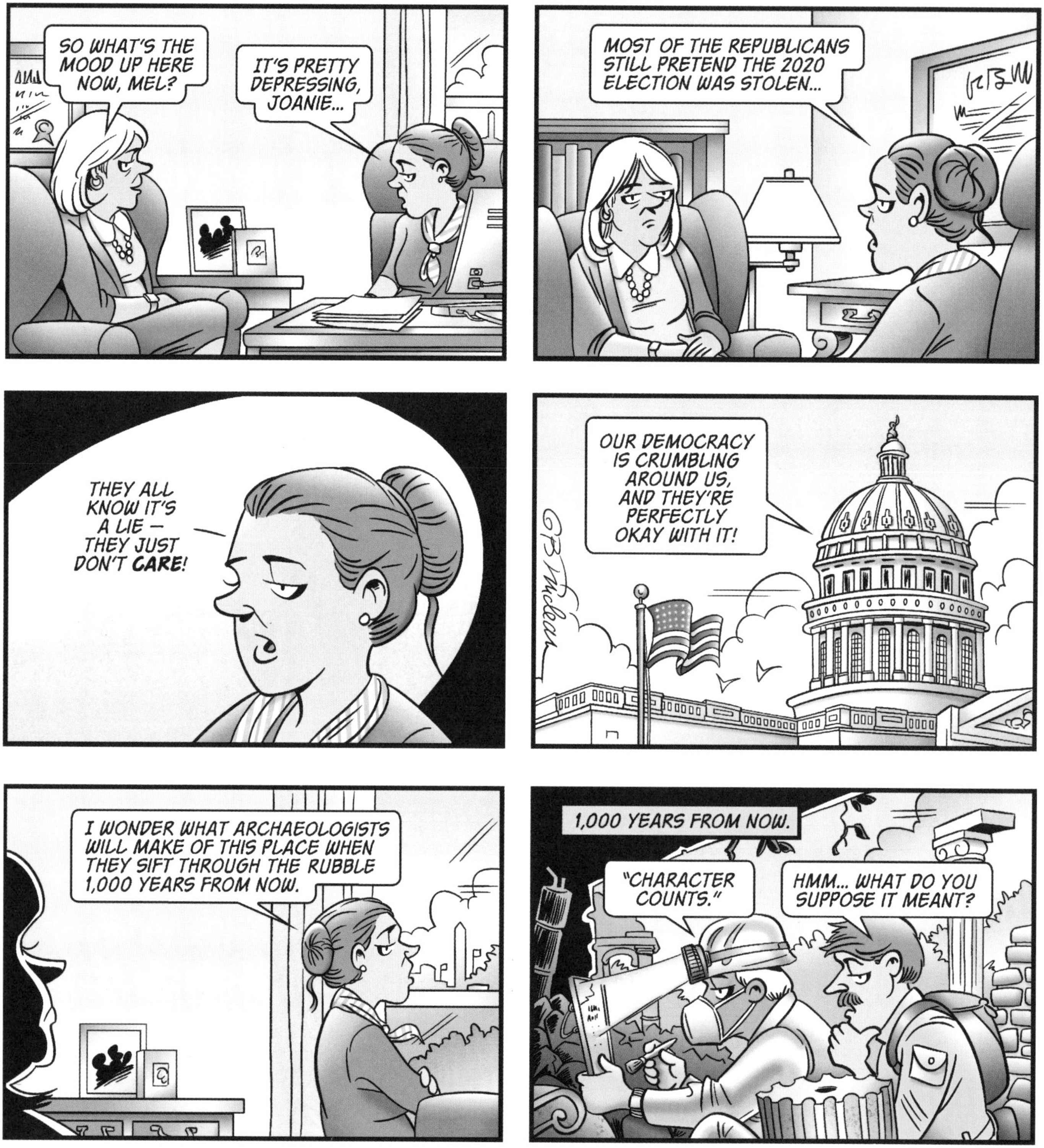
SO WHAT'S THE MOOD UP HERE NOW, MEL?
IT'S PRETTY DEPRESSING, JOANIE...
MOST OF THE REPUBLICANS STILL PRETEND THE 2020 ELECTION WAS STOLEN...
THEY ALL KNOW IT'S A LIE — THEY JUST DON'T **CARE**!
OUR DEMOCRACY IS CRUMBLING AROUND US, AND THEY'RE PERFECTLY OKAY WITH IT!
GB Trudeau
I WONDER WHAT ARCHAEOLOGISTS WILL MAKE OF THIS PLACE WHEN THEY SIFT THROUGH THE RUBBLE 1,000 YEARS FROM NOW.
1,000 YEARS FROM NOW.
"CHARACTER COUNTS."
HMM... WHAT DO YOU SUPPOSE IT MEANT?

August 7, 2022

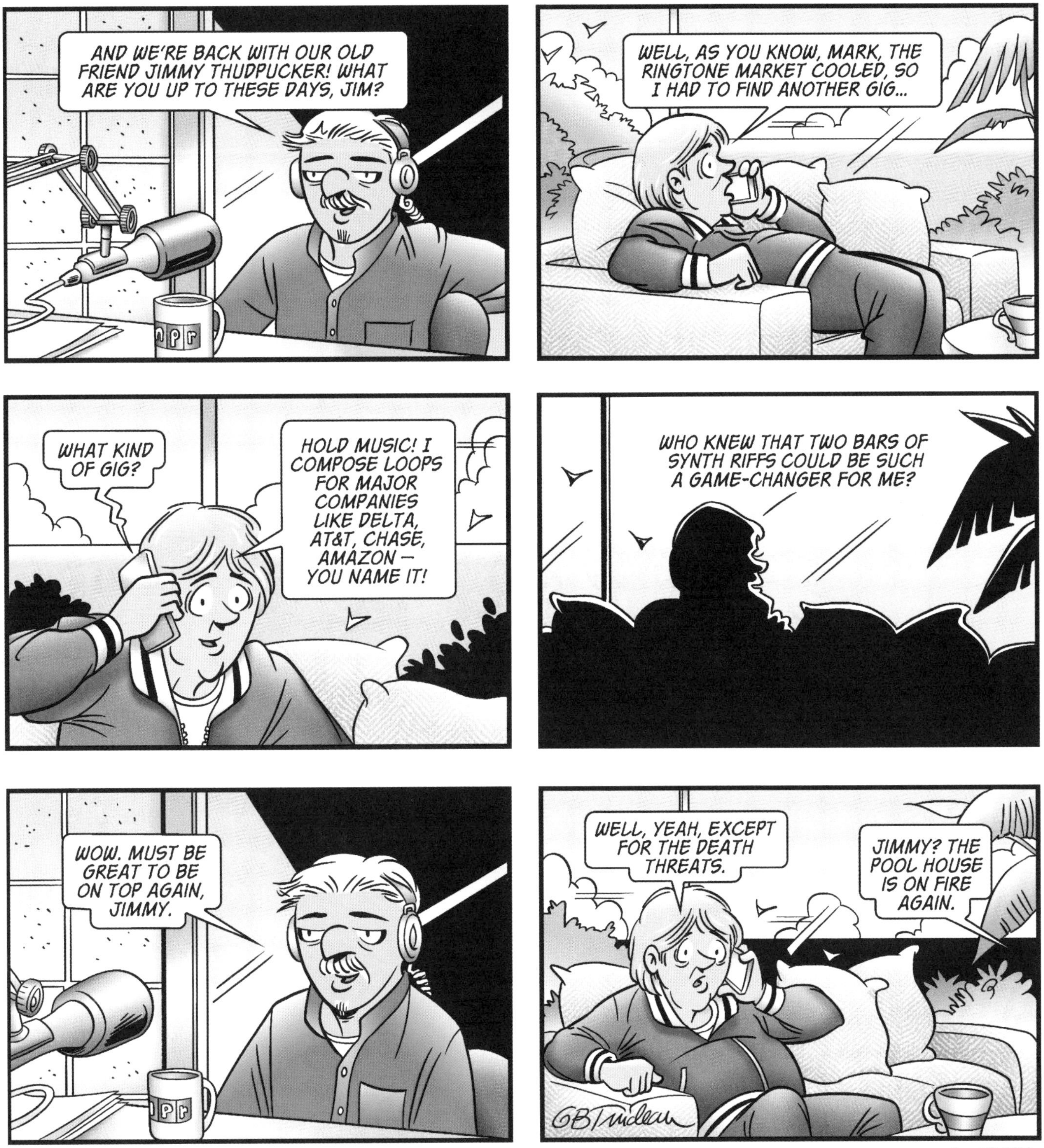
AND WE'RE BACK WITH OUR OLD FRIEND JIMMY THUDPUCKER! WHAT ARE YOU UP TO THESE DAYS, JIM?
WELL, AS YOU KNOW, MARK, THE RINGTONE MARKET COOLED, SO I HAD TO FIND ANOTHER GIG...
WHAT KIND OF GIG?
HOLD MUSIC! I COMPOSE LOOPS FOR MAJOR COMPANIES LIKE DELTA, AT&T, CHASE, AMAZON — YOU NAME IT!
WHO KNEW THAT TWO BARS OF SYNTH RIFFS COULD BE SUCH A GAME-CHANGER FOR ME?
WOW. MUST BE GREAT TO BE ON TOP AGAIN, JIMMY.
WELL, YEAH, EXCEPT FOR THE DEATH THREATS.
JIMMY? THE POOL HOUSE IS ON FIRE AGAIN.
npr
GBTrudeau

August 14, 2022

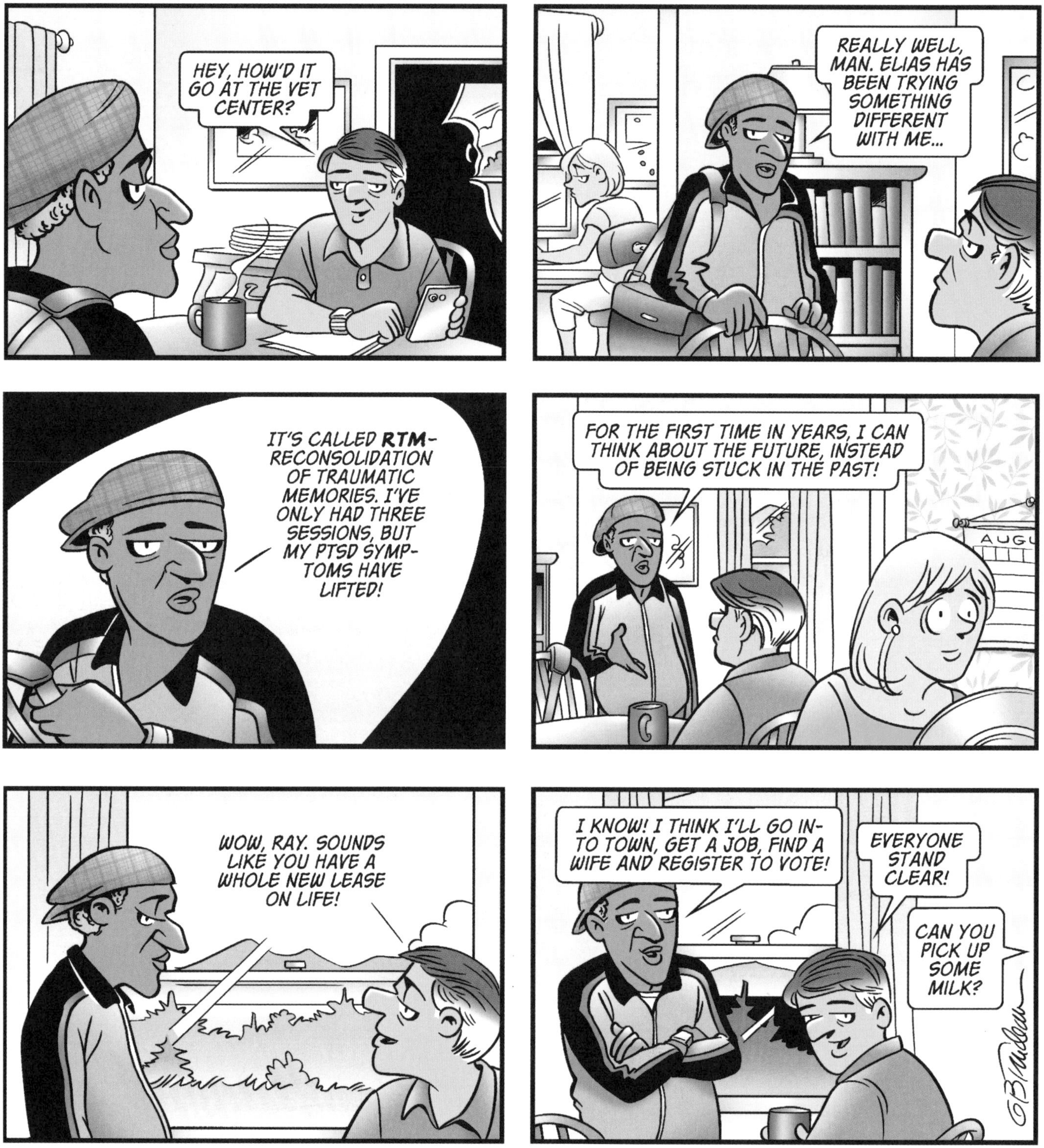
HEY, HOW'D IT GO AT THE VET CENTER?
REALLY WELL, MAN. ELIAS HAS BEEN TRYING SOMETHING DIFFERENT WITH ME...
IT'S CALLED **RTM**-RECONSOLIDATION OF TRAUMATIC MEMORIES. I'VE ONLY HAD THREE SESSIONS, BUT MY PTSD SYMPTOMS HAVE LIFTED!
FOR THE FIRST TIME IN YEARS, I CAN THINK ABOUT THE FUTURE, INSTEAD OF BEING STUCK IN THE PAST!
WOW, RAY. SOUNDS LIKE YOU HAVE A WHOLE NEW LEASE ON LIFE!
I KNOW! I THINK I'LL GO INTO TOWN, GET A JOB, FIND A WIFE AND REGISTER TO VOTE!
EVERYONE STAND CLEAR!
CAN YOU PICK UP SOME MILK?

August 21, 2022

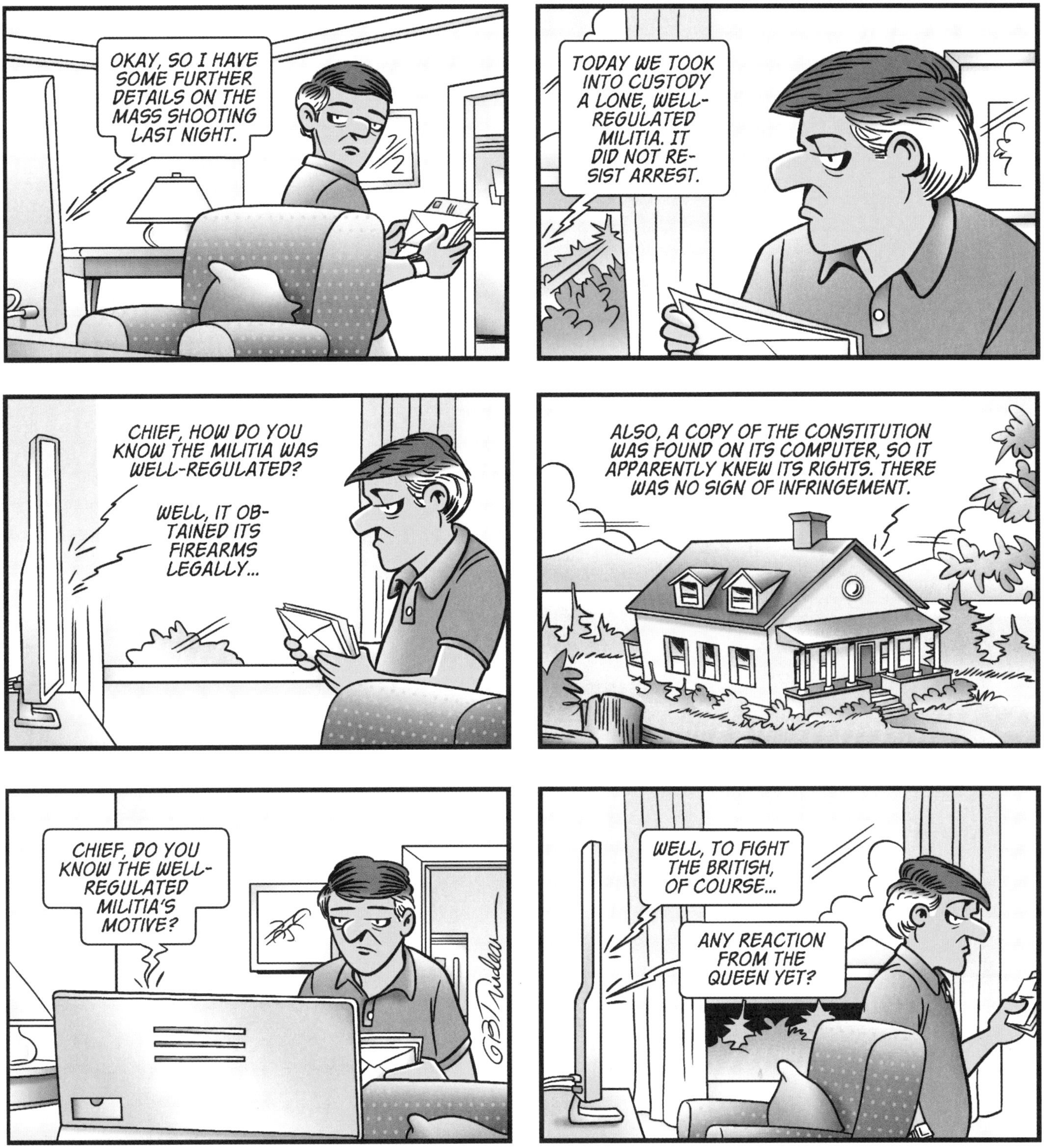
OKAY, SO I HAVE SOME FURTHER DETAILS ON THE MASS SHOOTING LAST NIGHT.
TODAY WE TOOK INTO CUSTODY A LONE, WELL-REGULATED MILITIA. IT DID NOT RESIST ARREST.
CHIEF, HOW DO YOU KNOW THE MILITIA WAS WELL-REGULATED?
WELL, IT OBTAINED ITS FIREARMS LEGALLY...
ALSO, A COPY OF THE CONSTITUTION WAS FOUND ON ITS COMPUTER, SO IT APPARENTLY KNEW ITS RIGHTS. THERE WAS NO SIGN OF INFRINGEMENT.
CHIEF, DO YOU KNOW THE WELL-REGULATED MILITIA'S MOTIVE?
GBTrudeau
WELL, TO FIGHT THE BRITISH, OF COURSE...
ANY REACTION FROM THE QUEEN YET?

August 28, 2022

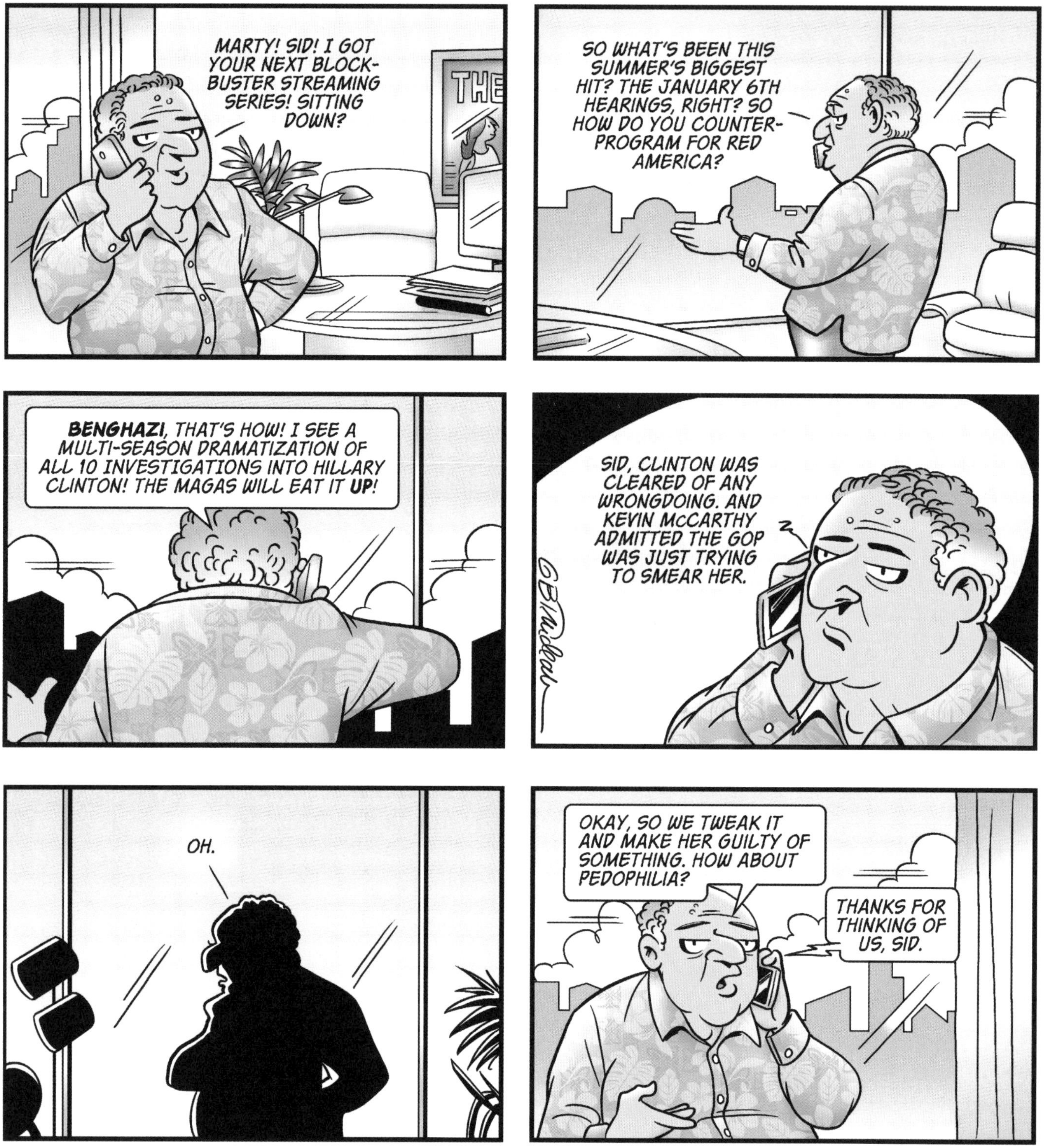
MARTY! SID! I GOT YOUR NEXT BLOCK-BUSTER STREAMING SERIES! SITTING DOWN?
THE
SO WHAT'S BEEN THIS SUMMER'S BIGGEST HIT? THE JANUARY 6TH HEARINGS, RIGHT? SO HOW DO YOU COUNTER-PROGRAM FOR RED AMERICA?
BENGHAZI, THAT'S HOW! I SEE A MULTI-SEASON DRAMATIZATION OF ALL 10 INVESTIGATIONS INTO HILLARY CLINTON! THE MAGAS WILL EAT IT UP!
SID, CLINTON WAS CLEARED OF ANY WRONGDOING. AND KEVIN McCARTHY ADMITTED THE GOP WAS JUST TRYING TO SMEAR HER.
OH.
OKAY, SO WE TWEAK IT AND MAKE HER GUILTY OF SOMETHING. HOW ABOUT PEDOPHILIA?
THANKS FOR THINKING OF US, SID.

September 4, 2022

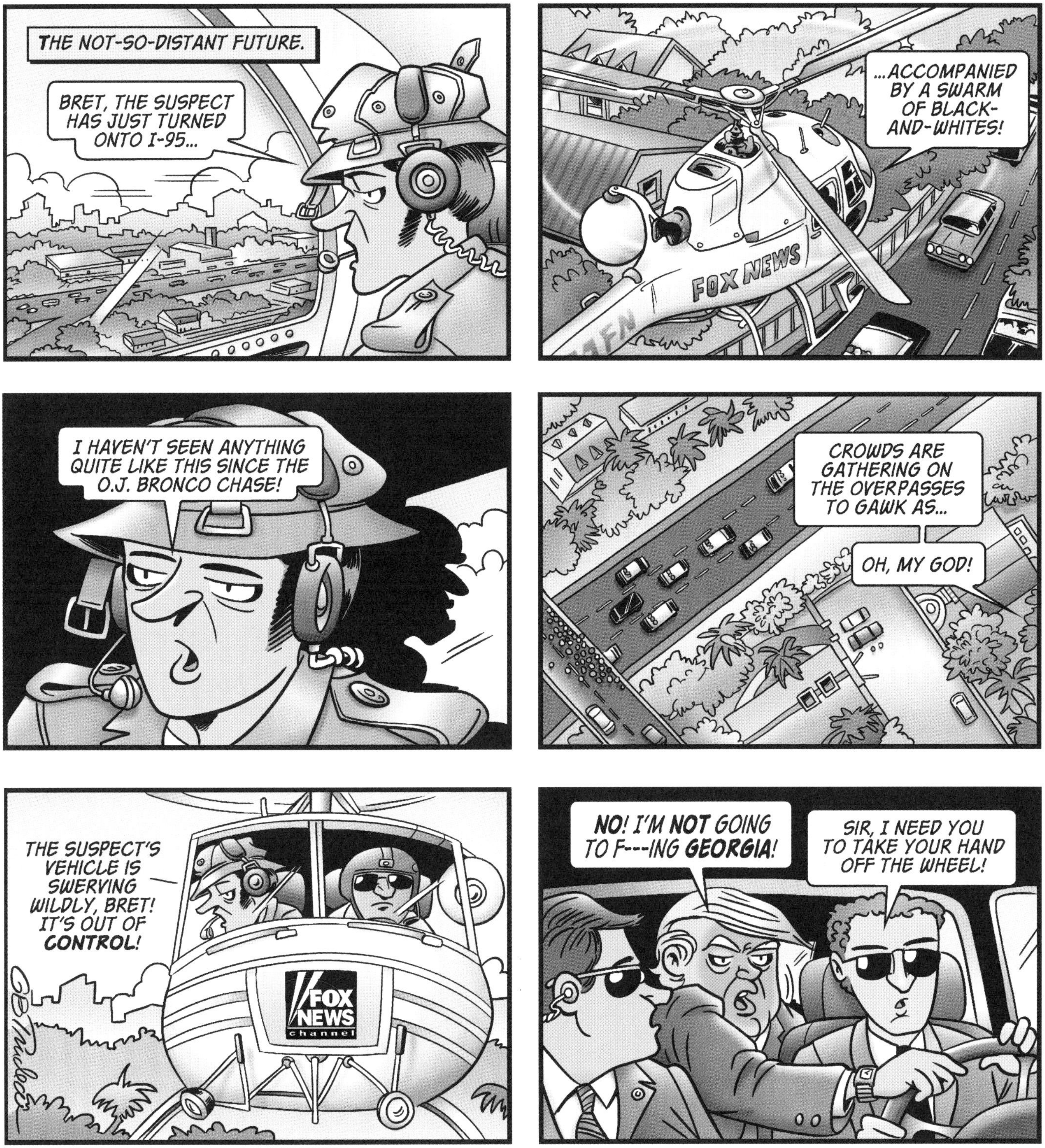
THE NOT-SO-DISTANT FUTURE.
BRET, THE SUSPECT HAS JUST TURNED ONTO I-95...
...ACCOMPANIED BY A SWARM OF BLACK-AND-WHITES!
FOX NEWS
I HAVEN'T SEEN ANYTHING QUITE LIKE THIS SINCE THE O.J. BRONCO CHASE!
CROWDS ARE GATHERING ON THE OVERPASSES TO GAWK AS...
OH, MY GOD!
THE SUSPECT'S VEHICLE IS SWERVING WILDLY, BRET! IT'S OUT OF **CONTROL**!
FOX NEWS channel
NO! I'M **NOT** GOING TO F---ING **GEORGIA**!
SIR, I NEED YOU TO TAKE YOUR HAND OFF THE WHEEL!

September 11, 2022

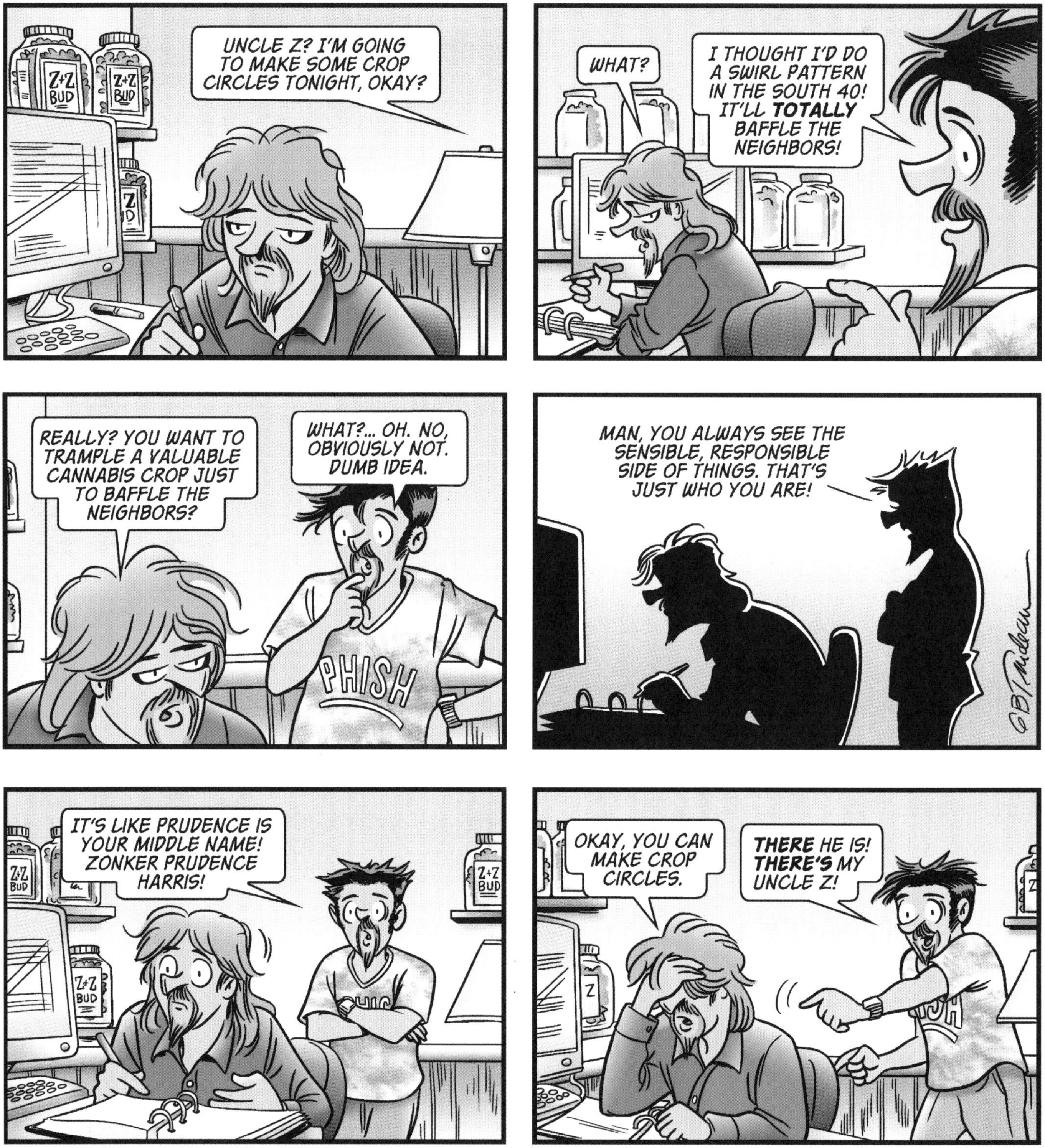
UNCLE Z? I'M GOING TO MAKE SOME CROP CIRCLES TONIGHT, OKAY?
Z+Z BUD
WHAT?
I THOUGHT I'D DO A SWIRL PATTERN IN THE SOUTH 40! IT'LL **TOTALLY** BAFFLE THE NEIGHBORS!
REALLY? YOU WANT TO TRAMPLE A VALUABLE CANNABIS CROP JUST TO BAFFLE THE NEIGHBORS?
WHAT?... OH. NO, OBVIOUSLY NOT. DUMB IDEA.
PHISH
MAN, YOU ALWAYS SEE THE SENSIBLE, RESPONSIBLE SIDE OF THINGS. THAT'S JUST WHO YOU ARE!
IT'S LIKE PRUDENCE IS YOUR MIDDLE NAME! ZONKER PRUDENCE HARRIS!
OKAY, YOU CAN MAKE CROP CIRCLES.
THERE HE IS! **THERE'S** MY UNCLE Z!

September 18, 2022

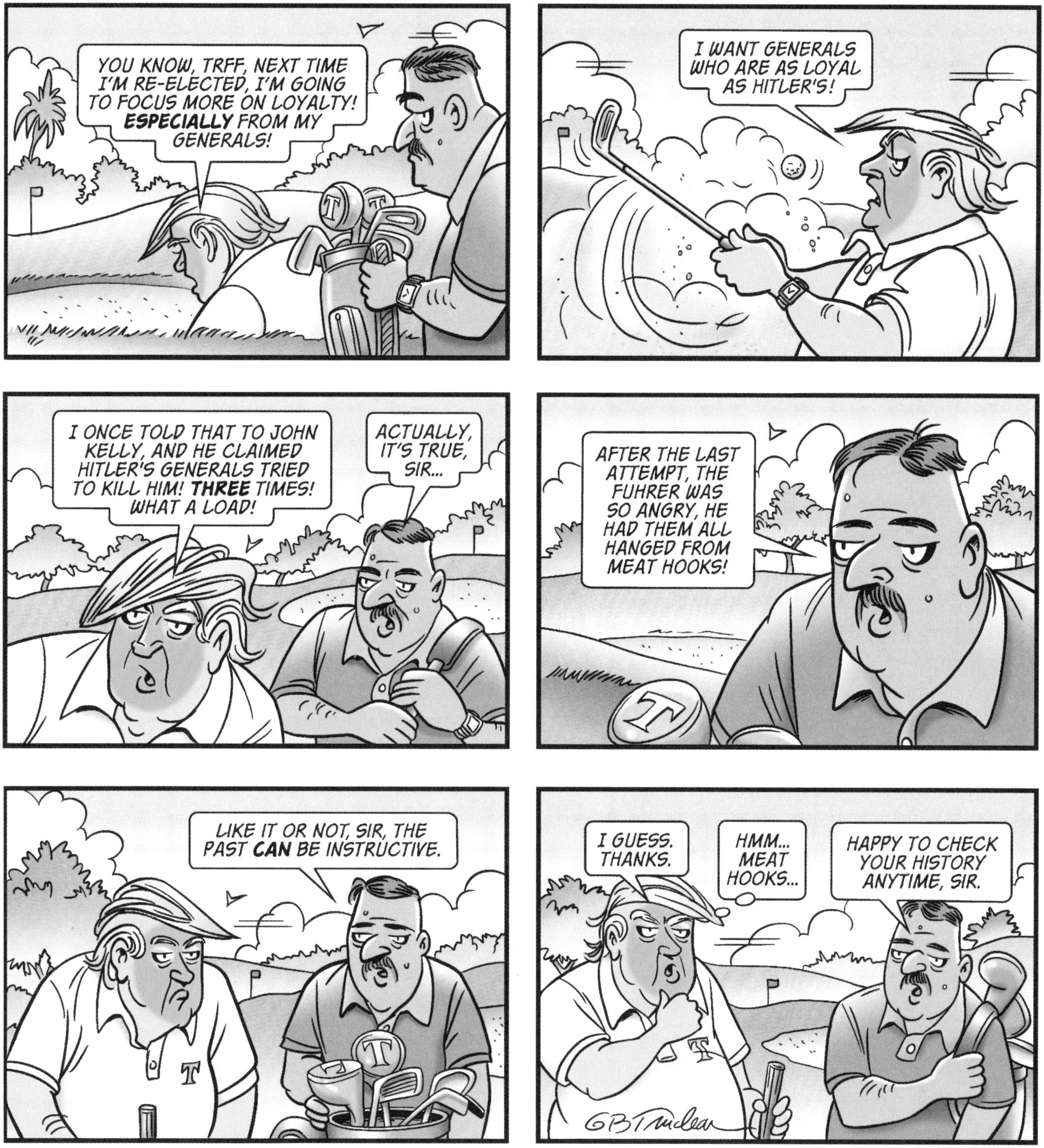
YOU KNOW, TRFF, NEXT TIME I'M RE-ELECTED, I'M GOING TO FOCUS MORE ON LOYALTY! **ESPECIALLY** FROM MY GENERALS!
I WANT GENERALS WHO ARE AS LOYAL AS HITLER'S!
I ONCE TOLD THAT TO JOHN KELLY, AND HE CLAIMED HITLER'S GENERALS TRIED TO KILL HIM! **THREE** TIMES! WHAT A LOAD!
ACTUALLY, IT'S TRUE, SIR...
AFTER THE LAST ATTEMPT, THE FUHRER WAS SO ANGRY, HE HAD THEM ALL HANGED FROM MEAT HOOKS!
LIKE IT OR NOT, SIR, THE PAST **CAN** BE INSTRUCTIVE.
I GUESS. THANKS.
HMM... MEAT HOOKS...
HAPPY TO CHECK YOUR HISTORY ANYTIME, SIR.
GBTrudeau

September 25, 2022

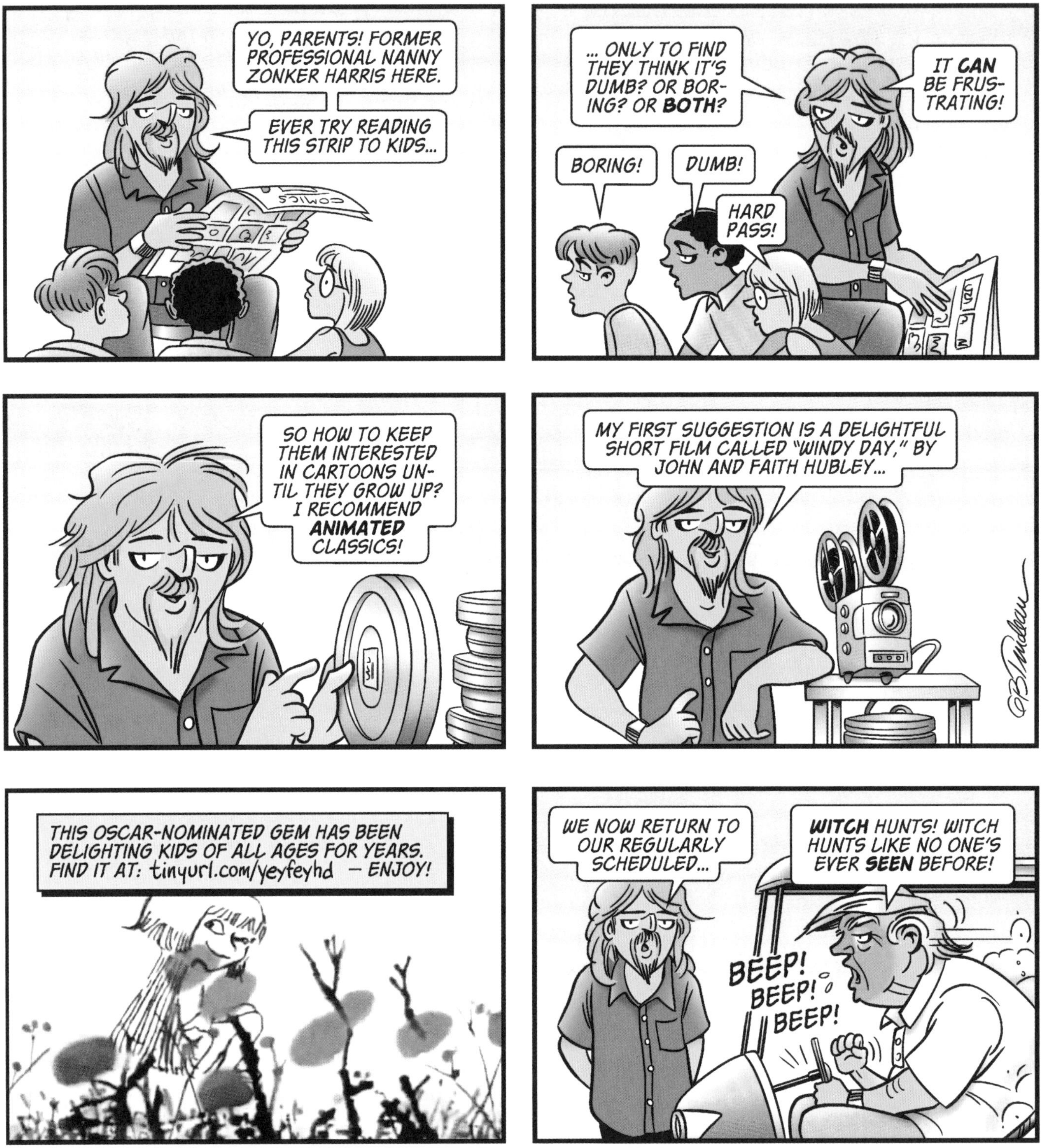
YO, PARENTS! FORMER PROFESSIONAL NANNY ZONKER HARRIS HERE.
EVER TRY READING THIS STRIP TO KIDS...
COMICS
... ONLY TO FIND THEY THINK IT'S DUMB? OR BOR-ING? OR **BOTH**?
IT **CAN** BE FRUS-TRATING!
BORING!
DUMB!
HARD PASS!
SO HOW TO KEEP THEM INTERESTED IN CARTOONS UN-TIL THEY GROW UP? I RECOMMEND **ANIMATED** CLASSICS!
MY FIRST SUGGESTION IS A DELIGHTFUL SHORT FILM CALLED "WINDY DAY," BY JOHN AND FAITH HUBLEY...
THIS OSCAR-NOMINATED GEM HAS BEEN DELIGHTING KIDS OF ALL AGES FOR YEARS. FIND IT AT: tinyurl.com/yeyfeyhd — ENJOY!
WE NOW RETURN TO OUR REGULARLY SCHEDULED...
WITCH HUNTS! WITCH HUNTS LIKE NO ONE'S EVER **SEEN** BEFORE!
BEEP! BEEP! BEEP!

October 2, 2022

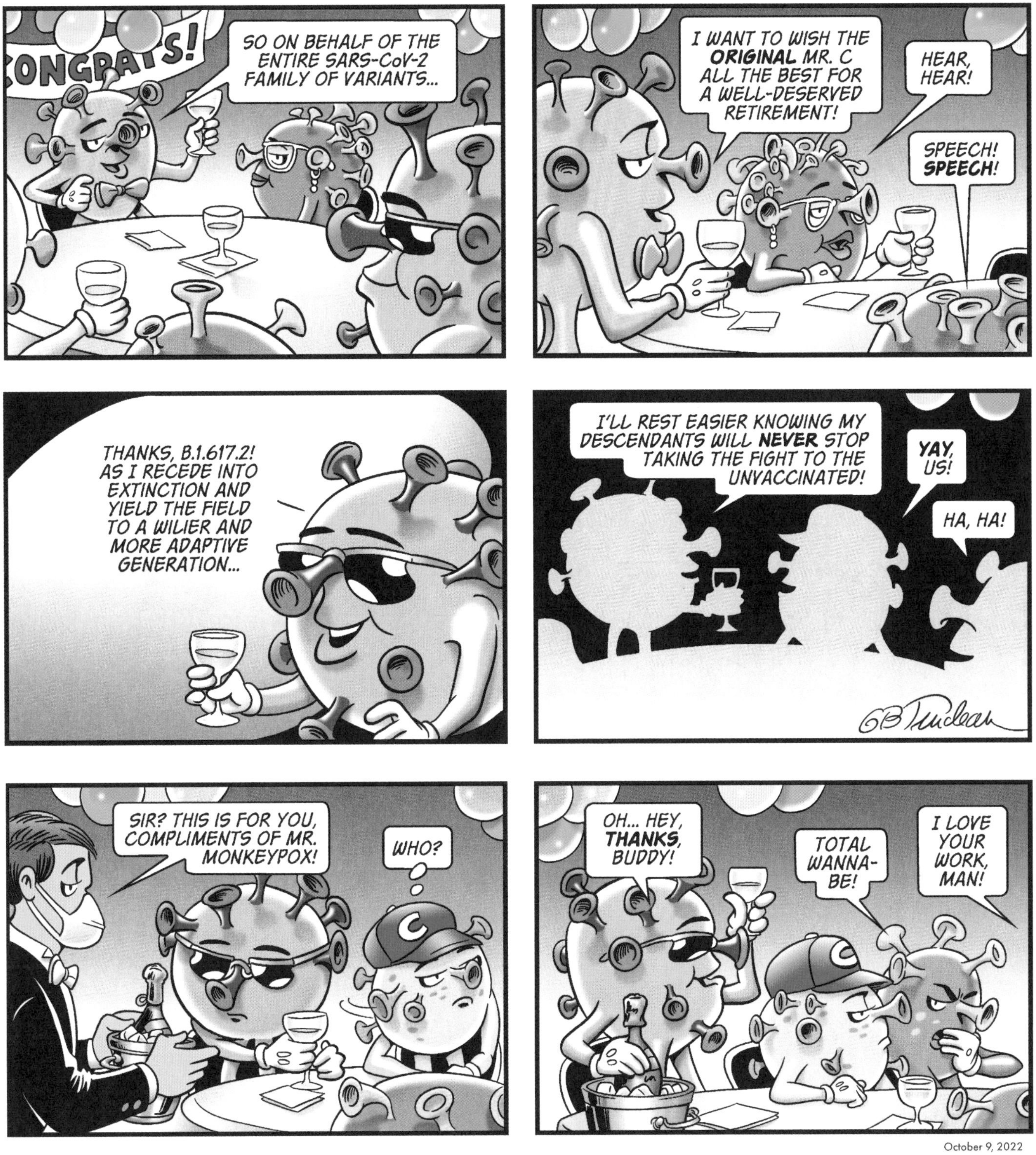
CONGRATS!
SO ON BEHALF OF THE ENTIRE SARS-CoV-2 FAMILY OF VARIANTS...
I WANT TO WISH THE **ORIGINAL** MR. C ALL THE BEST FOR A WELL-DESERVED RETIREMENT!
HEAR, HEAR!
SPEECH! **SPEECH!**
THANKS, B.1.617.2! AS I RECEDE INTO EXTINCTION AND YIELD THE FIELD TO A WILIER AND MORE ADAPTIVE GENERATION...
I'LL REST EASIER KNOWING MY DESCENDANTS WILL **NEVER** STOP TAKING THE FIGHT TO THE UNVACCINATED!
YAY, US!
HA, HA!
SIR? THIS IS FOR YOU, COMPLIMENTS OF MR. MONKEYPOX!
WHO?
OH... HEY, **THANKS,** BUDDY!
TOTAL WANNA-BE!
I LOVE YOUR WORK, MAN!

October 9, 2022

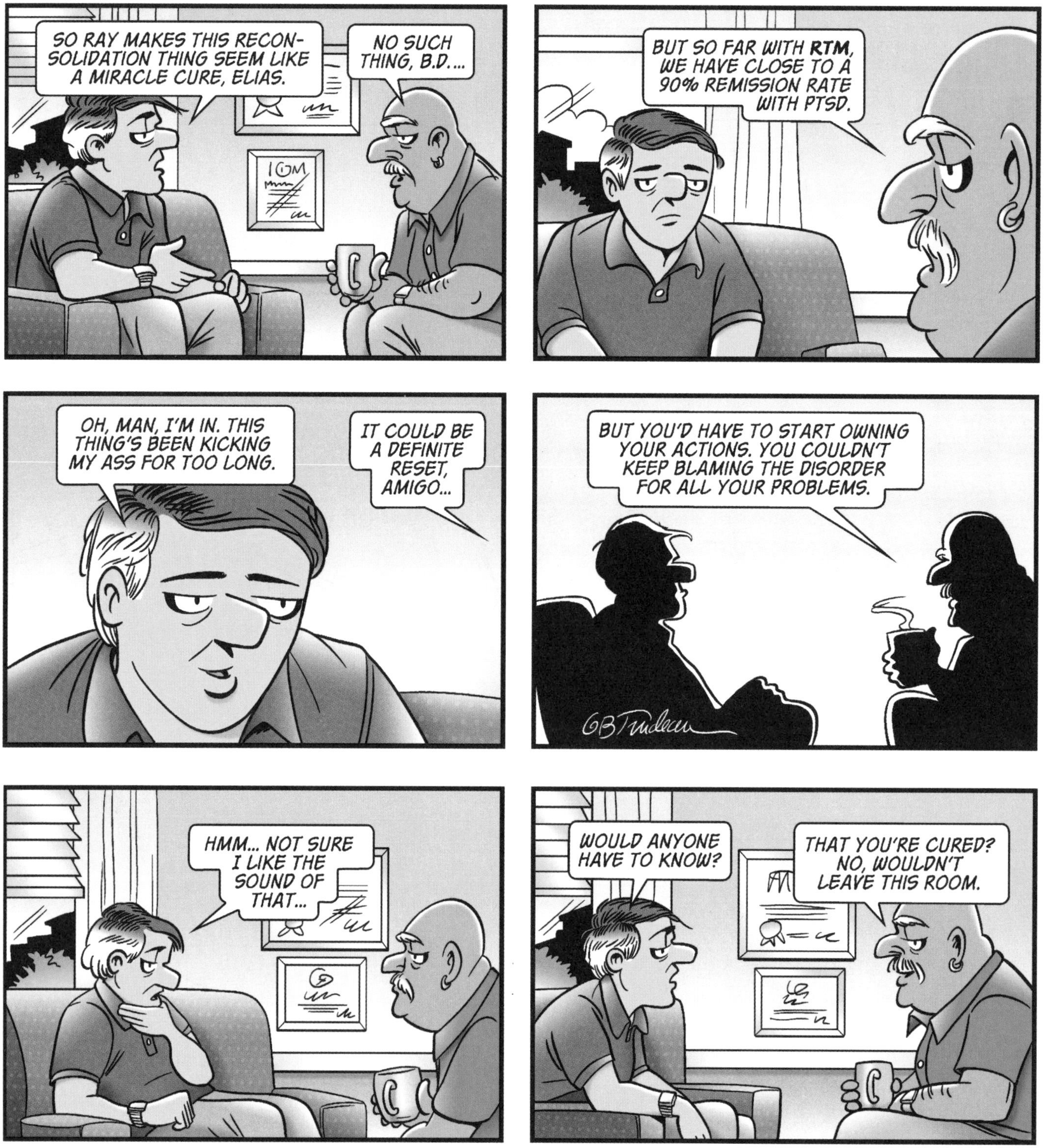
SO RAY MAKES THIS RECON-SOLIDATION THING SEEM LIKE A MIRACLE CURE, ELIAS.
NO SUCH THING, B.D....
BUT SO FAR WITH **RTM**, WE HAVE CLOSE TO A 90% REMISSION RATE WITH PTSD.
OH, MAN, I'M IN. THIS THING'S BEEN KICKING MY ASS FOR TOO LONG.
IT COULD BE A DEFINITE RESET, AMIGO...
BUT YOU'D HAVE TO START OWNING YOUR ACTIONS. YOU COULDN'T KEEP BLAMING THE DISORDER FOR ALL YOUR PROBLEMS.
GBTrudeau
HMM... NOT SURE I LIKE THE SOUND OF THAT...
WOULD ANYONE HAVE TO KNOW?
THAT YOU'RE CURED? NO, WOULDN'T LEAVE THIS ROOM.

October 16, 2022

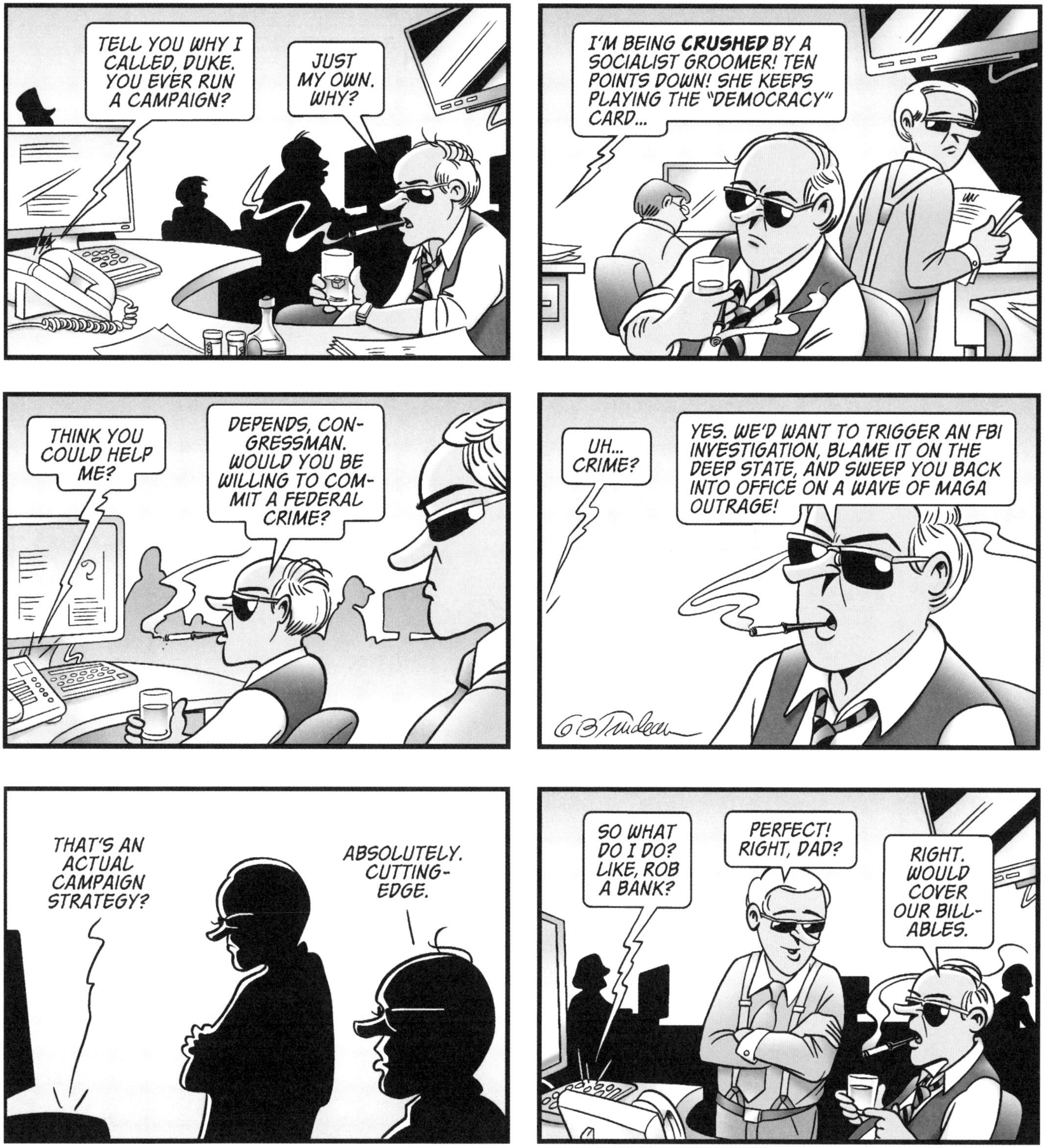

TELL YOU WHY I CALLED, DUKE. YOU EVER RUN A CAMPAIGN?
JUST MY OWN. WHY?
I'M BEING **CRUSHED** BY A SOCIALIST GROOMER! TEN POINTS DOWN! SHE KEEPS PLAYING THE "DEMOCRACY" CARD...
THINK YOU COULD HELP ME?
DEPENDS, CONGRESSMAN. WOULD YOU BE WILLING TO COMMIT A FEDERAL CRIME?
UH... CRIME?
YES. WE'D WANT TO TRIGGER AN FBI INVESTIGATION, BLAME IT ON THE DEEP STATE, AND SWEEP YOU BACK INTO OFFICE ON A WAVE OF MAGA OUTRAGE!
G B Trudeau
THAT'S AN ACTUAL CAMPAIGN STRATEGY?
ABSOLUTELY. CUTTING-EDGE.
SO WHAT DO I DO? LIKE, ROB A BANK?
PERFECT! RIGHT, DAD?
RIGHT. WOULD COVER OUR BILLABLES.

October 23, 2022

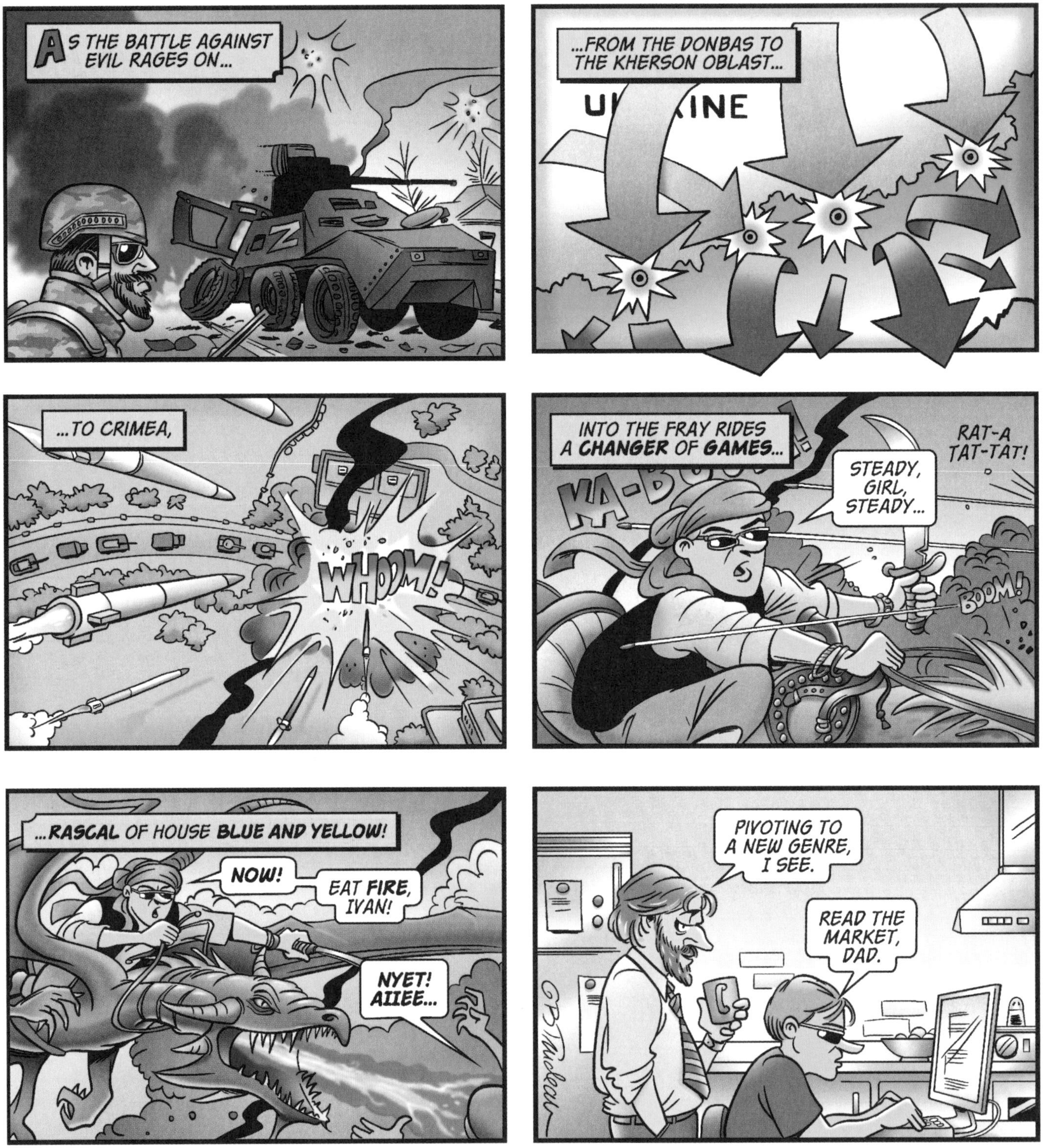
AS THE BATTLE AGAINST EVIL RAGES ON...
Z
...FROM THE DONBAS TO THE KHERSON OBLAST...
...TO CRIMEA,
WHOOM!
INTO THE FRAY RIDES A **CHANGER** OF **GAMES**...
RAT-A TAT-TAT!
STEADY, GIRL, STEADY...
BOOM!
...**RASCAL** OF HOUSE **BLUE AND YELLOW**!
NOW!
EAT **FIRE**, IVAN!
NYET! AIIEE...
PIVOTING TO A NEW GENRE, I SEE.
READ THE MARKET, DAD.
GBTrudeau

October 30, 2022

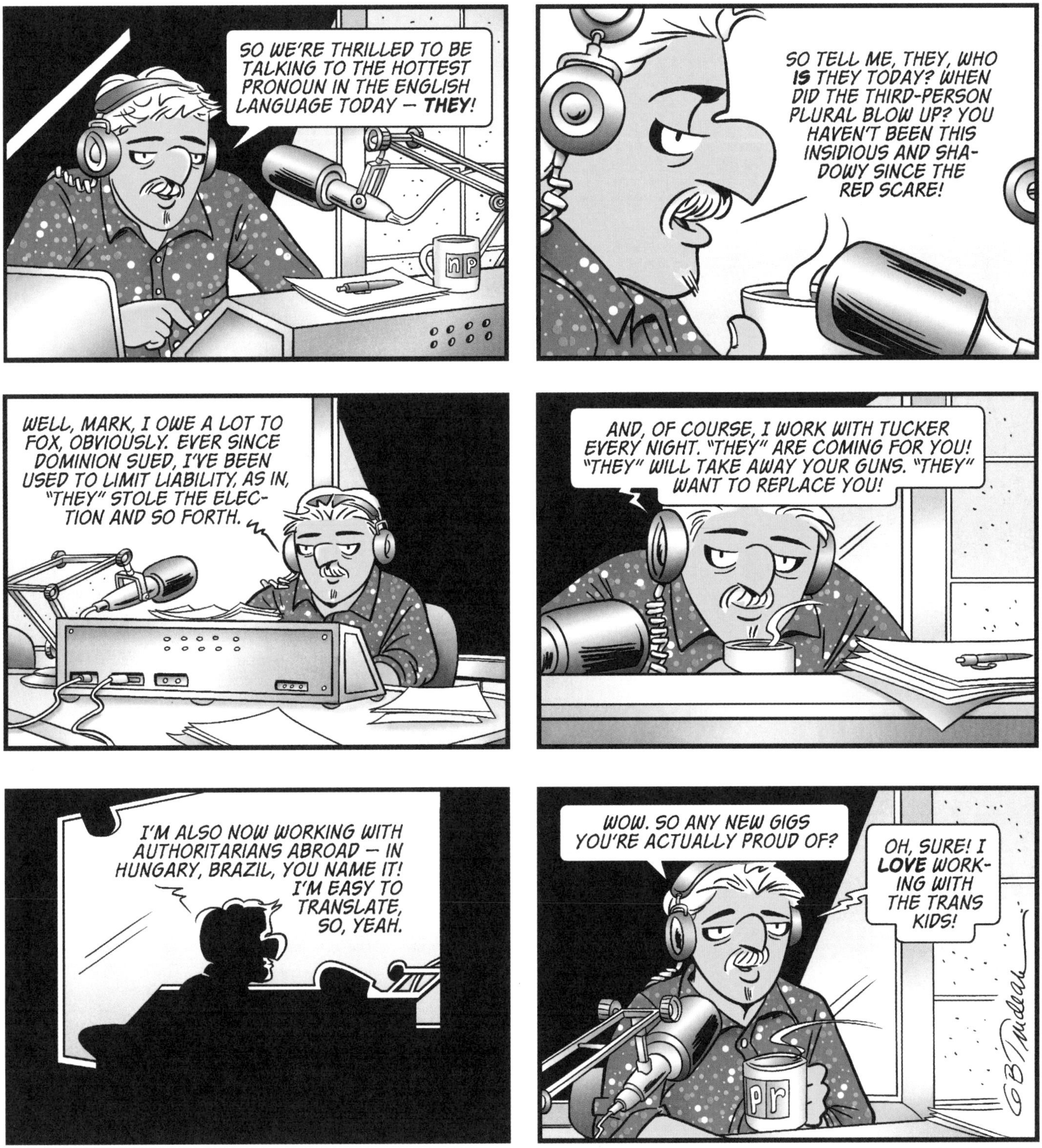
SO WE'RE THRILLED TO BE TALKING TO THE HOTTEST PRONOUN IN THE ENGLISH LANGUAGE TODAY — THEY!
SO TELL ME, THEY, WHO IS THEY TODAY? WHEN DID THE THIRD-PERSON PLURAL BLOW UP? YOU HAVEN'T BEEN THIS INSIDIOUS AND SHADOWY SINCE THE RED SCARE!
WELL, MARK, I OWE A LOT TO FOX, OBVIOUSLY. EVER SINCE DOMINION SUED, I'VE BEEN USED TO LIMIT LIABILITY, AS IN, "THEY" STOLE THE ELECTION AND SO FORTH.
AND, OF COURSE, I WORK WITH TUCKER EVERY NIGHT. "THEY" ARE COMING FOR YOU! "THEY" WILL TAKE AWAY YOUR GUNS. "THEY" WANT TO REPLACE YOU!
I'M ALSO NOW WORKING WITH AUTHORITARIANS ABROAD — IN HUNGARY, BRAZIL, YOU NAME IT! I'M EASY TO TRANSLATE, SO, YEAH.
WOW. SO ANY NEW GIGS YOU'RE ACTUALLY PROUD OF?
OH, SURE! I LOVE WORKING WITH THE TRANS KIDS!
GBTrudeau

November 6, 2022

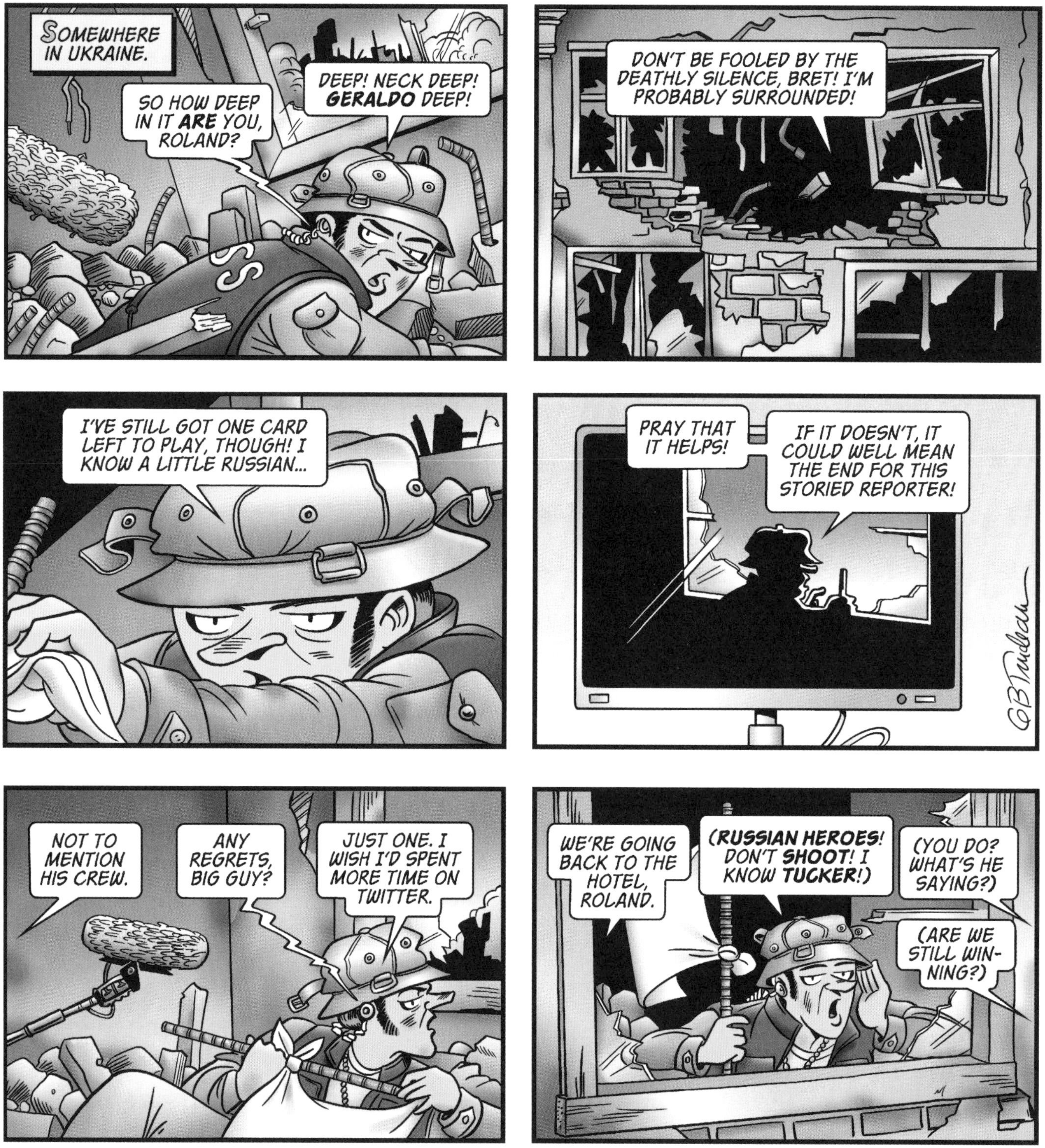
SOMEWHERE IN UKRAINE.
SO HOW DEEP IN IT ARE YOU, ROLAND?
DEEP! NECK DEEP! GERALDO DEEP!
DON'T BE FOOLED BY THE DEATHLY SILENCE, BRET! I'M PROBABLY SURROUNDED!
I'VE STILL GOT ONE CARD LEFT TO PLAY, THOUGH! I KNOW A LITTLE RUSSIAN...
PRAY THAT IT HELPS!
IF IT DOESN'T, IT COULD WELL MEAN THE END FOR THIS STORIED REPORTER!
GBTrudeau
NOT TO MENTION HIS CREW.
ANY REGRETS, BIG GUY?
JUST ONE. I WISH I'D SPENT MORE TIME ON TWITTER.
WE'RE GOING BACK TO THE HOTEL, ROLAND.
(RUSSIAN HEROES! DON'T SHOOT! I KNOW TUCKER!)
(YOU DO? WHAT'S HE SAYING?)
(ARE WE STILL WIN-NING?)

November 13, 2022

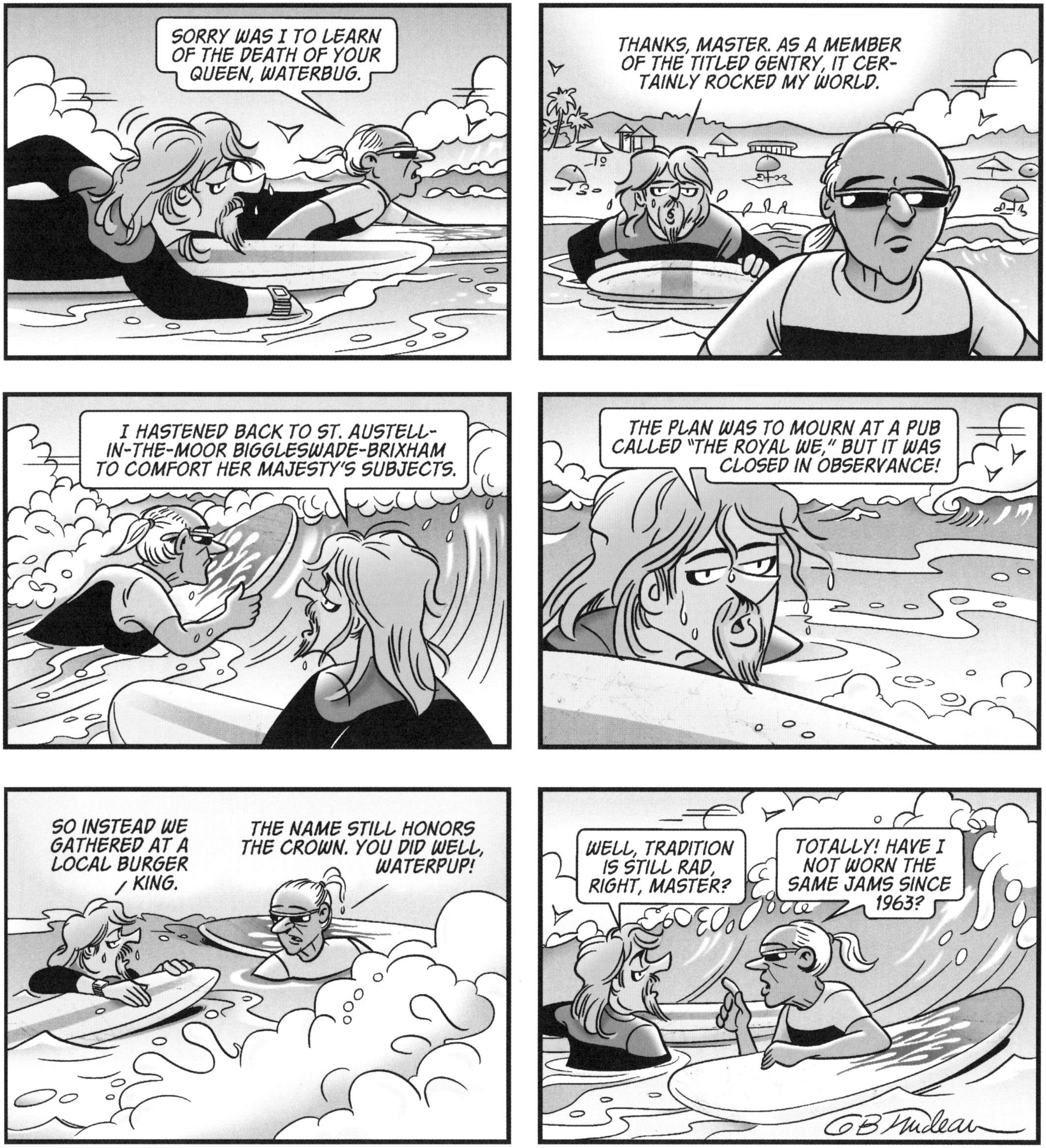
SORRY WAS I TO LEARN OF THE DEATH OF YOUR QUEEN, WATERBUG.
THANKS, MASTER. AS A MEMBER OF THE TITLED GENTRY, IT CERTAINLY ROCKED MY WORLD.
I HASTENED BACK TO ST. AUSTELL-IN-THE-MOOR BIGGLESWADE-BRIXHAM TO COMFORT HER MAJESTY'S SUBJECTS.
THE PLAN WAS TO MOURN AT A PUB CALLED "THE ROYAL WE," BUT IT WAS CLOSED IN OBSERVANCE!
SO INSTEAD WE GATHERED AT A LOCAL BURGER KING.
THE NAME STILL HONORS THE CROWN. YOU DID WELL, WATERPUP!
WELL, TRADITION IS STILL RAD, RIGHT, MASTER?
TOTALLY! HAVE I NOT WORN THE SAME JAMS SINCE 1963?
GB Trudeau

November 20, 2022

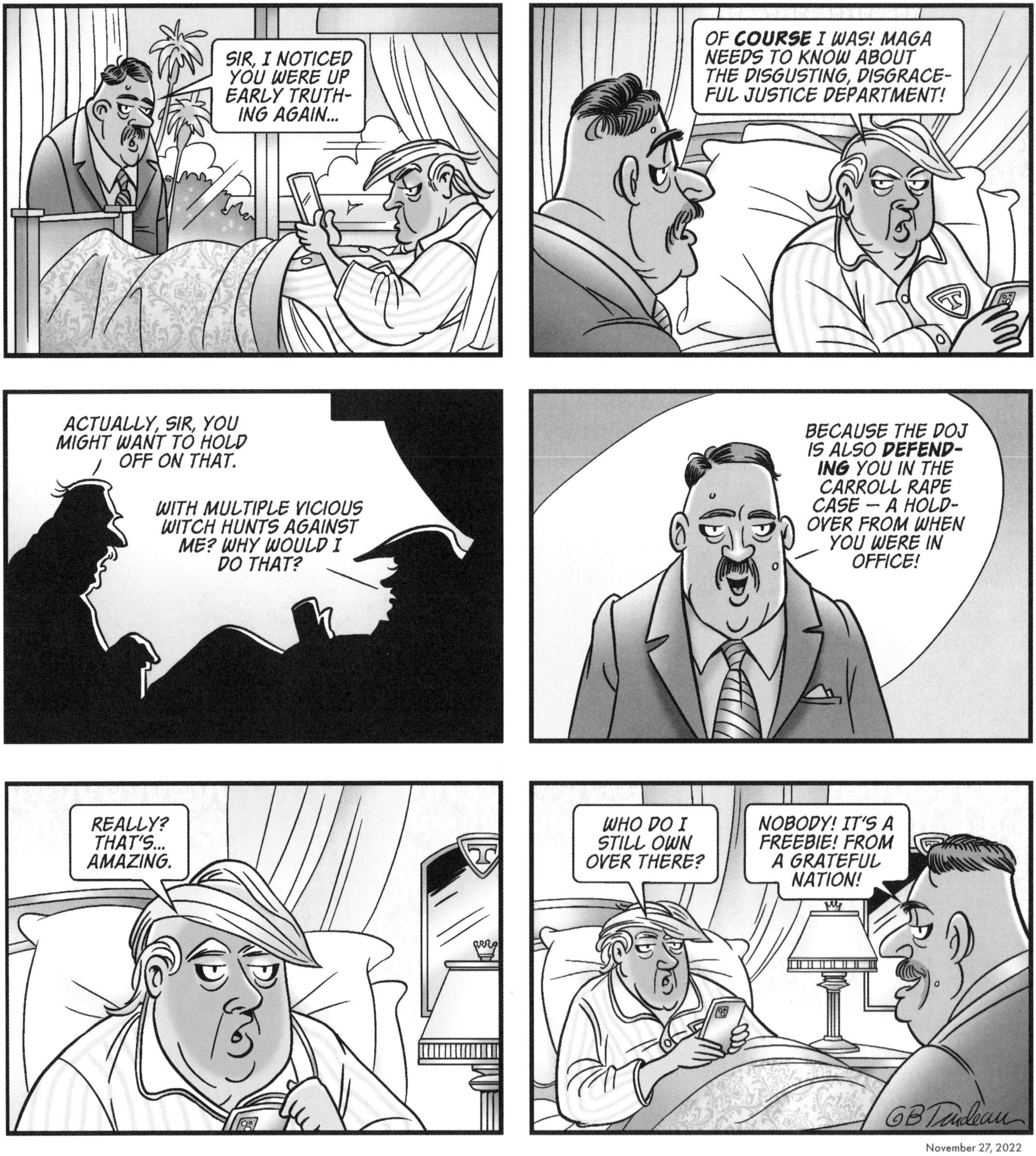
SIR, I NOTICED YOU WERE UP EARLY TRUTH-ING AGAIN...
OF COURSE I WAS! MAGA NEEDS TO KNOW ABOUT THE DISGUSTING, DISGRACE-FUL JUSTICE DEPARTMENT!
ACTUALLY, SIR, YOU MIGHT WANT TO HOLD OFF ON THAT.
WITH MULTIPLE VICIOUS WITCH HUNTS AGAINST ME? WHY WOULD I DO THAT?
BECAUSE THE DOJ IS ALSO DEFEND-ING YOU IN THE CARROLL RAPE CASE — A HOLD-OVER FROM WHEN YOU WERE IN OFFICE!
REALLY? THAT'S... AMAZING.
WHO DO I STILL OWN OVER THERE?
NOBODY! IT'S A FREEBIE! FROM A GRATEFUL NATION!
GB Trudeau

November 27, 2022

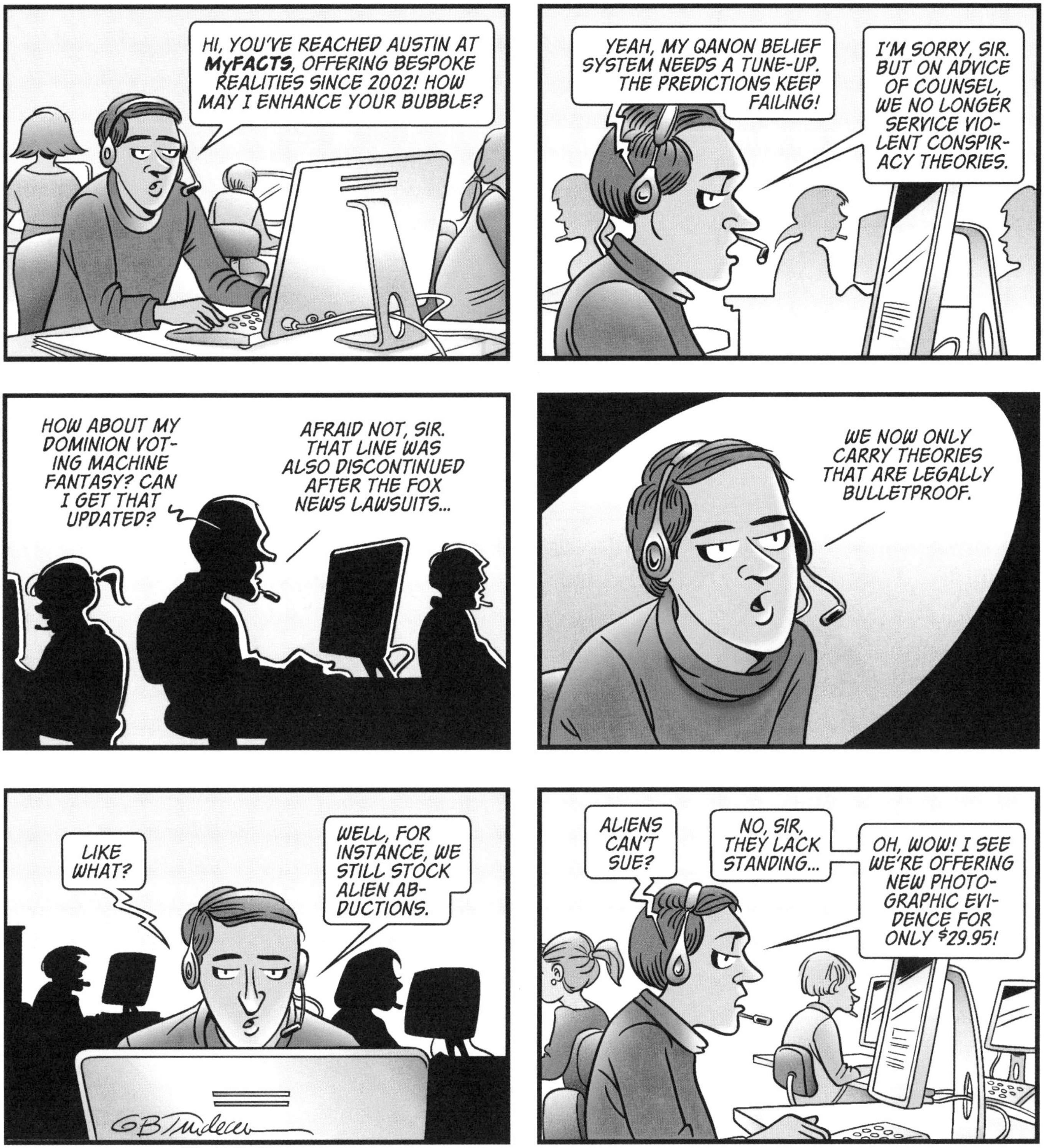
HI, YOU'VE REACHED AUSTIN AT MyFACTS, OFFERING BESPOKE REALITIES SINCE 2002! HOW MAY I ENHANCE YOUR BUBBLE?
YEAH, MY QANON BELIEF SYSTEM NEEDS A TUNE-UP. THE PREDICTIONS KEEP FAILING!
I'M SORRY, SIR. BUT ON ADVICE OF COUNSEL, WE NO LONGER SERVICE VIOLENT CONSPIRACY THEORIES.
HOW ABOUT MY DOMINION VOTING MACHINE FANTASY? CAN I GET THAT UPDATED?
AFRAID NOT, SIR. THAT LINE WAS ALSO DISCONTINUED AFTER THE FOX NEWS LAWSUITS...
WE NOW ONLY CARRY THEORIES THAT ARE LEGALLY BULLETPROOF.
LIKE WHAT?
WELL, FOR INSTANCE, WE STILL STOCK ALIEN ABDUCTIONS.
ALIENS CAN'T SUE?
NO, SIR, THEY LACK STANDING...
OH, WOW! I SEE WE'RE OFFERING NEW PHOTOGRAPHIC EVIDENCE FOR ONLY $29.95!
GBTrudeau

December 4, 2022

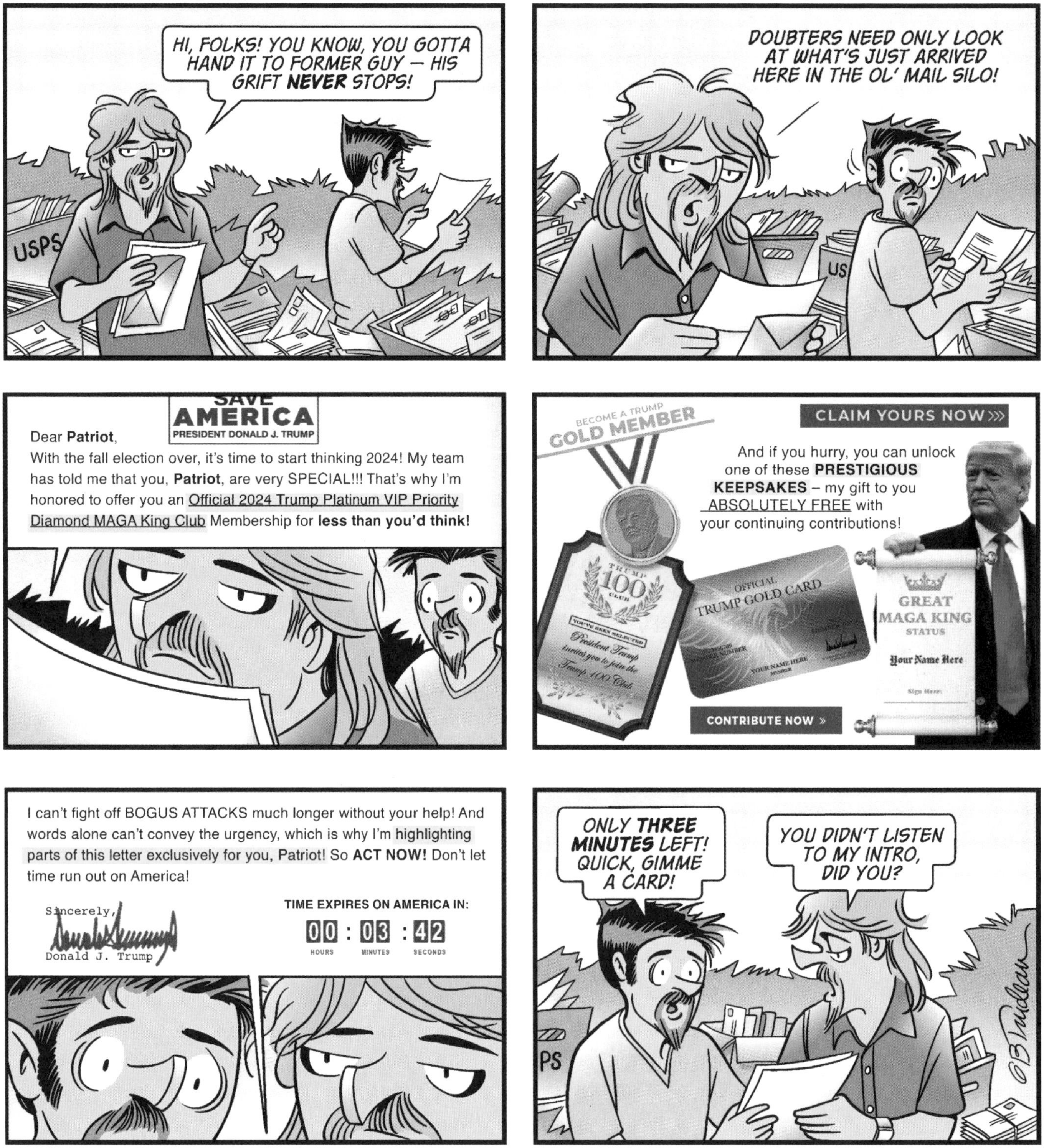
HI, FOLKS! YOU KNOW, YOU GOTTA HAND IT TO FORMER GUY — HIS GRIFT **NEVER** STOPS!
USPS
DOUBTERS NEED ONLY LOOK AT WHAT'S JUST ARRIVED HERE IN THE OL' MAIL SILO!
SAVE AMERICA
PRESIDENT DONALD J. TRUMP
Dear **Patriot**,
With the fall election over, it's time to start thinking 2024! My team has told me that you, **Patriot**, are very SPECIAL!!! That's why I'm honored to offer you an Official 2024 Trump Platinum VIP Priority Diamond MAGA King Club Membership for **less than you'd think!**
BECOME A TRUMP GOLD MEMBER
CLAIM YOURS NOW »»
And if you hurry, you can unlock one of these **PRESTIGIOUS KEEPSAKES** – my gift to you ABSOLUTELY FREE with your continuing contributions!
TRUMP 100 CLUB
YOU'VE BEEN SELECTED
President Trump invites you to join the Trump 100 Club
OFFICIAL TRUMP GOLD CARD
YOUR NAME HERE
GREAT MAGA KING STATUS
Your Name Here
CONTRIBUTE NOW »
I can't fight off BOGUS ATTACKS much longer without your help! And words alone can't convey the urgency, which is why I'm highlighting parts of this letter exclusively for you, Patriot! So **ACT NOW!** Don't let time run out on America!
Sincerely,
Donald J. Trump
TIME EXPIRES ON AMERICA IN:
00 : 03 : 42
HOURS MINUTES SECONDS
ONLY **THREE MINUTES** LEFT! QUICK, GIMME A CARD!
YOU DIDN'T LISTEN TO MY INTRO, DID YOU?
PS

December 11, 2022

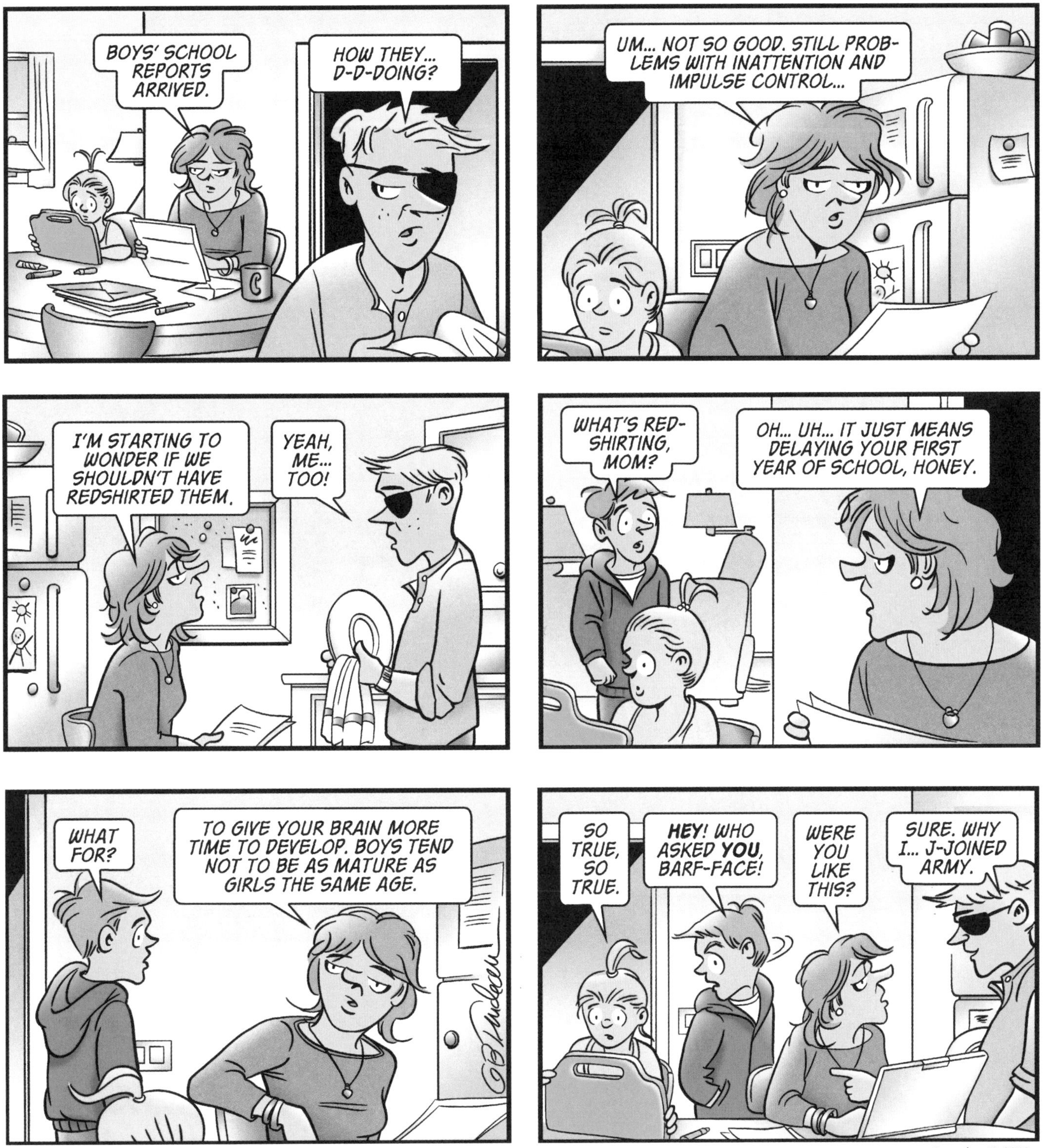
BOYS' SCHOOL REPORTS ARRIVED.
HOW THEY... D-D-DOING?
UM... NOT SO GOOD. STILL PROBLEMS WITH INATTENTION AND IMPULSE CONTROL...
I'M STARTING TO WONDER IF WE SHOULDN'T HAVE REDSHIRTED THEM.
YEAH, ME... TOO!
WHAT'S RED-SHIRTING, MOM?
OH... UH... IT JUST MEANS DELAYING YOUR FIRST YEAR OF SCHOOL, HONEY.
WHAT FOR?
TO GIVE YOUR BRAIN MORE TIME TO DEVELOP. BOYS TEND NOT TO BE AS MATURE AS GIRLS THE SAME AGE.
SO TRUE, SO TRUE.
HEY! WHO ASKED **YOU**, BARF-FACE!
WERE YOU LIKE THIS?
SURE. WHY I... J-JOINED ARMY.

December 18, 2022

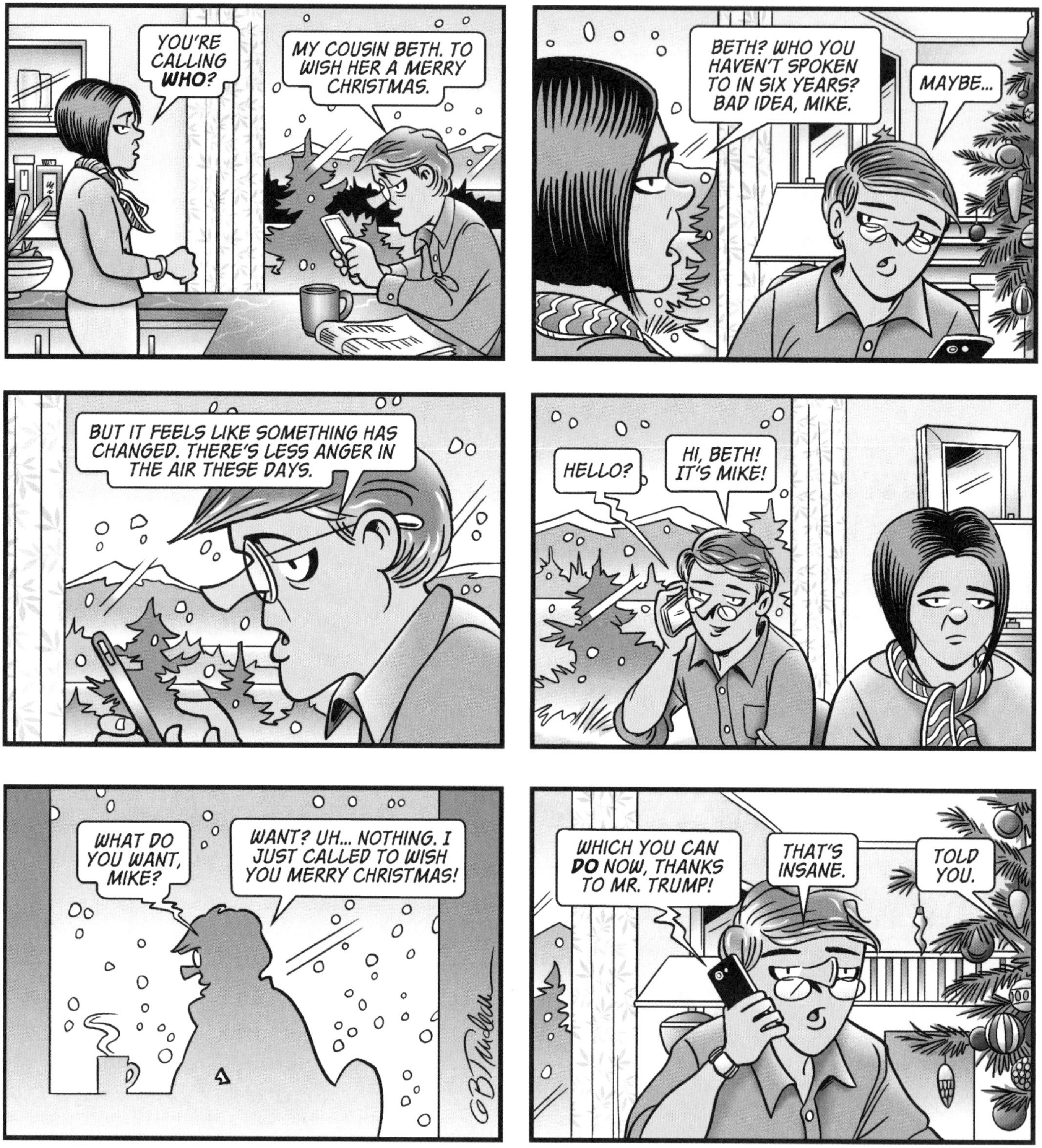
YOU'RE CALLING WHO?
MY COUSIN BETH. TO WISH HER A MERRY CHRISTMAS.
BETH? WHO YOU HAVEN'T SPOKEN TO IN SIX YEARS? BAD IDEA, MIKE.
MAYBE...
BUT IT FEELS LIKE SOMETHING HAS CHANGED. THERE'S LESS ANGER IN THE AIR THESE DAYS.
HELLO?
HI, BETH! IT'S MIKE!
WHAT DO YOU WANT, MIKE?
WANT? UH... NOTHING. I JUST CALLED TO WISH YOU MERRY CHRISTMAS!
WHICH YOU CAN DO NOW, THANKS TO MR. TRUMP!
THAT'S INSANE.
TOLD YOU.
GBTrudeau

December 25, 2022

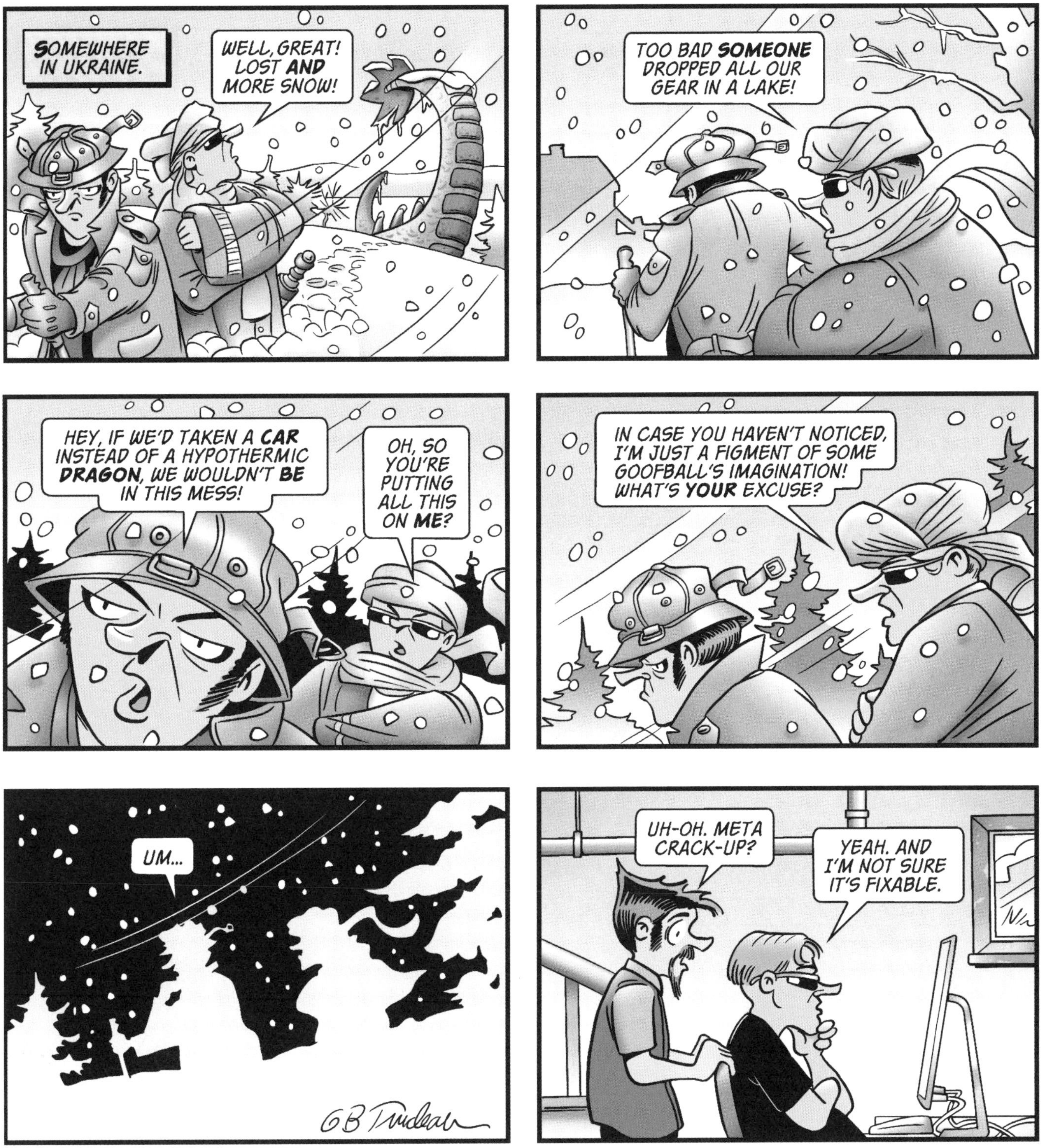
SOMEWHERE IN UKRAINE.
WELL, GREAT! LOST AND MORE SNOW!
TOO BAD SOMEONE DROPPED ALL OUR GEAR IN A LAKE!
HEY, IF WE'D TAKEN A CAR INSTEAD OF A HYPOTHERMIC DRAGON, WE WOULDN'T BE IN THIS MESS!
OH, SO YOU'RE PUTTING ALL THIS ON ME?
IN CASE YOU HAVEN'T NOTICED, I'M JUST A FIGMENT OF SOME GOOFBALL'S IMAGINATION! WHAT'S YOUR EXCUSE?
UM...
UH-OH. META CRACK-UP?
YEAH. AND I'M NOT SURE IT'S FIXABLE.
GB Trudeau

January 1, 2023

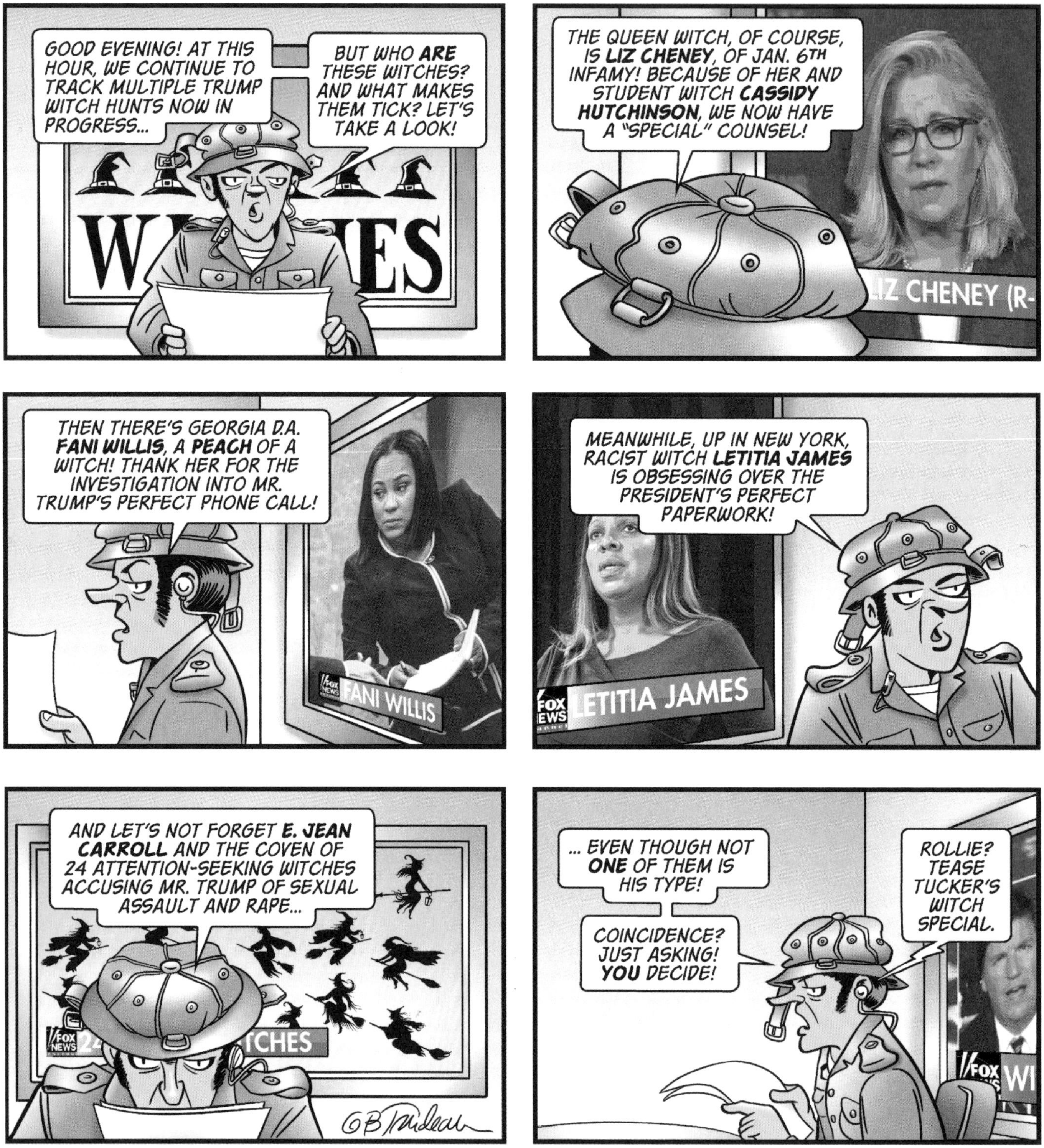
GOOD EVENING! AT THIS HOUR, WE CONTINUE TO TRACK MULTIPLE TRUMP WITCH HUNTS NOW IN PROGRESS...
BUT WHO **ARE** THESE WITCHES? AND WHAT MAKES THEM TICK? LET'S TAKE A LOOK!
THE QUEEN WITCH, OF COURSE, IS **LIZ CHENEY**, OF JAN. 6TH INFAMY! BECAUSE OF HER AND STUDENT WITCH **CASSIDY HUTCHINSON**, WE NOW HAVE A "SPECIAL" COUNSEL!
LIZ CHENEY (R-
THEN THERE'S GEORGIA D.A. **FANI WILLIS**, A **PEACH** OF A WITCH! THANK HER FOR THE INVESTIGATION INTO MR. TRUMP'S PERFECT PHONE CALL!
FOX NEWS FANI WILLIS
MEANWHILE, UP IN NEW YORK, RACIST WITCH **LETITIA JAMES** IS OBSESSING OVER THE PRESIDENT'S PERFECT PAPERWORK!
FOX NEWS LETITIA JAMES
AND LET'S NOT FORGET **E. JEAN CARROLL** AND THE COVEN OF 24 ATTENTION-SEEKING WITCHES ACCUSING MR. TRUMP OF SEXUAL ASSAULT AND RAPE...
FOX NEWS 24 TCHES
GB Trudeau
... EVEN THOUGH NOT **ONE** OF THEM IS HIS TYPE!
COINCIDENCE? JUST ASKING! **YOU** DECIDE!
ROLLIE? TEASE TUCKER'S WITCH SPECIAL.
FOX NEWS WI

January 8, 2023

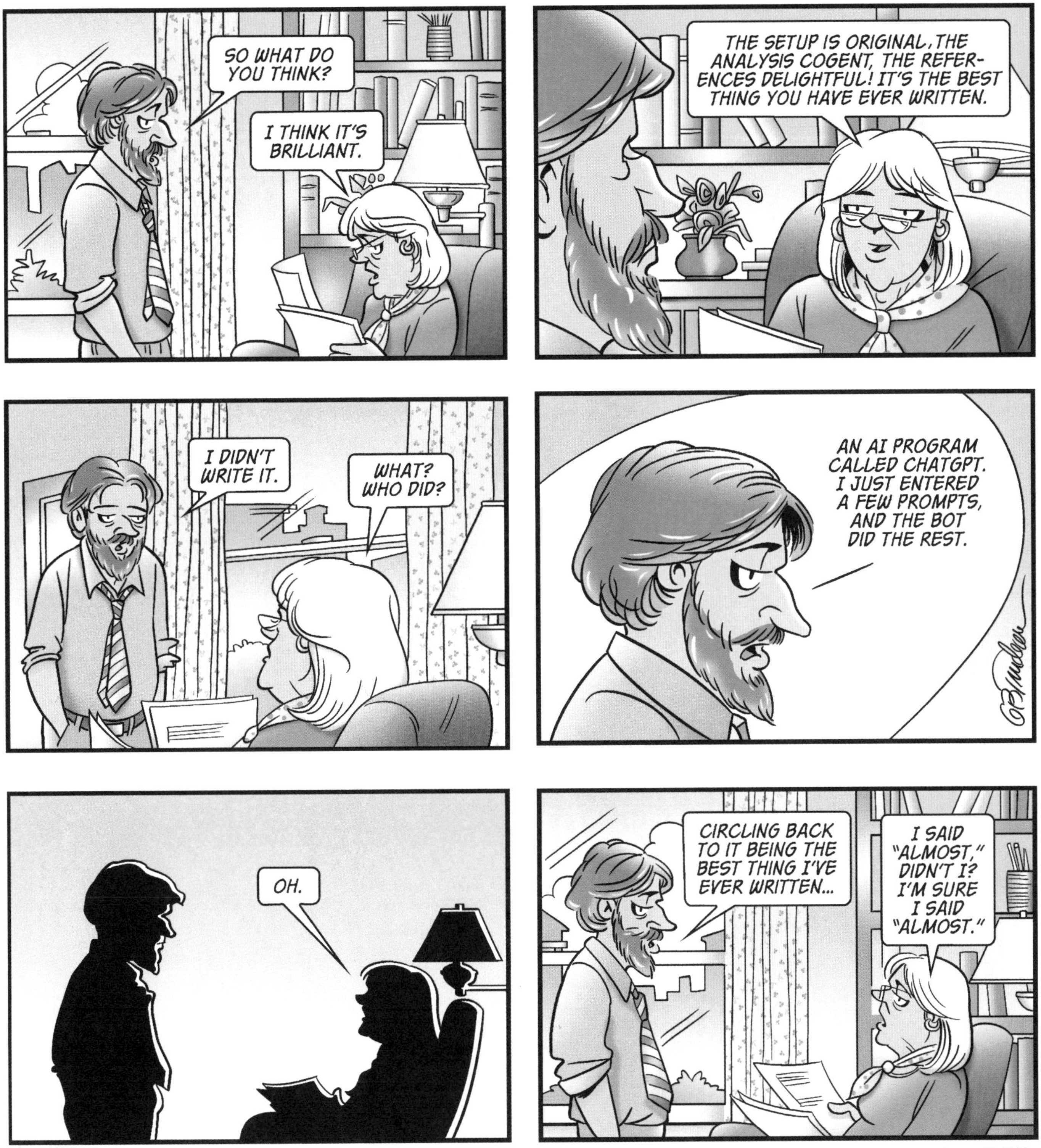
SO WHAT DO YOU THINK?
I THINK IT'S BRILLIANT.
THE SETUP IS ORIGINAL, THE ANALYSIS COGENT, THE REFERENCES DELIGHTFUL! IT'S THE BEST THING YOU HAVE EVER WRITTEN.
I DIDN'T WRITE IT.
WHAT? WHO DID?
AN AI PROGRAM CALLED CHATGPT. I JUST ENTERED A FEW PROMPTS, AND THE BOT DID THE REST.
OH.
CIRCLING BACK TO IT BEING THE BEST THING I'VE EVER WRITTEN...
I SAID "ALMOST," DIDN'T I? I'M SURE I SAID "ALMOST."

January 15, 2023

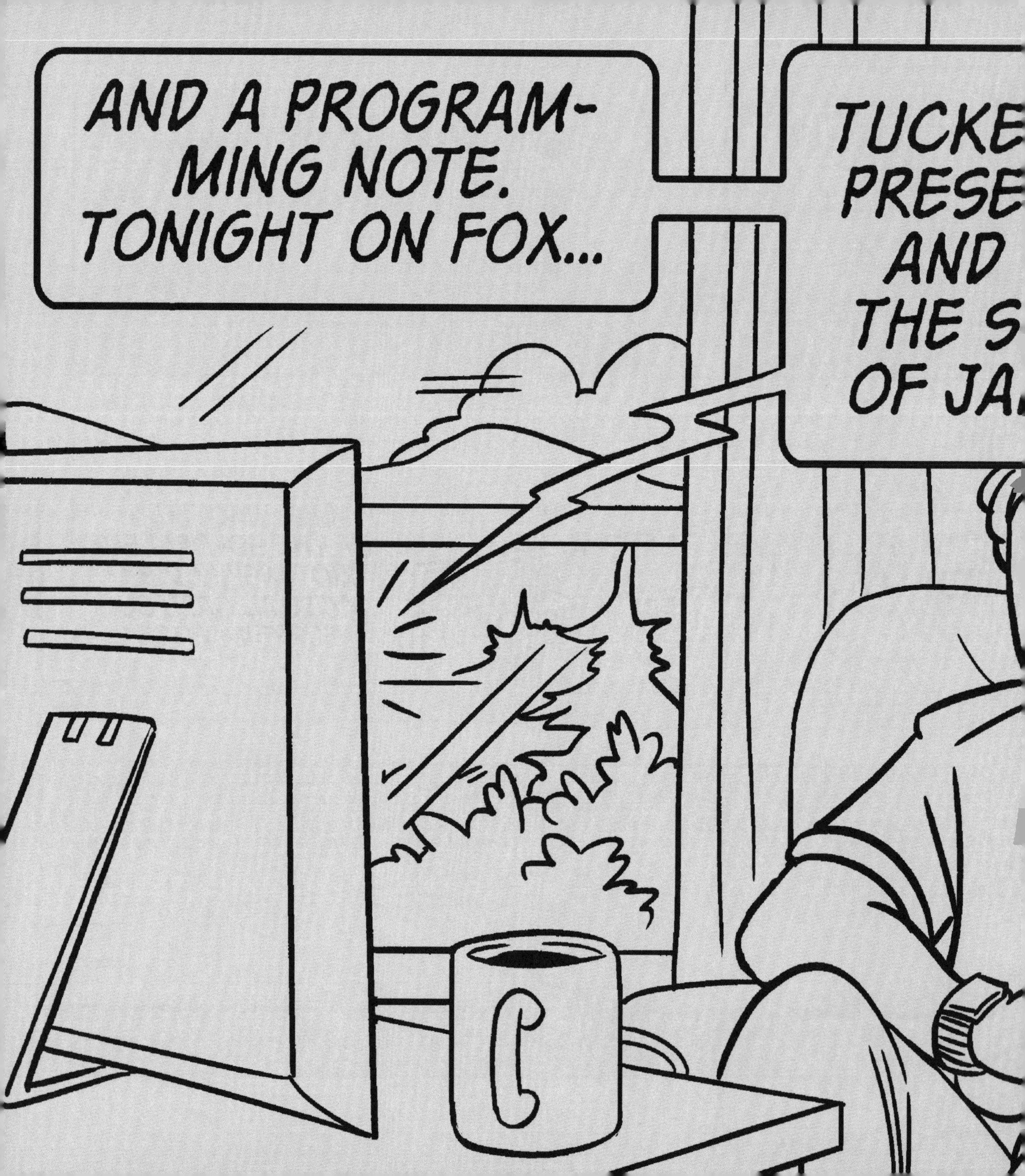
AND A PROGRAM-MING NOTE. TONIGHT ON FOX...
TUCKE
PRESE
AND
THE S
OF JA

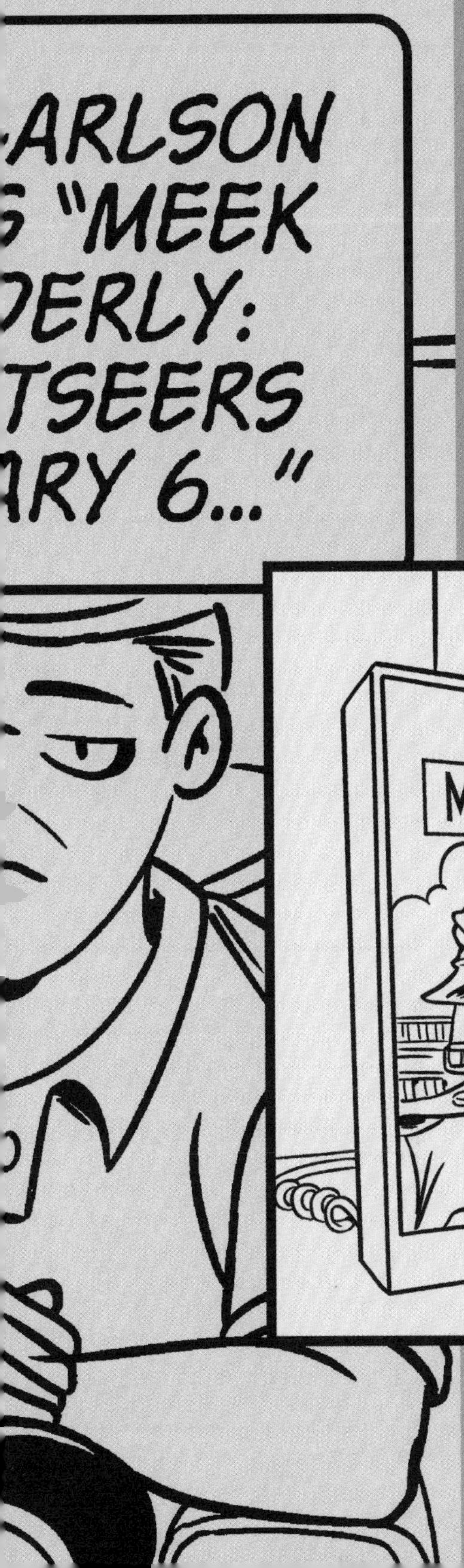

ARLSON
S "MEEK
DERLY:
TSEERS
ARY 6..."

PART 2

The Sightseers of January 6th

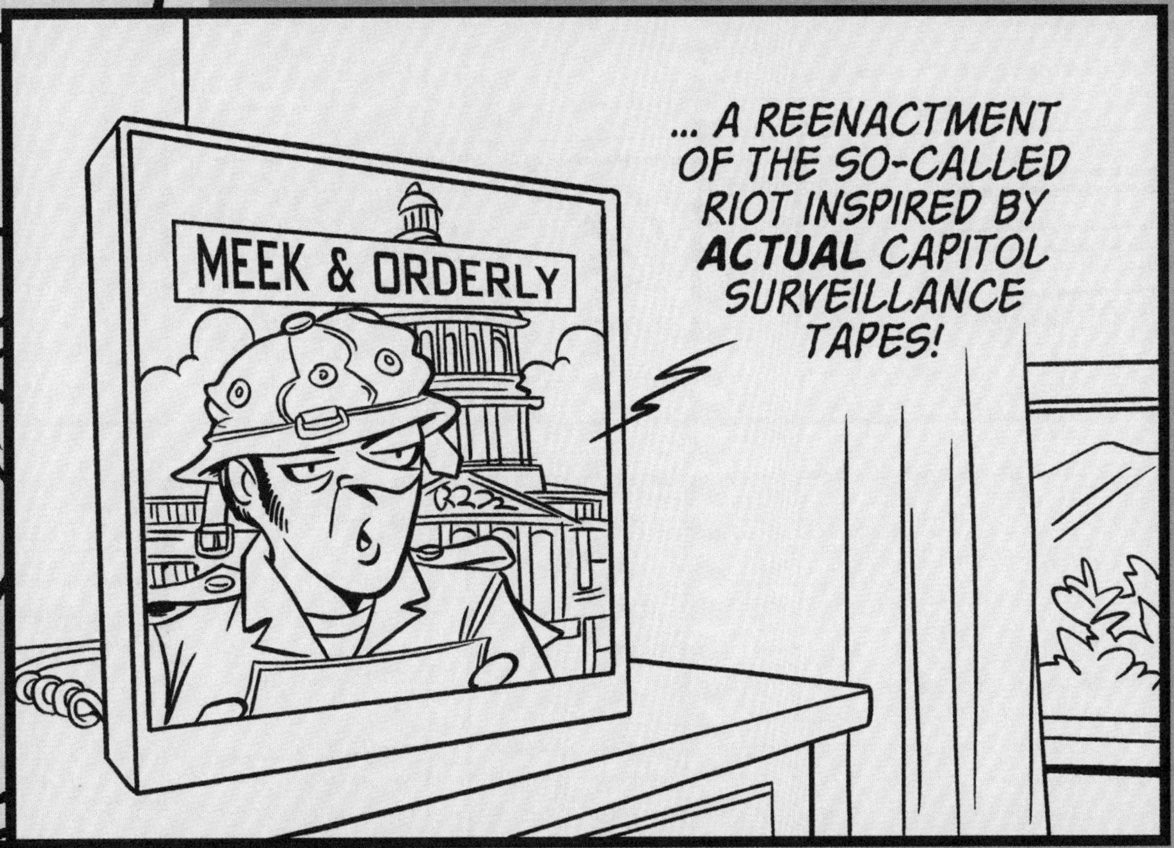

MEEK & ORDERLY
... A REENACTMENT OF THE SO-CALLED RIOT INSPIRED BY **ACTUAL** CAPITOL SURVEILLANCE TAPES!

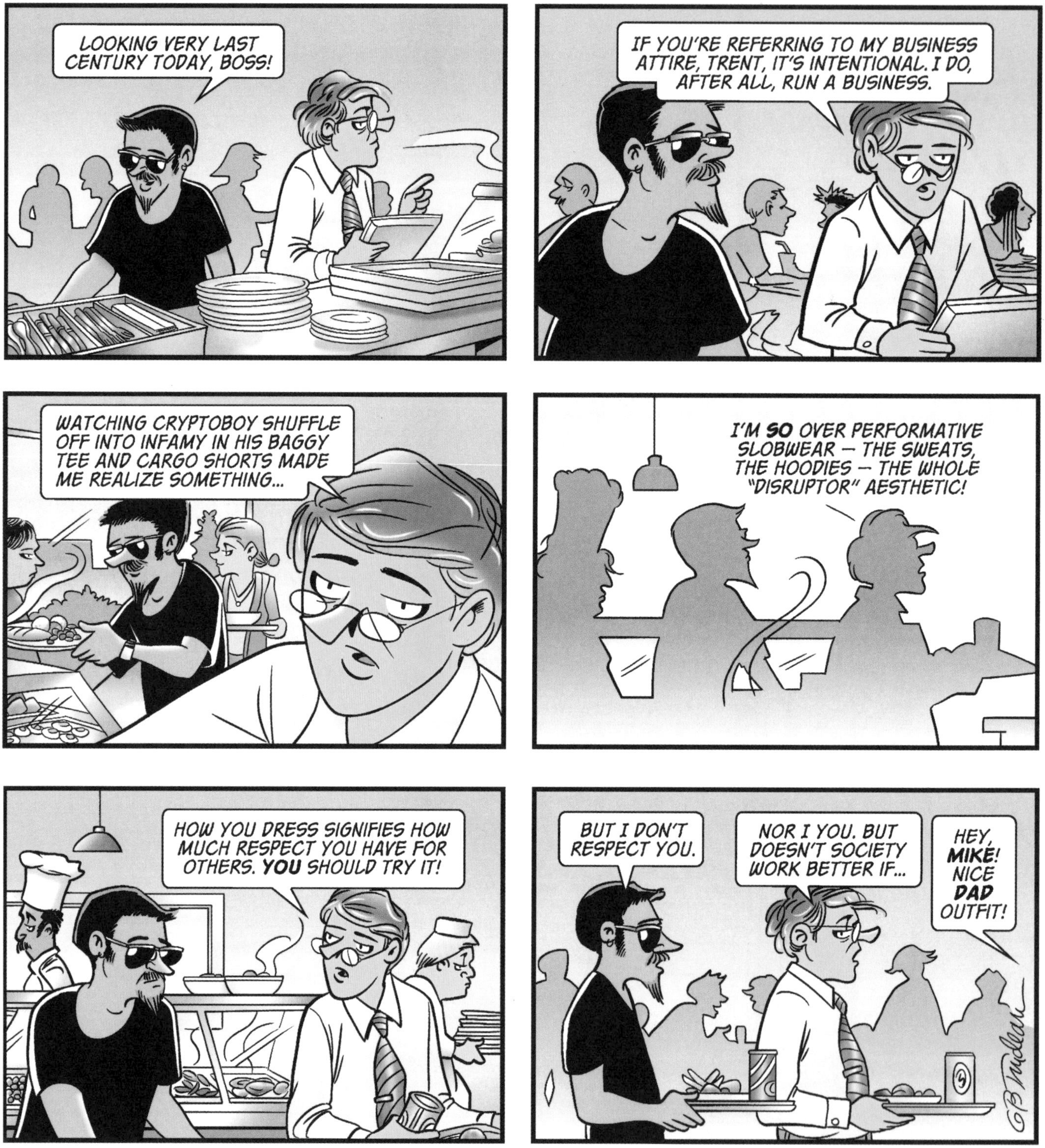
LOOKING VERY LAST CENTURY TODAY, BOSS!
IF YOU'RE REFERRING TO MY BUSINESS ATTIRE, TRENT, IT'S INTENTIONAL. I DO, AFTER ALL, RUN A BUSINESS.
WATCHING CRYPTOBOY SHUFFLE OFF INTO INFAMY IN HIS BAGGY TEE AND CARGO SHORTS MADE ME REALIZE SOMETHING...
I'M SO OVER PERFORMATIVE SLOBWEAR — THE SWEATS, THE HOODIES — THE WHOLE "DISRUPTOR" AESTHETIC!
HOW YOU DRESS SIGNIFIES HOW MUCH RESPECT YOU HAVE FOR OTHERS. YOU SHOULD TRY IT!
BUT I DON'T RESPECT YOU.
NOR I YOU. BUT DOESN'T SOCIETY WORK BETTER IF...
HEY, MIKE! NICE DAD OUTFIT!
GBTrudeau

January 22, 2023

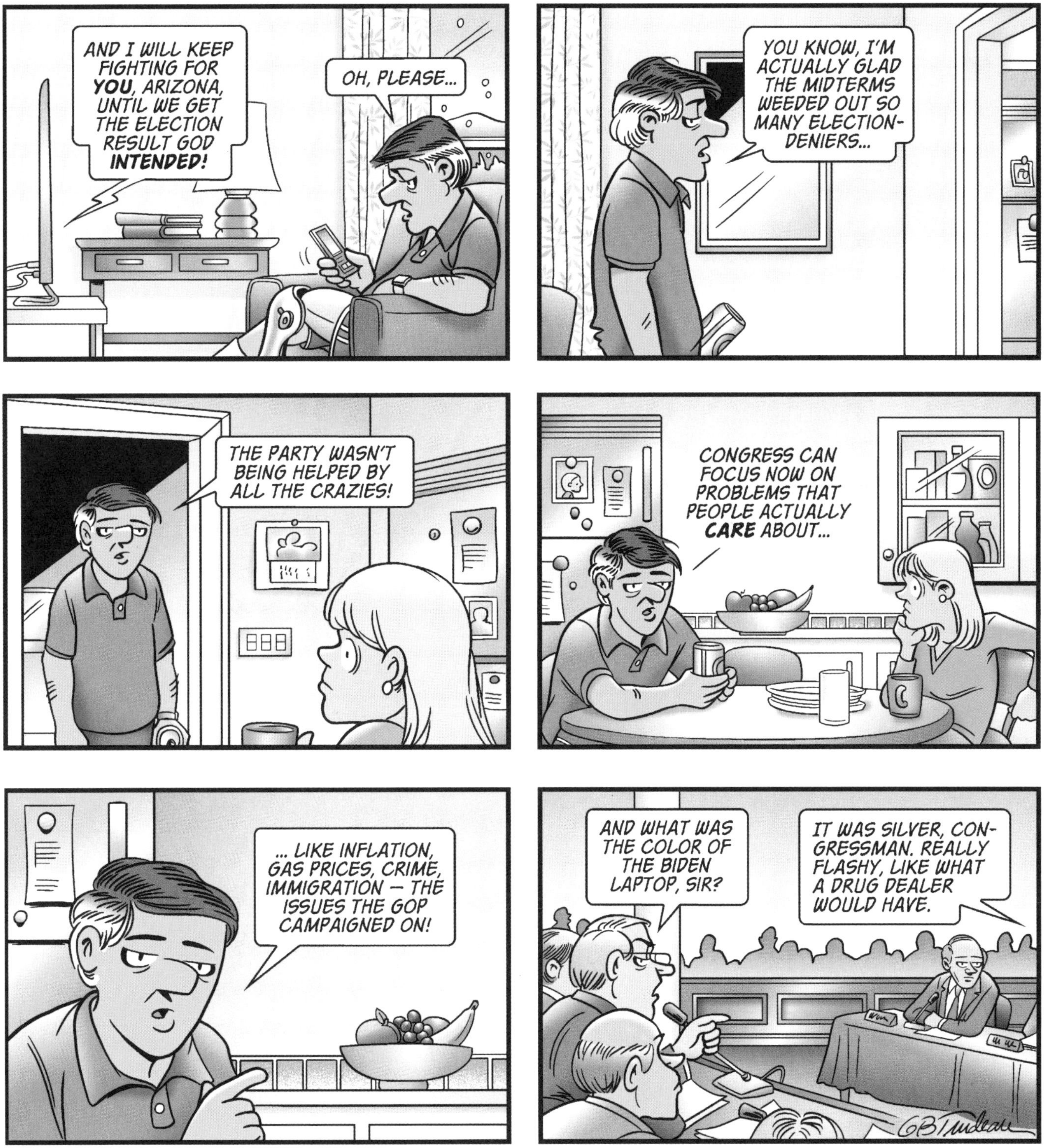
AND I WILL KEEP FIGHTING FOR YOU, ARIZONA, UNTIL WE GET THE ELECTION RESULT GOD INTENDED!
OH, PLEASE...
YOU KNOW, I'M ACTUALLY GLAD THE MIDTERMS WEEDED OUT SO MANY ELECTION-DENIERS...
THE PARTY WASN'T BEING HELPED BY ALL THE CRAZIES!
CONGRESS CAN FOCUS NOW ON PROBLEMS THAT PEOPLE ACTUALLY CARE ABOUT...
... LIKE INFLATION, GAS PRICES, CRIME, IMMIGRATION — THE ISSUES THE GOP CAMPAIGNED ON!
AND WHAT WAS THE COLOR OF THE BIDEN LAPTOP, SIR?
IT WAS SILVER, CONGRESSMAN. REALLY FLASHY, LIKE WHAT A DRUG DEALER WOULD HAVE.
GBTrudeau

January 29, 2023

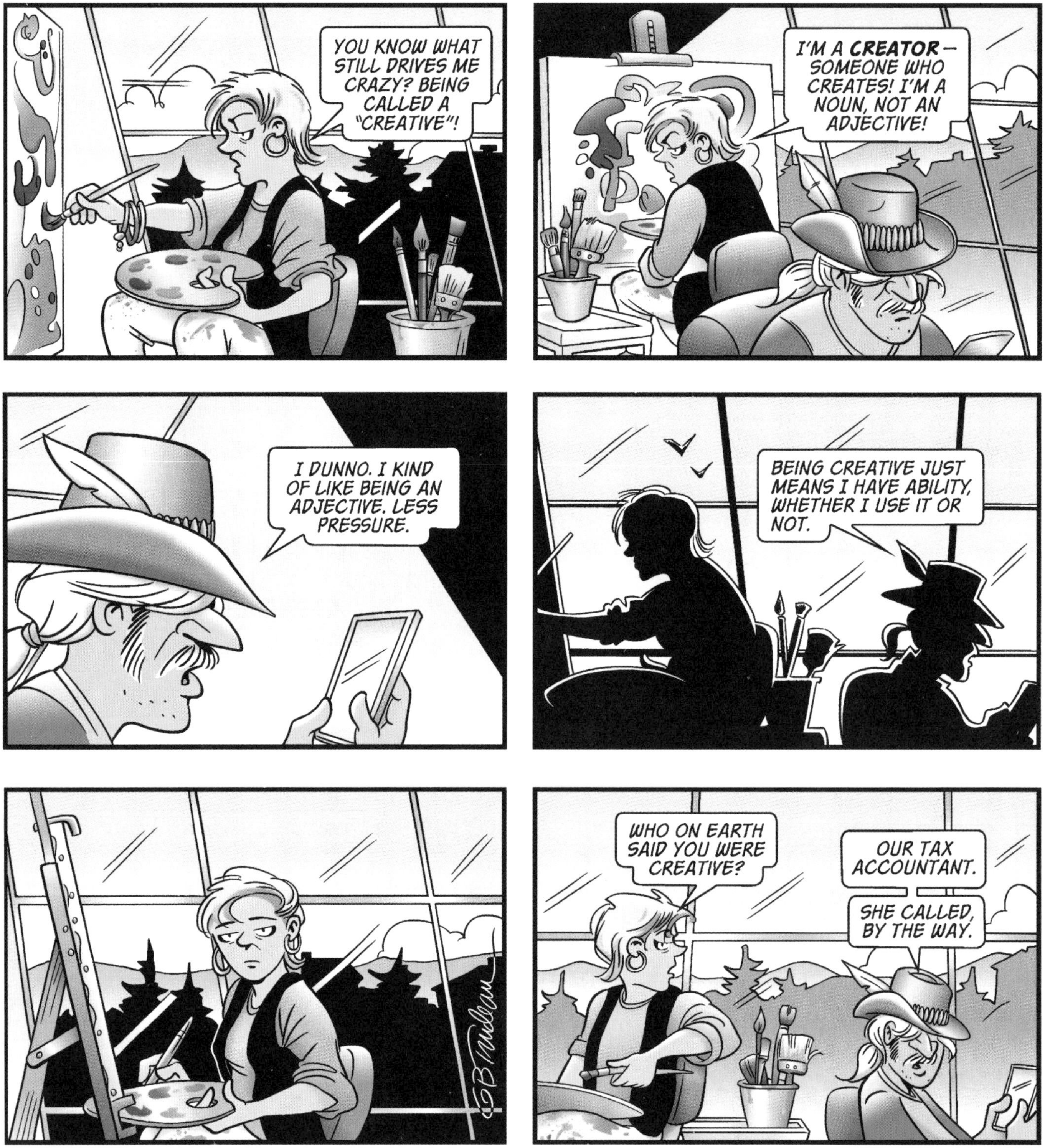
YOU KNOW WHAT STILL DRIVES ME CRAZY? BEING CALLED A "CREATIVE"!
I'M A **CREATOR** — SOMEONE WHO CREATES! I'M A NOUN, NOT AN ADJECTIVE!
I DUNNO. I KIND OF LIKE BEING AN ADJECTIVE. LESS PRESSURE.
BEING CREATIVE JUST MEANS I HAVE ABILITY, WHETHER I USE IT OR NOT.
WHO ON EARTH SAID YOU WERE CREATIVE?
OUR TAX ACCOUNTANT.
SHE CALLED, BY THE WAY.
GBTrudeau

February 5, 2023

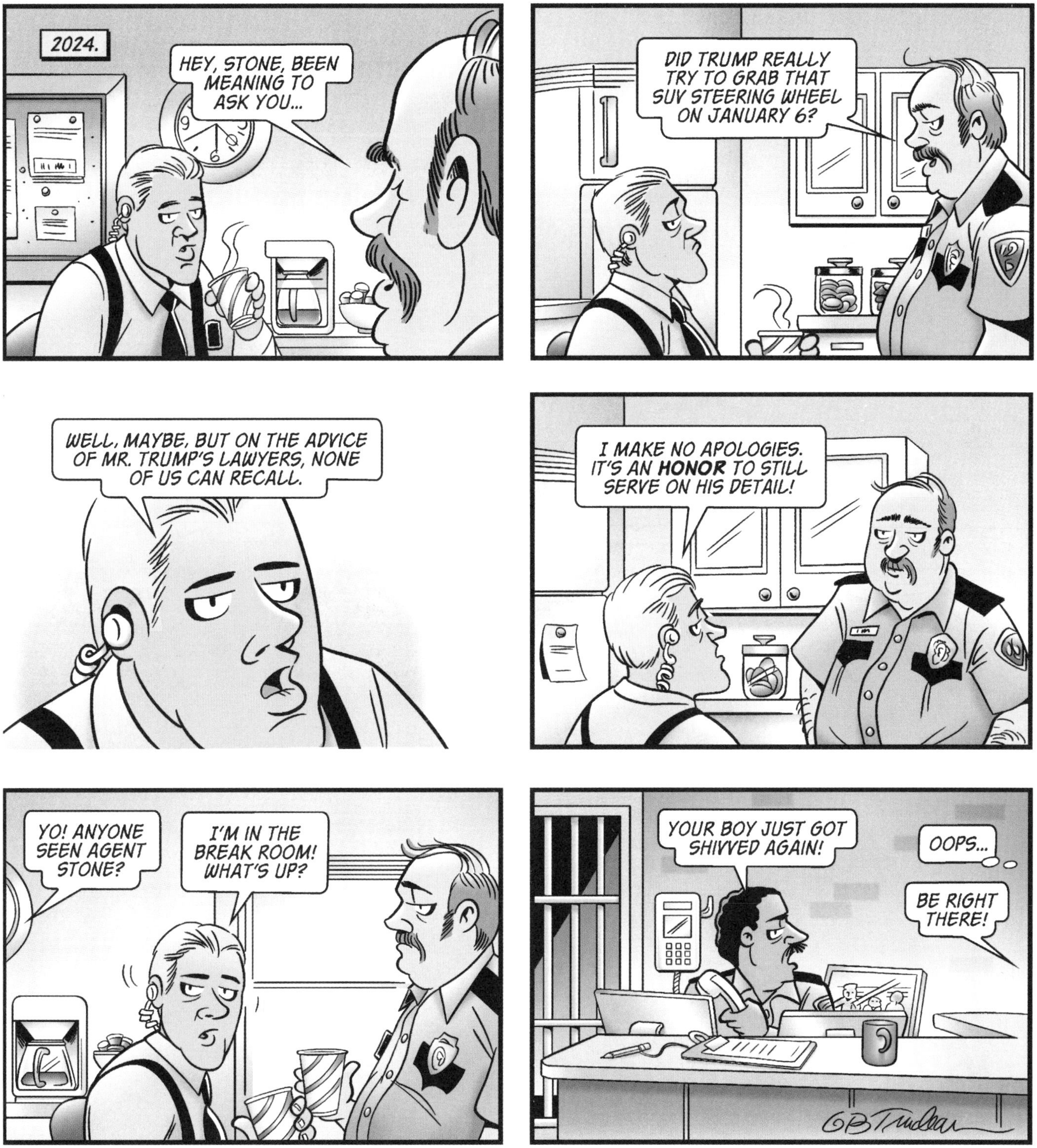
2024.
HEY, STONE, BEEN MEANING TO ASK YOU...
DID TRUMP REALLY TRY TO GRAB THAT SUV STEERING WHEEL ON JANUARY 6?
WELL, MAYBE, BUT ON THE ADVICE OF MR. TRUMP'S LAWYERS, NONE OF US CAN RECALL.
I MAKE NO APOLOGIES. IT'S AN **HONOR** TO STILL SERVE ON HIS DETAIL!
YO! ANYONE SEEN AGENT STONE?
I'M IN THE BREAK ROOM! WHAT'S UP?
YOUR BOY JUST GOT SHIVVED AGAIN!
OOPS...
BE RIGHT THERE!
GB Trudeau

February 12, 2023

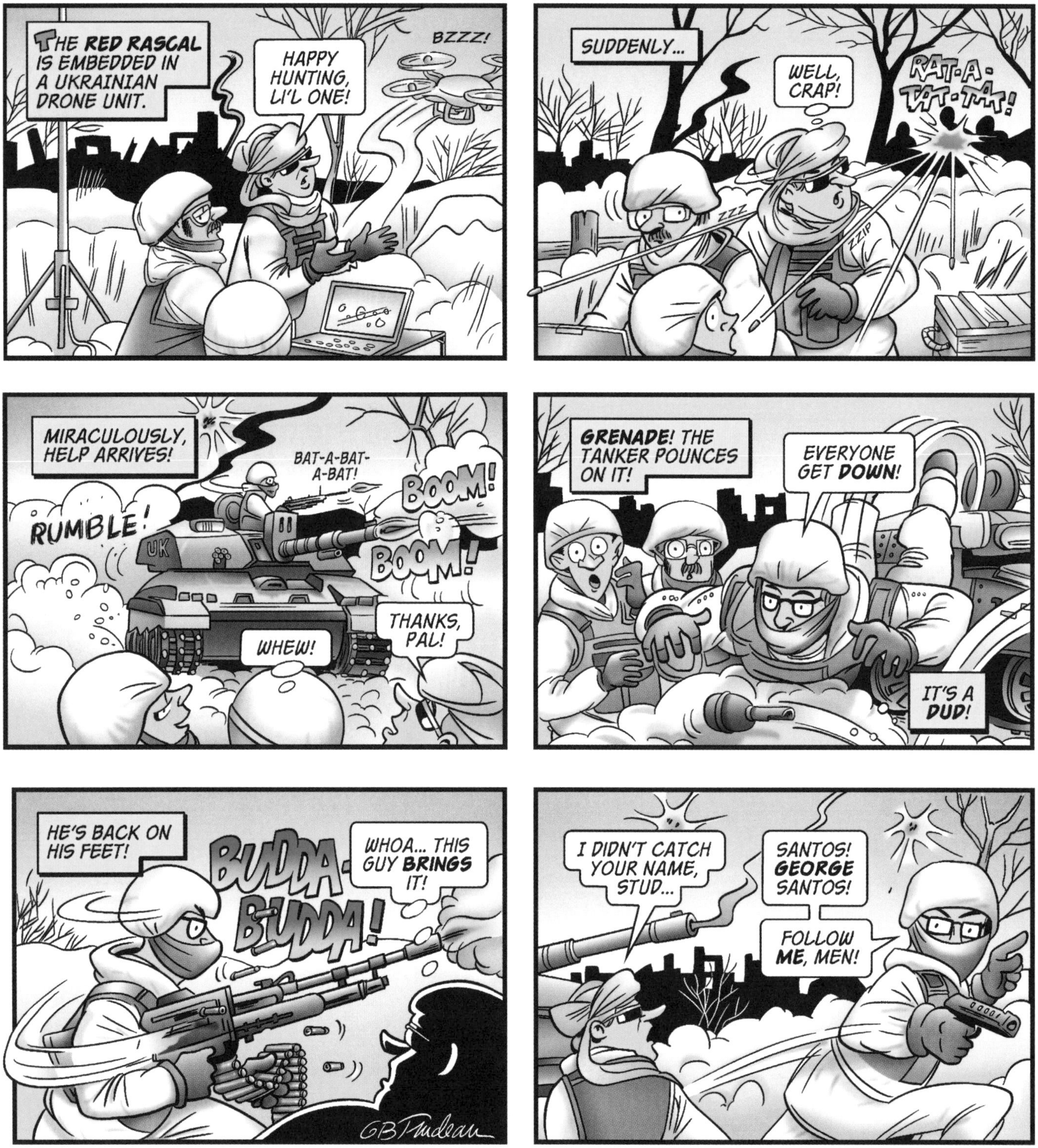
THE RED RASCAL IS EMBEDDED IN A UKRAINIAN DRONE UNIT.
HAPPY HUNTING, LI'L ONE!
BZZZ!
SUDDENLY...
WELL, CRAP!
RAT-A-TAT-TAT!
ZZZ
ZZIP
MIRACULOUSLY, HELP ARRIVES!
BAT-A-BAT-A-BAT!
BOOM!
RUMBLE!
UK
BOOM!
THANKS, PAL!
WHEW!
GRENADE! THE TANKER POUNCES ON IT!
EVERYONE GET DOWN!
IT'S A DUD!
HE'S BACK ON HIS FEET!
BUDDA-BUDDA!
WHOA... THIS GUY BRINGS IT!
GBTrudeau
I DIDN'T CATCH YOUR NAME, STUD...
SANTOS! GEORGE SANTOS!
FOLLOW ME, MEN!

February 19, 2023

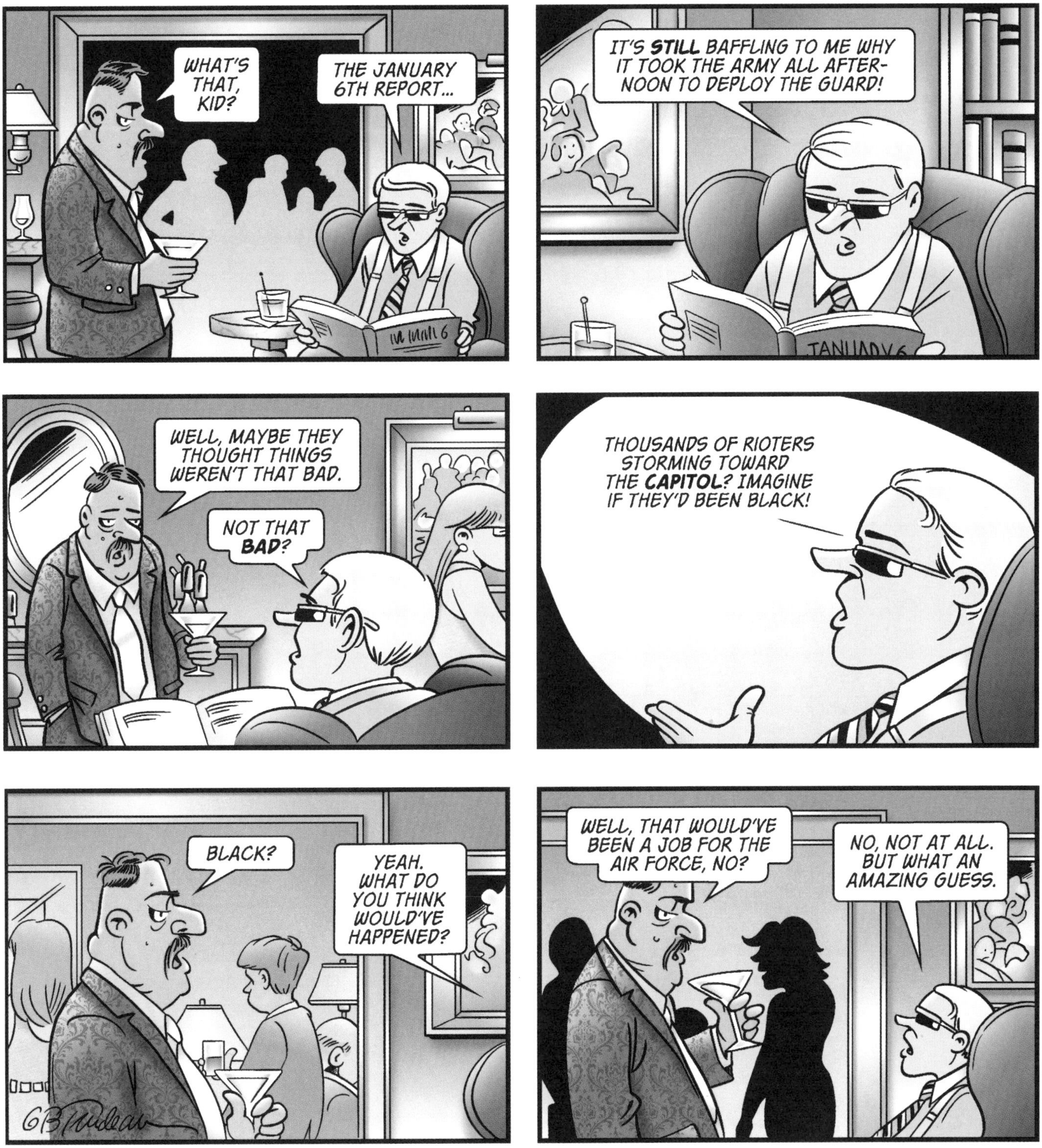

WHAT'S THAT, KID?
THE JANUARY 6TH REPORT...
IT'S STILL BAFFLING TO ME WHY IT TOOK THE ARMY ALL AFTERNOON TO DEPLOY THE GUARD!
WELL, MAYBE THEY THOUGHT THINGS WEREN'T THAT BAD.
NOT THAT BAD?
THOUSANDS OF RIOTERS STORMING TOWARD THE CAPITOL? IMAGINE IF THEY'D BEEN BLACK!
BLACK?
YEAH. WHAT DO YOU THINK WOULD'VE HAPPENED?
WELL, THAT WOULD'VE BEEN A JOB FOR THE AIR FORCE, NO?
NO, NOT AT ALL. BUT WHAT AN AMAZING GUESS.
GBTrudeau

February 26, 2023

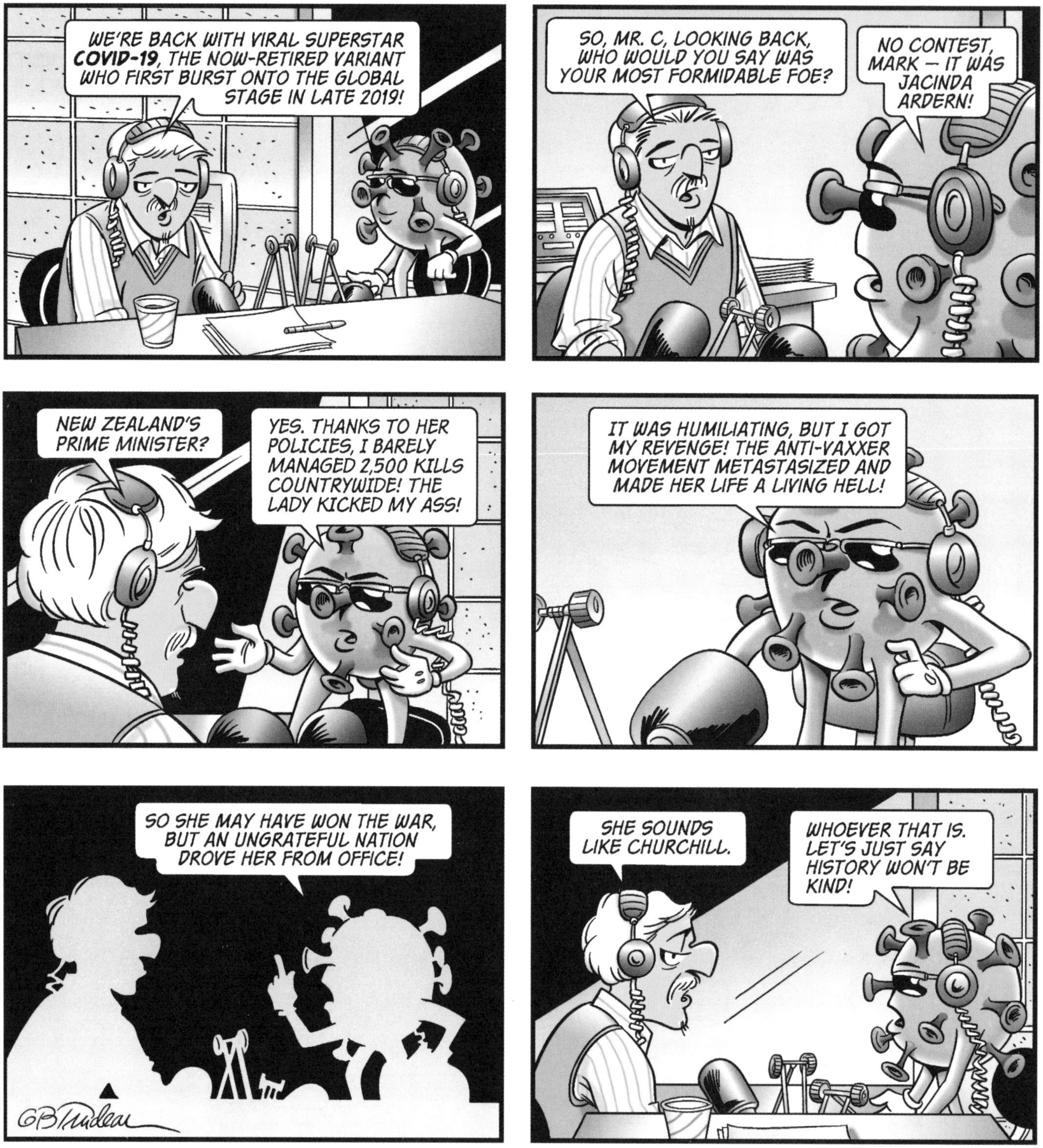
WE'RE BACK WITH VIRAL SUPERSTAR COVID-19, THE NOW-RETIRED VARIANT WHO FIRST BURST ONTO THE GLOBAL STAGE IN LATE 2019!
SO, MR. C, LOOKING BACK, WHO WOULD YOU SAY WAS YOUR MOST FORMIDABLE FOE?
NO CONTEST, MARK — IT WAS JACINDA ARDERN!
NEW ZEALAND'S PRIME MINISTER?
YES. THANKS TO HER POLICIES, I BARELY MANAGED 2,500 KILLS COUNTRYWIDE! THE LADY KICKED MY ASS!
IT WAS HUMILIATING, BUT I GOT MY REVENGE! THE ANTI-VAXXER MOVEMENT METASTASIZED AND MADE HER LIFE A LIVING HELL!
SO SHE MAY HAVE WON THE WAR, BUT AN UNGRATEFUL NATION DROVE HER FROM OFFICE!
GBTrudeau
SHE SOUNDS LIKE CHURCHILL.
WHOEVER THAT IS. LET'S JUST SAY HISTORY WON'T BE KIND!

March 5, 2023

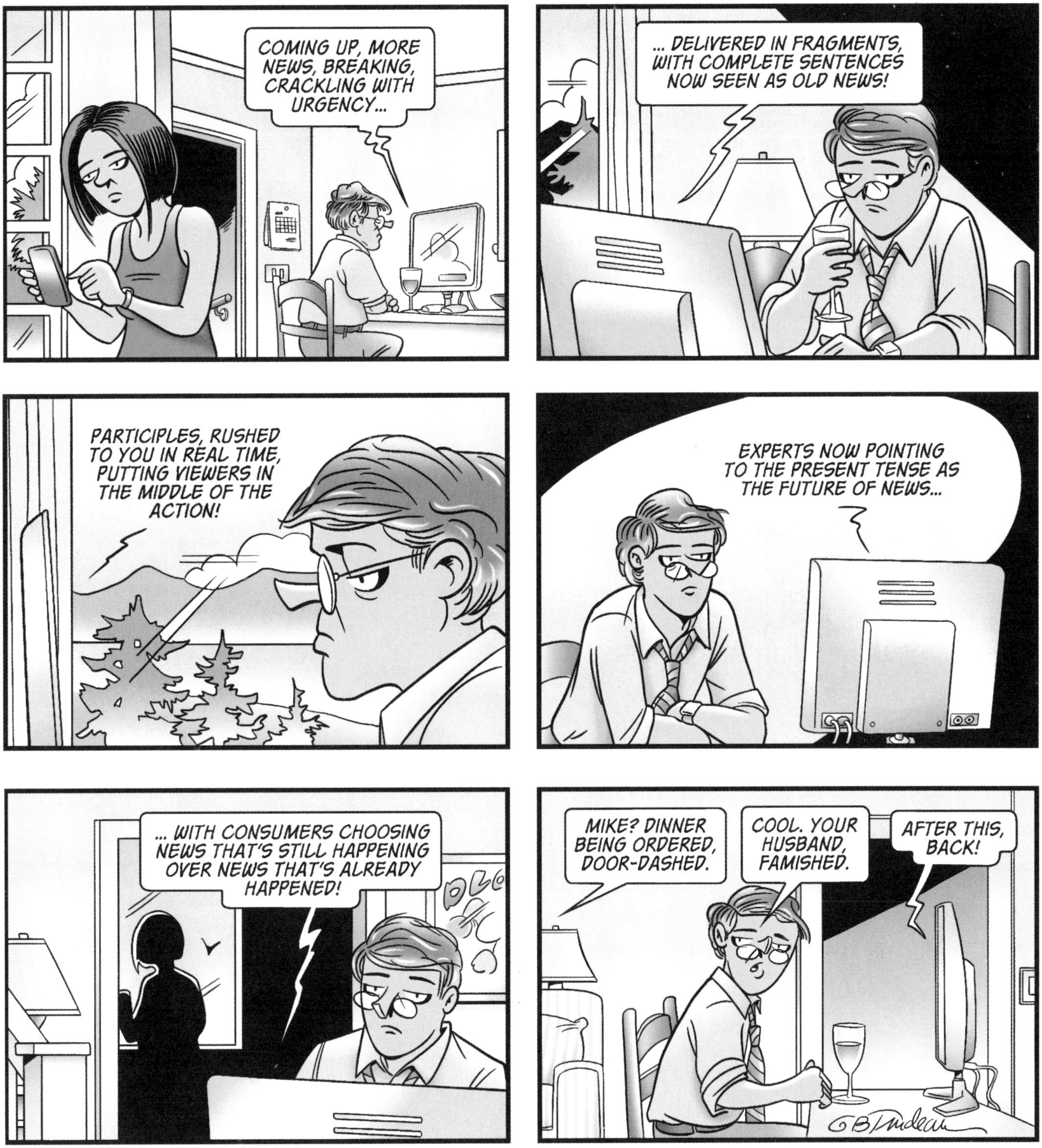
COMING UP, MORE NEWS, BREAKING, CRACKLING WITH URGENCY...
... DELIVERED IN FRAGMENTS, WITH COMPLETE SENTENCES NOW SEEN AS OLD NEWS!
PARTICIPLES, RUSHED TO YOU IN REAL TIME, PUTTING VIEWERS IN THE MIDDLE OF THE ACTION!
EXPERTS NOW POINTING TO THE PRESENT TENSE AS THE FUTURE OF NEWS...
... WITH CONSUMERS CHOOSING NEWS THAT'S STILL HAPPENING OVER NEWS THAT'S ALREADY HAPPENED!
MIKE? DINNER BEING ORDERED, DOOR-DASHED.
COOL. YOUR HUSBAND, FAMISHED.
AFTER THIS, BACK!
G B Trudeau

March 12, 2023

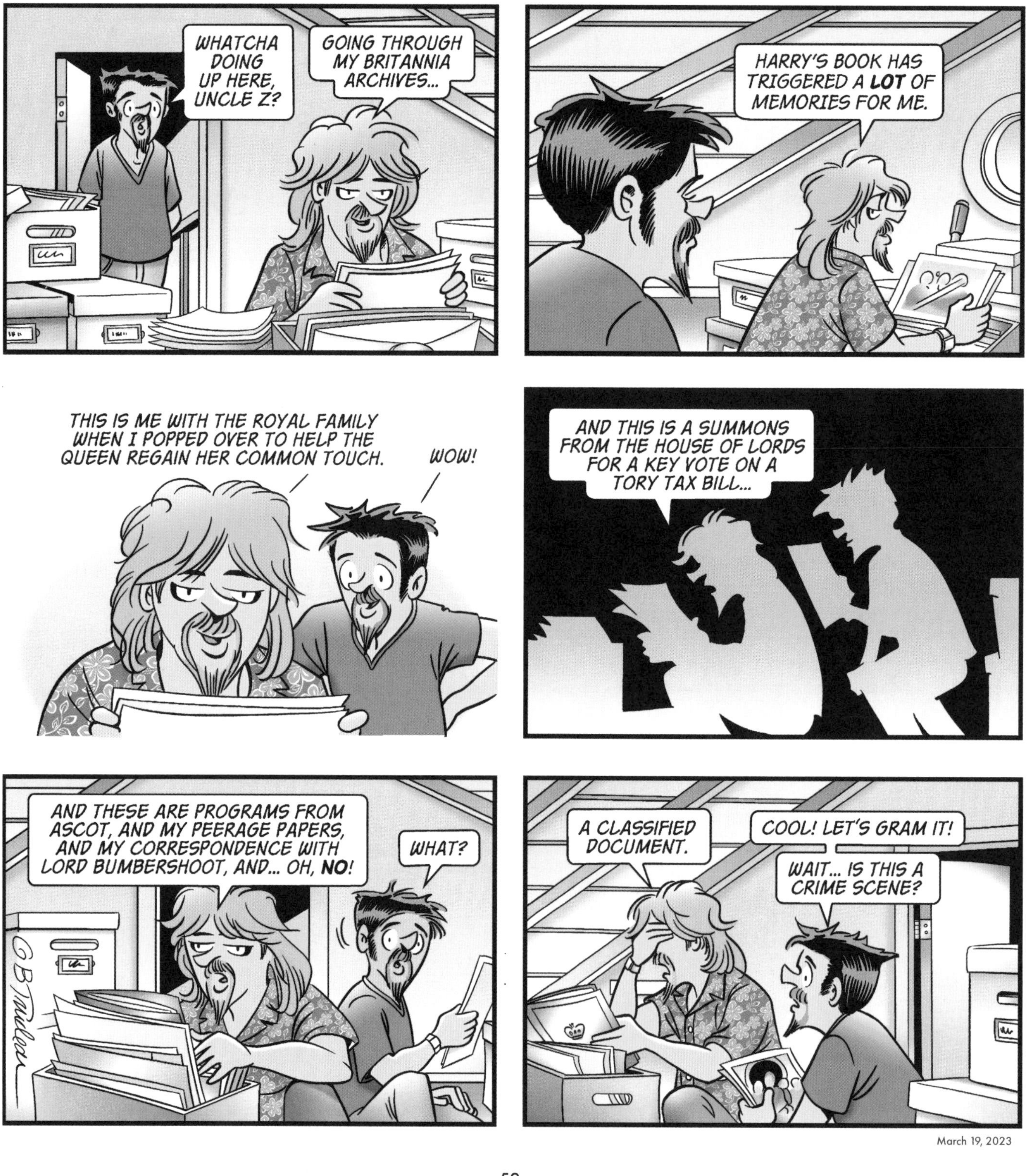
WHATCHA DOING UP HERE, UNCLE Z?
GOING THROUGH MY BRITANNIA ARCHIVES...
HARRY'S BOOK HAS TRIGGERED A **LOT** OF MEMORIES FOR ME.
THIS IS ME WITH THE ROYAL FAMILY WHEN I POPPED OVER TO HELP THE QUEEN REGAIN HER COMMON TOUCH.
WOW!
AND THIS IS A SUMMONS FROM THE HOUSE OF LORDS FOR A KEY VOTE ON A TORY TAX BILL...
AND THESE ARE PROGRAMS FROM ASCOT, AND MY PEERAGE PAPERS, AND MY CORRESPONDENCE WITH LORD BUMBERSHOOT, AND... OH, **NO**!
WHAT?
A CLASSIFIED DOCUMENT.
COOL! LET'S GRAM IT!
WAIT... IS THIS A CRIME SCENE?
G B Trudeau

March 19, 2023

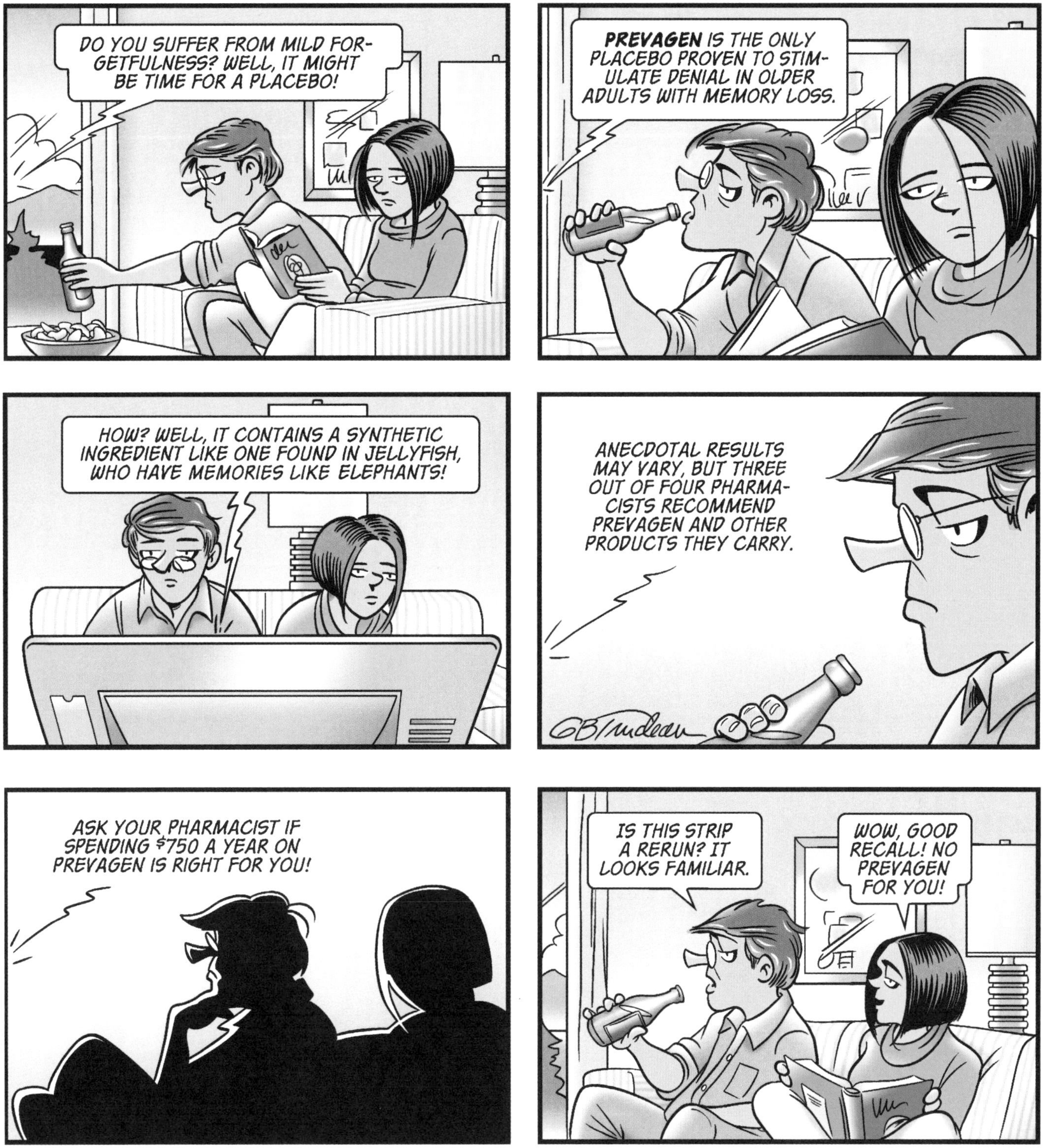
DO YOU SUFFER FROM MILD FORGETFULNESS? WELL, IT MIGHT BE TIME FOR A PLACEBO!
PREVAGEN IS THE ONLY PLACEBO PROVEN TO STIMULATE DENIAL IN OLDER ADULTS WITH MEMORY LOSS.
HOW? WELL, IT CONTAINS A SYNTHETIC INGREDIENT LIKE ONE FOUND IN JELLYFISH, WHO HAVE MEMORIES LIKE ELEPHANTS!
ANECDOTAL RESULTS MAY VARY, BUT THREE OUT OF FOUR PHARMACISTS RECOMMEND PREVAGEN AND OTHER PRODUCTS THEY CARRY.
GBTrudeau
ASK YOUR PHARMACIST IF SPENDING $750 A YEAR ON PREVAGEN IS RIGHT FOR YOU!
IS THIS STRIP A RERUN? IT LOOKS FAMILIAR.
WOW, GOOD RECALL! NO PREVAGEN FOR YOU!

March 26, 2023

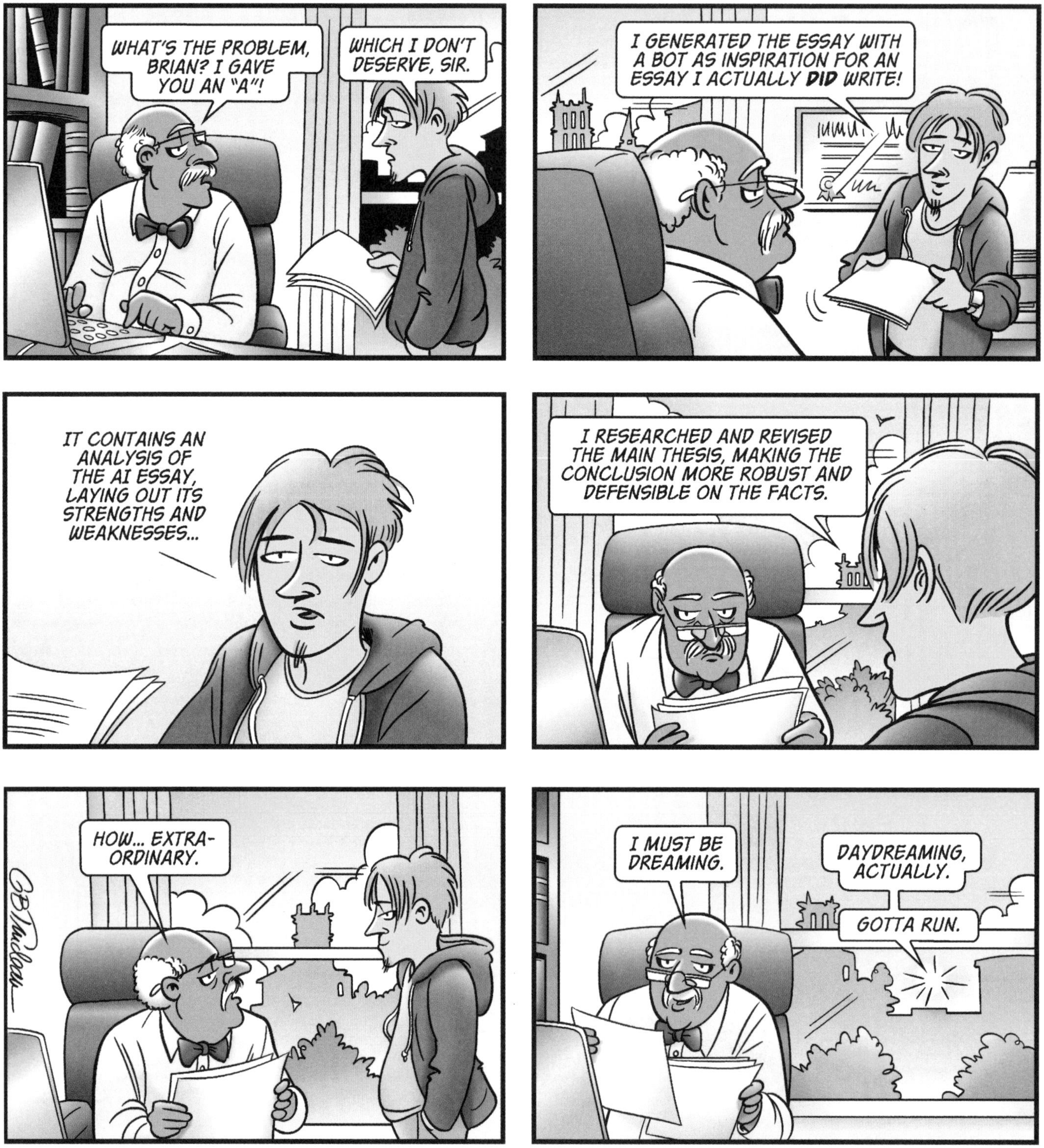
WHAT'S THE PROBLEM, BRIAN? I GAVE YOU AN "A"!
WHICH I DON'T DESERVE, SIR.
I GENERATED THE ESSAY WITH A BOT AS INSPIRATION FOR AN ESSAY I ACTUALLY **DID** WRITE!
IT CONTAINS AN ANALYSIS OF THE AI ESSAY, LAYING OUT ITS STRENGTHS AND WEAKNESSES...
I RESEARCHED AND REVISED THE MAIN THESIS, MAKING THE CONCLUSION MORE ROBUST AND DEFENSIBLE ON THE FACTS.
HOW... EXTRA-ORDINARY.
I MUST BE DREAMING.
DAYDREAMING, ACTUALLY.
GOTTA RUN.

April 2, 2023

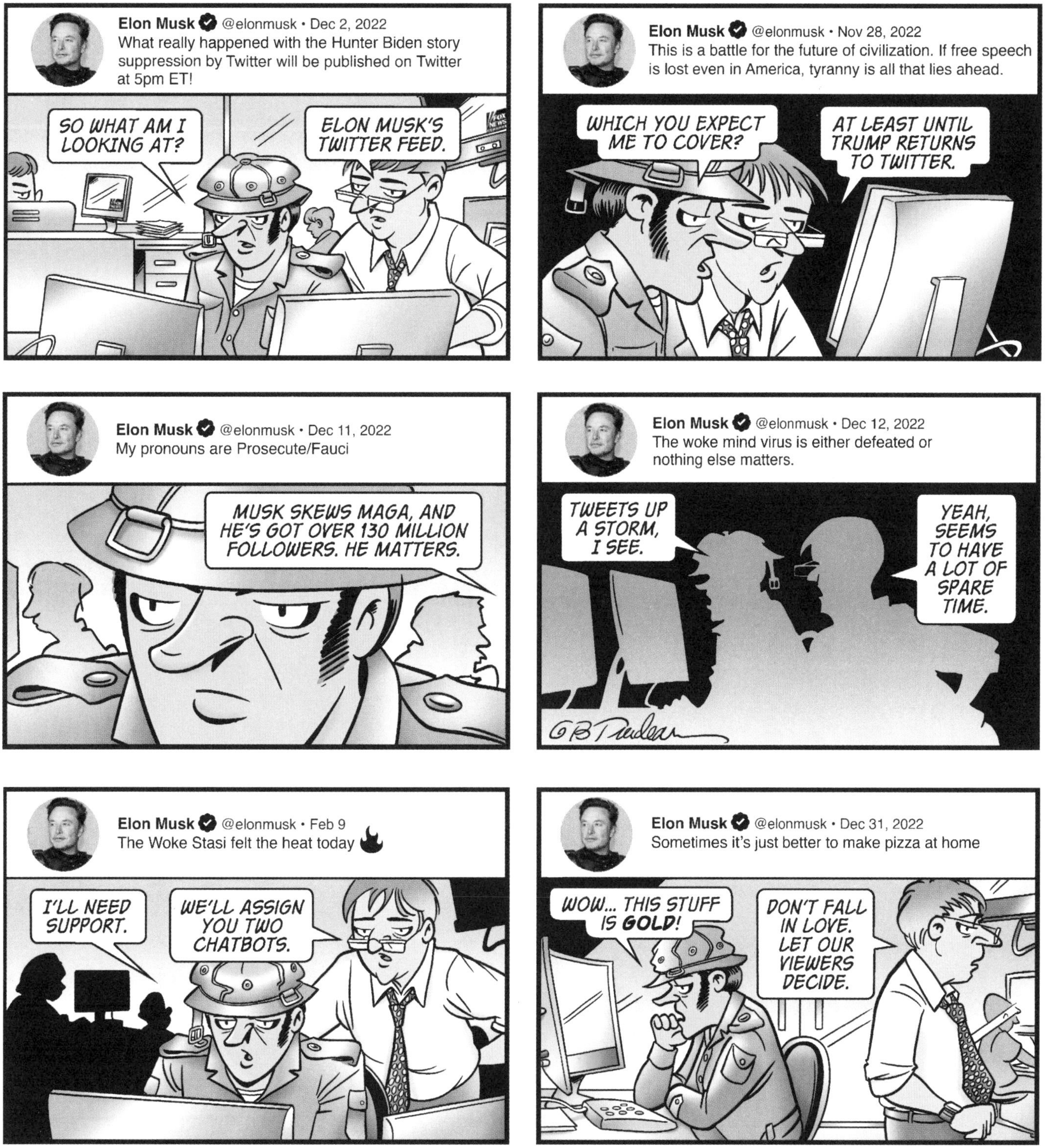
Elon Musk @elonmusk • Dec 2, 2022
What really happened with the Hunter Biden story suppression by Twitter will be published on Twitter at 5pm ET!
SO WHAT AM I LOOKING AT?
ELON MUSK'S TWITTER FEED.
Elon Musk @elonmusk • Nov 28, 2022
This is a battle for the future of civilization. If free speech is lost even in America, tyranny is all that lies ahead.
WHICH YOU EXPECT ME TO COVER?
AT LEAST UNTIL TRUMP RETURNS TO TWITTER.
Elon Musk @elonmusk • Dec 11, 2022
My pronouns are Prosecute/Fauci
MUSK SKEWS MAGA, AND HE'S GOT OVER 130 MILLION FOLLOWERS. HE MATTERS.
Elon Musk @elonmusk • Dec 12, 2022
The woke mind virus is either defeated or nothing else matters.
TWEETS UP A STORM, I SEE.
YEAH, SEEMS TO HAVE A LOT OF SPARE TIME.
GB Trudeau
Elon Musk @elonmusk • Feb 9
The Woke Stasi felt the heat today
I'LL NEED SUPPORT.
WE'LL ASSIGN YOU TWO CHATBOTS.
Elon Musk @elonmusk • Dec 31, 2022
Sometimes it's just better to make pizza at home
WOW... THIS STUFF IS GOLD!
DON'T FALL IN LOVE. LET OUR VIEWERS DECIDE.

April 16, 2023

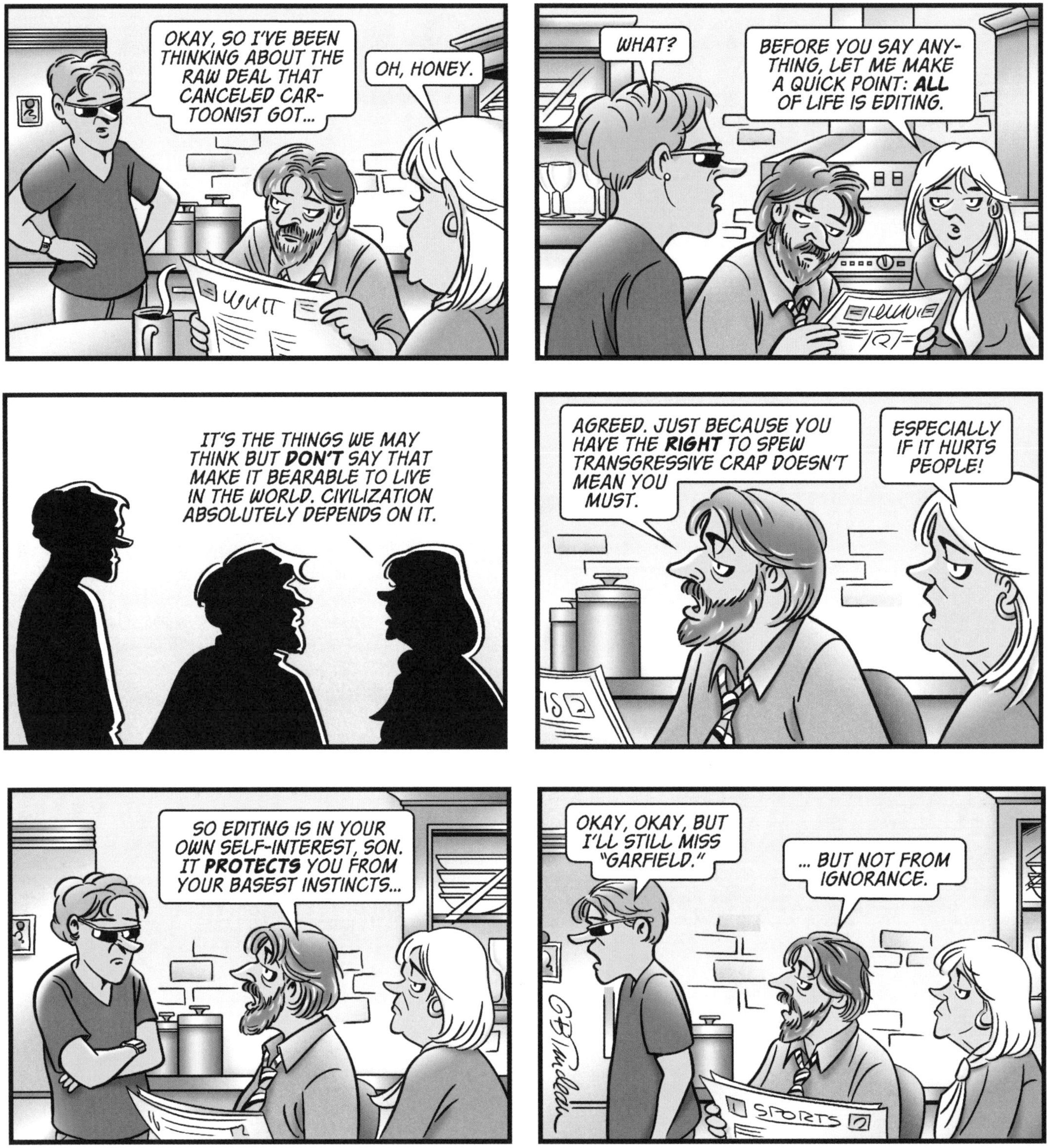

OKAY, SO I'VE BEEN THINKING ABOUT THE RAW DEAL THAT CANCELED CAR-TOONIST GOT...
OH, HONEY.
WHAT?
BEFORE YOU SAY ANY-THING, LET ME MAKE A QUICK POINT: **ALL** OF LIFE IS EDITING.
IT'S THE THINGS WE MAY THINK BUT **DON'T** SAY THAT MAKE IT BEARABLE TO LIVE IN THE WORLD. CIVILIZATION ABSOLUTELY DEPENDS ON IT.
AGREED. JUST BECAUSE YOU HAVE THE **RIGHT** TO SPEW TRANSGRESSIVE CRAP DOESN'T MEAN YOU MUST.
ESPECIALLY IF IT HURTS PEOPLE!
SO EDITING IS IN YOUR OWN SELF-INTEREST, SON. IT **PROTECTS** YOU FROM YOUR BASEST INSTINCTS...
OKAY, OKAY, BUT I'LL STILL MISS "GARFIELD."
... BUT NOT FROM IGNORANCE.
SPORTS

April 9, 2022

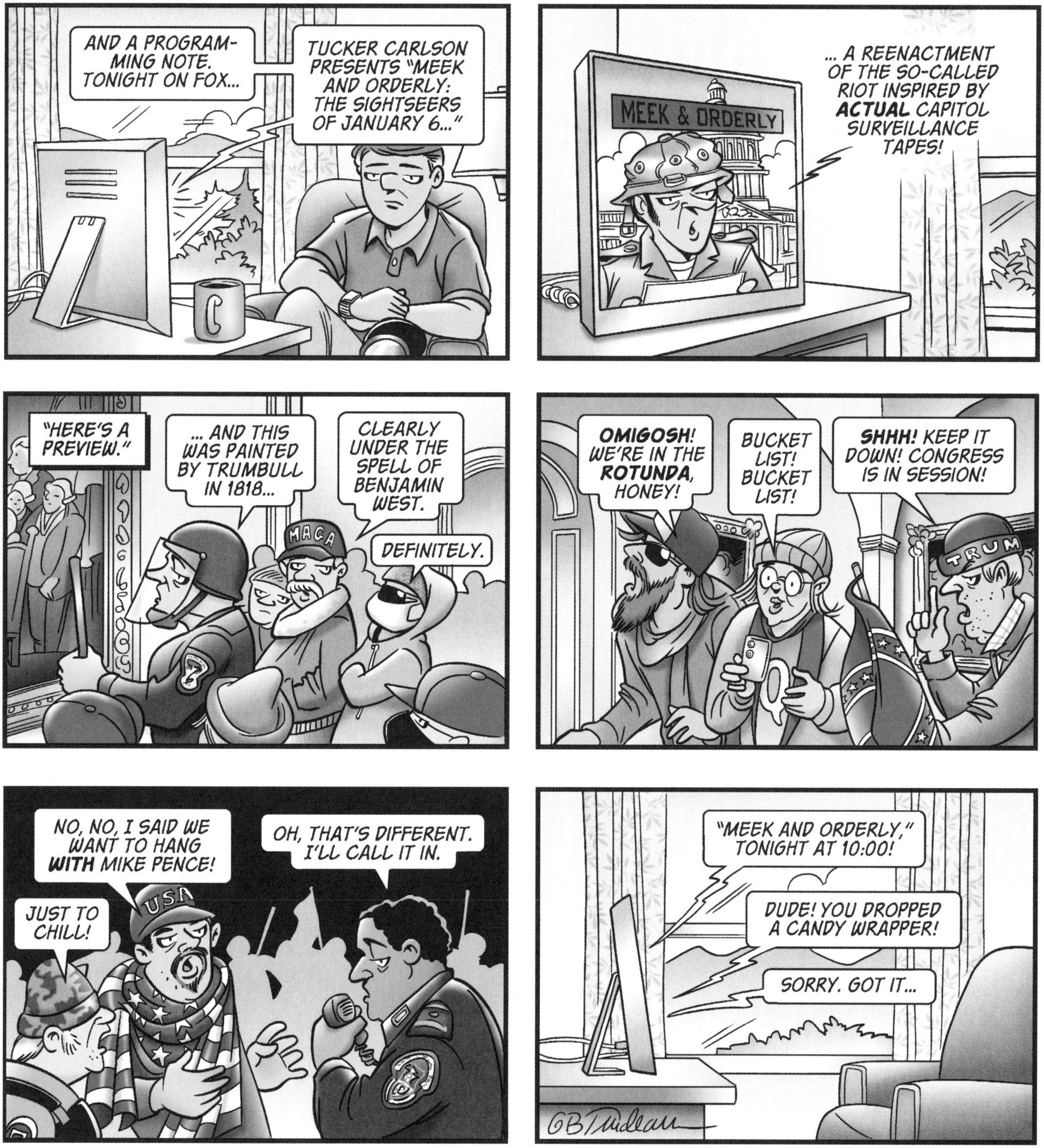
AND A PROGRAM-MING NOTE. TONIGHT ON FOX...
TUCKER CARLSON PRESENTS "MEEK AND ORDERLY: THE SIGHTSEERS OF JANUARY 6..."
MEEK & ORDERLY
... A REENACTMENT OF THE SO-CALLED RIOT INSPIRED BY **ACTUAL** CAPITOL SURVEILLANCE TAPES!
"HERE'S A PREVIEW."
... AND THIS WAS PAINTED BY TRUMBULL IN 1818...
MAGA
CLEARLY UNDER THE SPELL OF BENJAMIN WEST.
DEFINITELY.
OMIGOSH! WE'RE IN THE **ROTUNDA**, HONEY!
BUCKET LIST! BUCKET LIST!
SHHH! KEEP IT DOWN! CONGRESS IS IN SESSION!
TRUM
NO, NO, I SAID WE WANT TO HANG **WITH** MIKE PENCE!
USA
JUST TO CHILL!
OH, THAT'S DIFFERENT. I'LL CALL IT IN.
"MEEK AND ORDERLY," TONIGHT AT 10:00!
DUDE! YOU DROPPED A CANDY WRAPPER!
SORRY. GOT IT...
GBTrudeau

April 23, 2023

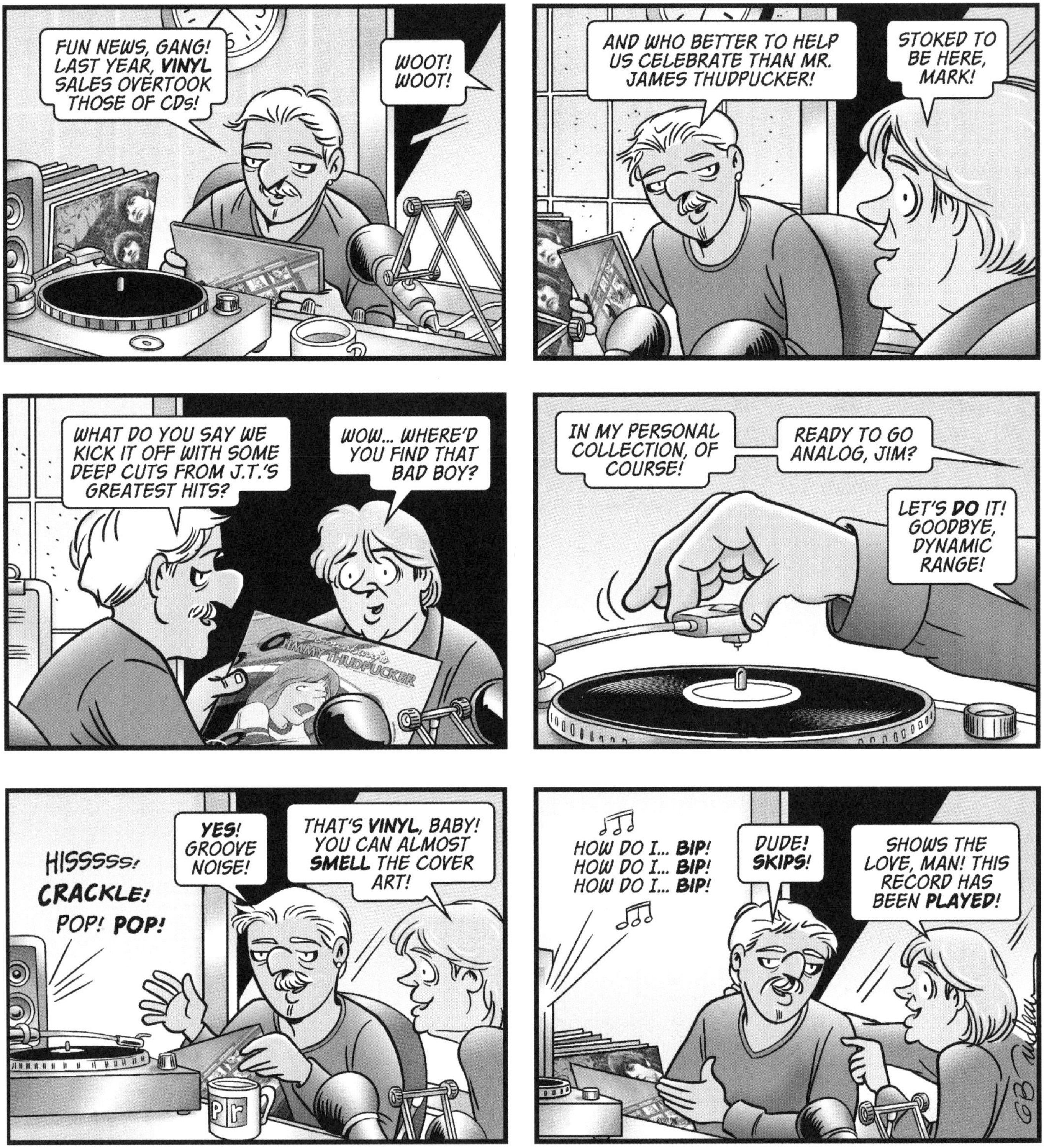
FUN NEWS, GANG! LAST YEAR, VINYL SALES OVERTOOK THOSE OF CDs!
WOOT! WOOT!
AND WHO BETTER TO HELP US CELEBRATE THAN MR. JAMES THUDPUCKER!
STOKED TO BE HERE, MARK!
WHAT DO YOU SAY WE KICK IT OFF WITH SOME DEEP CUTS FROM J.T.'S GREATEST HITS?
WOW... WHERE'D YOU FIND THAT BAD BOY?
JIMMY THUDPUCKER
IN MY PERSONAL COLLECTION, OF COURSE!
READY TO GO ANALOG, JIM?
LET'S DO IT! GOODBYE, DYNAMIC RANGE!
HISSSSS!
CRACKLE!
POP! POP!
YES! GROOVE NOISE!
THAT'S VINYL, BABY! YOU CAN ALMOST SMELL THE COVER ART!
HOW DO I... BIP! HOW DO I... BIP! HOW DO I... BIP!
DUDE! SKIPS!
SHOWS THE LOVE, MAN! THIS RECORD HAS BEEN PLAYED!

April 30, 2023

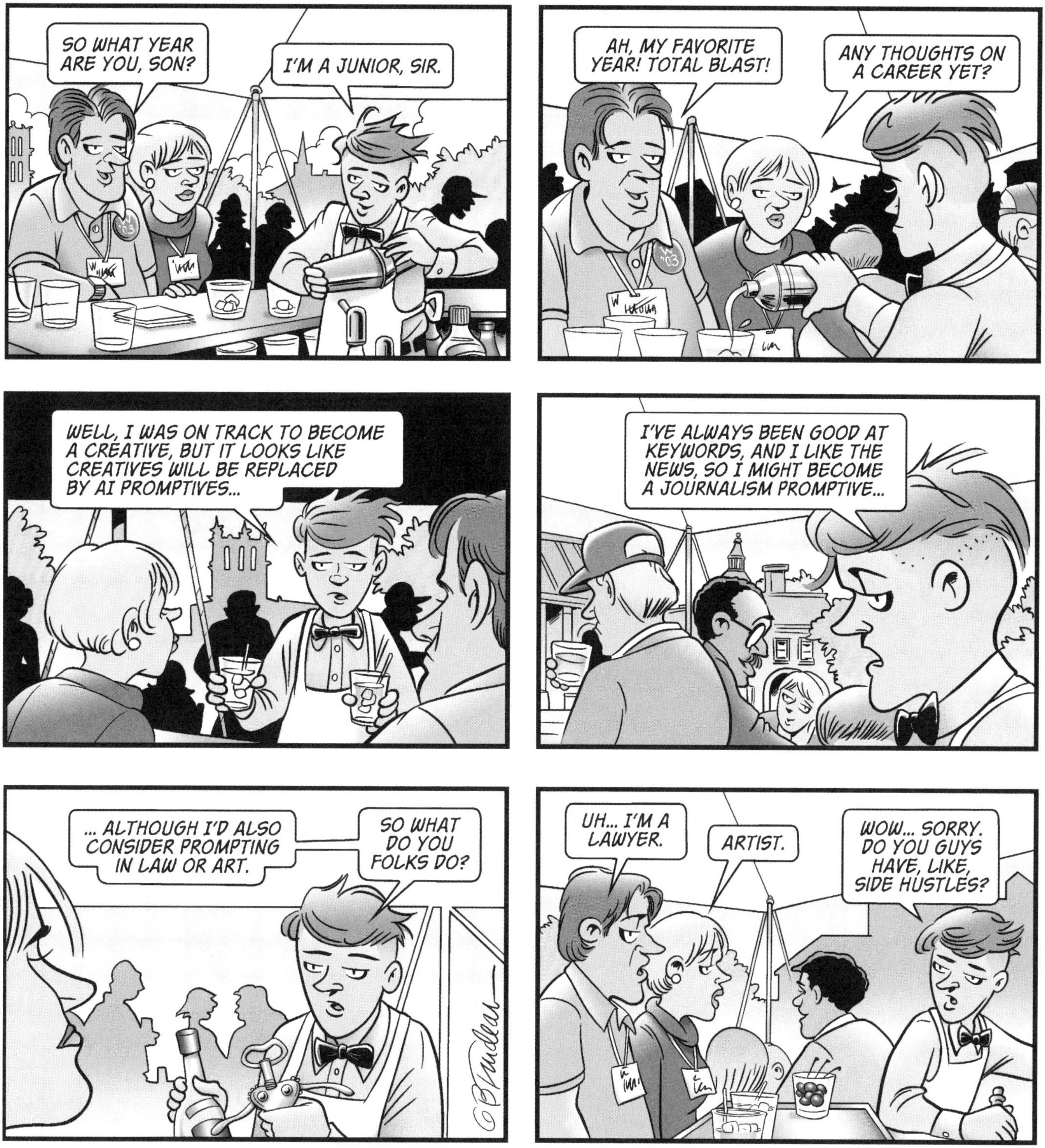
SO WHAT YEAR ARE YOU, SON?
I'M A JUNIOR, SIR.
AH, MY FAVORITE YEAR! TOTAL BLAST!
ANY THOUGHTS ON A CAREER YET?
WELL, I WAS ON TRACK TO BECOME A CREATIVE, BUT IT LOOKS LIKE CREATIVES WILL BE REPLACED BY AI PROMPTIVES...
I'VE ALWAYS BEEN GOOD AT KEYWORDS, AND I LIKE THE NEWS, SO I MIGHT BECOME A JOURNALISM PROMPTIVE...
... ALTHOUGH I'D ALSO CONSIDER PROMPTING IN LAW OR ART.
SO WHAT DO YOU FOLKS DO?
UH... I'M A LAWYER.
ARTIST.
WOW... SORRY. DO YOU GUYS HAVE, LIKE, SIDE HUSTLES?
©BTrudeau

May 7, 2023

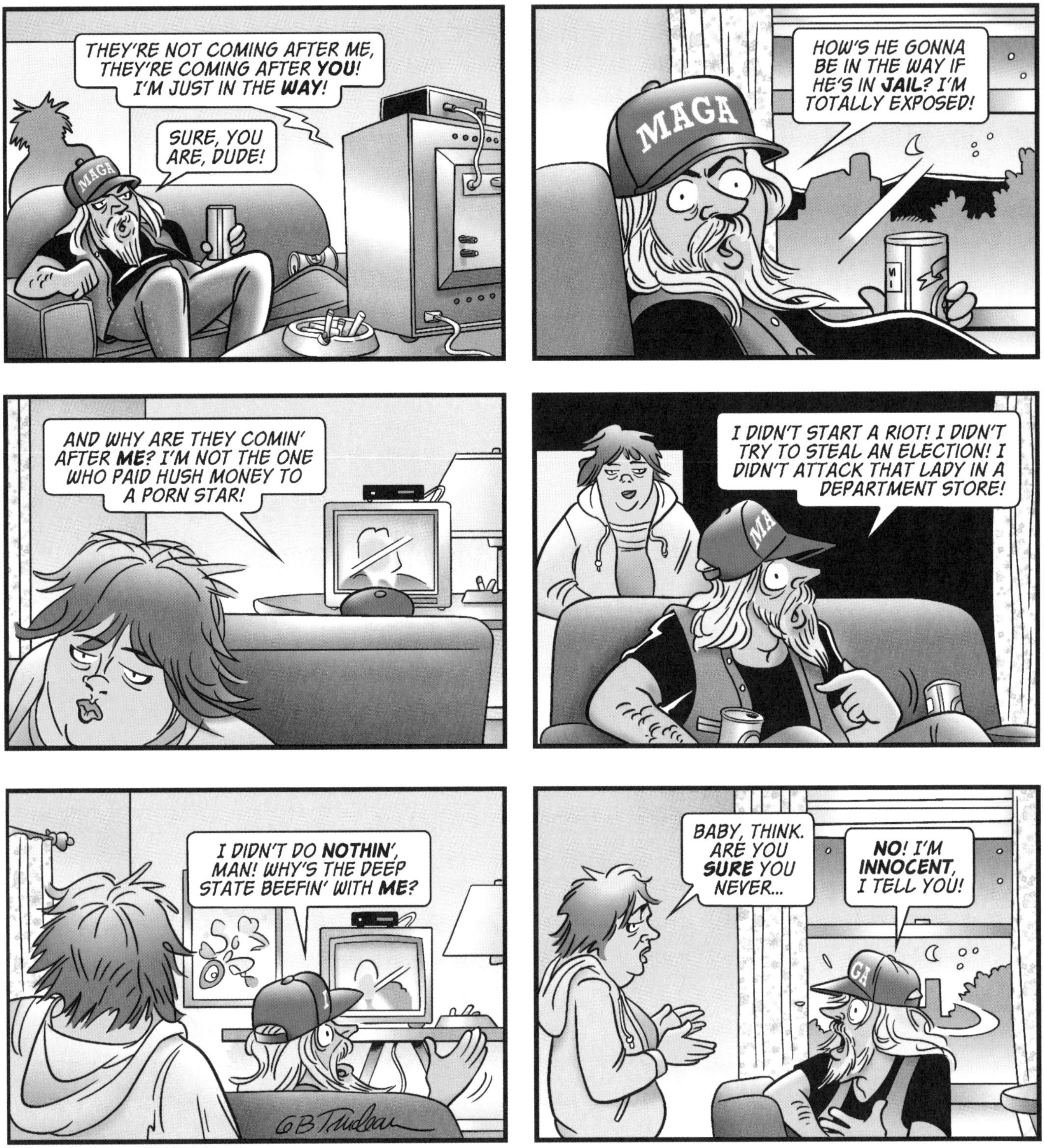
THEY'RE NOT COMING AFTER ME, THEY'RE COMING AFTER **YOU**! I'M JUST IN THE **WAY**!
SURE, YOU ARE, DUDE!
MAGA
HOW'S HE GONNA BE IN THE WAY IF HE'S IN **JAIL**? I'M TOTALLY EXPOSED!
MAGA
AND WHY ARE THEY COMIN' AFTER **ME**? I'M NOT THE ONE WHO PAID HUSH MONEY TO A PORN STAR!
I DIDN'T START A RIOT! I DIDN'T TRY TO STEAL AN ELECTION! I DIDN'T ATTACK THAT LADY IN A DEPARTMENT STORE!
I DIDN'T DO **NOTHIN'**, MAN! WHY'S THE DEEP STATE BEEFIN' WITH **ME**?
BABY, THINK. ARE YOU **SURE** YOU NEVER...
NO! I'M **INNOCENT**, I TELL YOU!

May 14, 2023

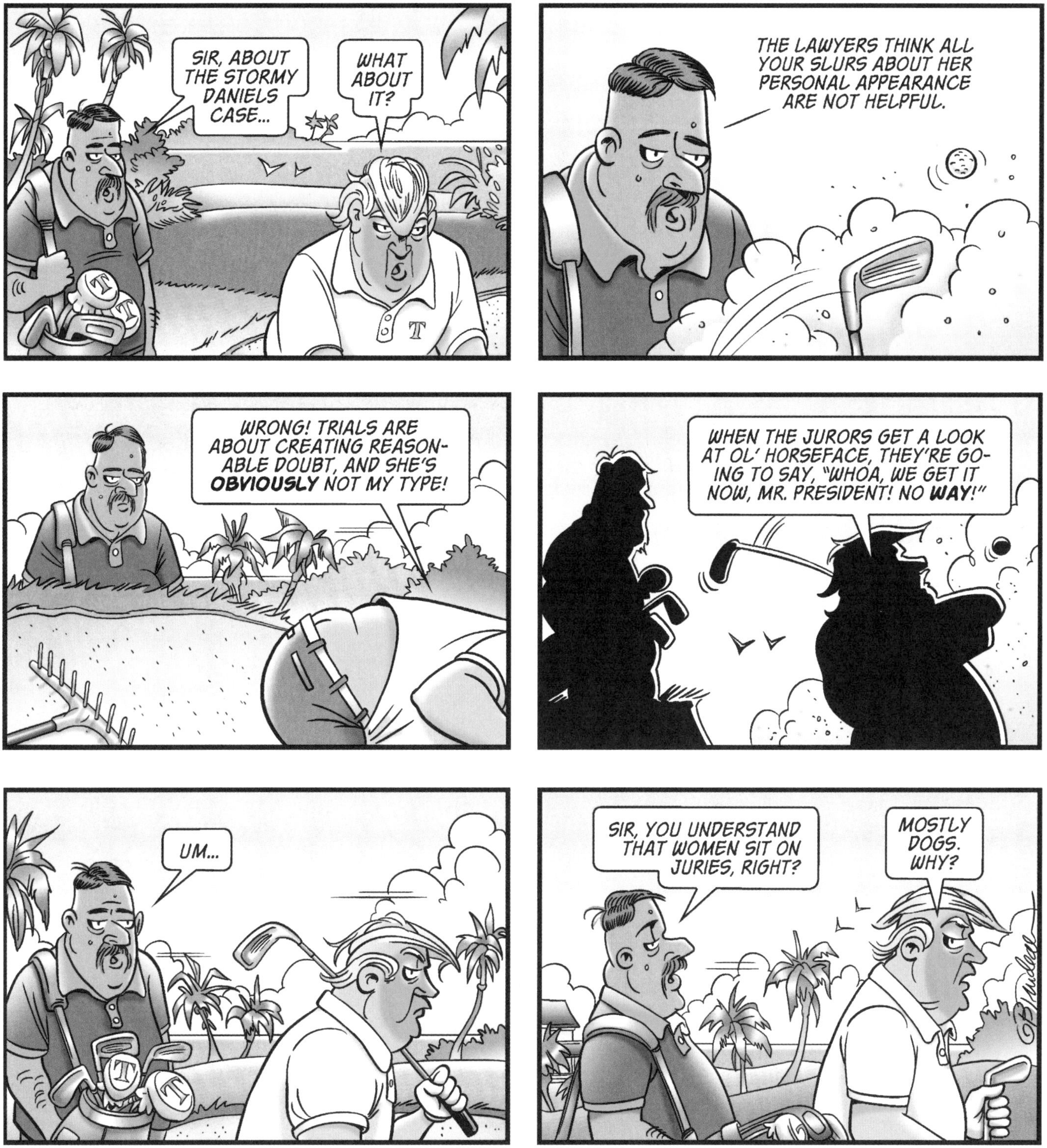
SIR, ABOUT THE STORMY DANIELS CASE...
WHAT ABOUT IT?
THE LAWYERS THINK ALL YOUR SLURS ABOUT HER PERSONAL APPEARANCE ARE NOT HELPFUL.
WRONG! TRIALS ARE ABOUT CREATING REASONABLE DOUBT, AND SHE'S **OBVIOUSLY** NOT MY TYPE!
WHEN THE JURORS GET A LOOK AT OL' HORSEFACE, THEY'RE GOING TO SAY, "WHOA, WE GET IT NOW, MR. PRESIDENT! NO **WAY**!"
UM...
SIR, YOU UNDERSTAND THAT WOMEN SIT ON JURIES, RIGHT?
MOSTLY DOGS. WHY?

May 21, 2023

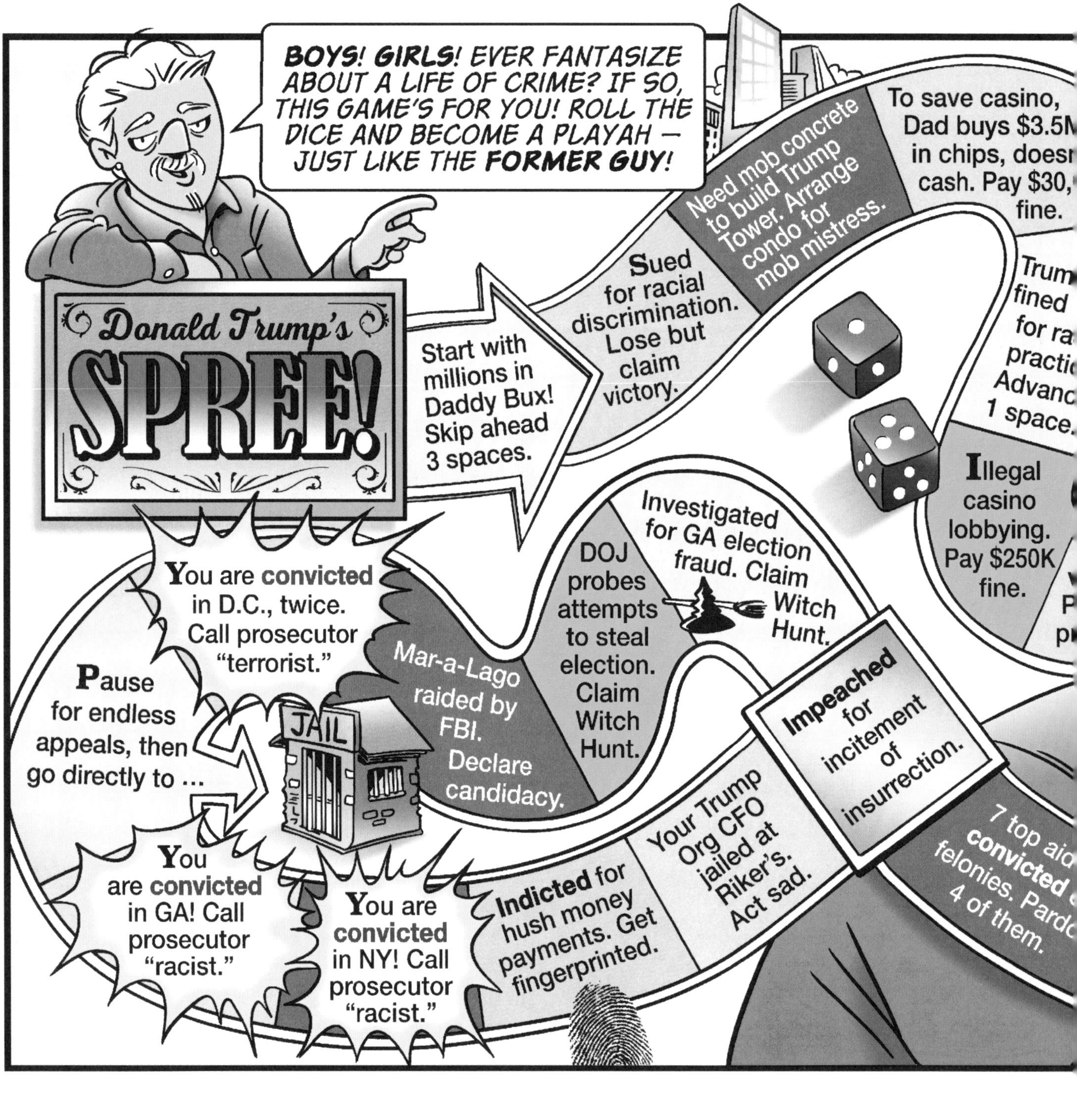

BOYS! GIRLS! EVER FANTASIZE ABOUT A LIFE OF CRIME? IF SO, THIS GAME'S FOR YOU! ROLL THE DICE AND BECOME A PLAYAH — JUST LIKE THE FORMER GUY!
Donald Trump's SPREE!
Start with millions in Daddy Bux! Skip ahead 3 spaces.
Sued for racial discrimination. Lose but claim victory.
Need mob concrete to build Trump Tower. Arrange condo for mob mistress.
To save casino, Dad buys $3.5
in chips, does
cash. Pay $30,
fine.
fined
for ra
Advan
1 space.
Illegal casino lobbying. Pay $250K fine.
Investigated for GA election fraud. Claim Witch Hunt.
DOJ probes attempts to steal election. Claim Witch Hunt.
Mar-a-Lago raided by FBI. Declare candidacy.
You are convicted in D.C., twice. Call prosecutor "terrorist."
Pause for endless appeals, then go directly to ...
JAIL
You are convicted in GA! Call prosecutor "racist."
You are convicted in NY! Call prosecutor "racist."
Indicted for hush money payments. Get fingerprinted.
Your Trump Org CFO jailed at Riker's. Act sad.
Impeached for incitement of insurrection.
7 top
convicted
felonies.
4 of them.

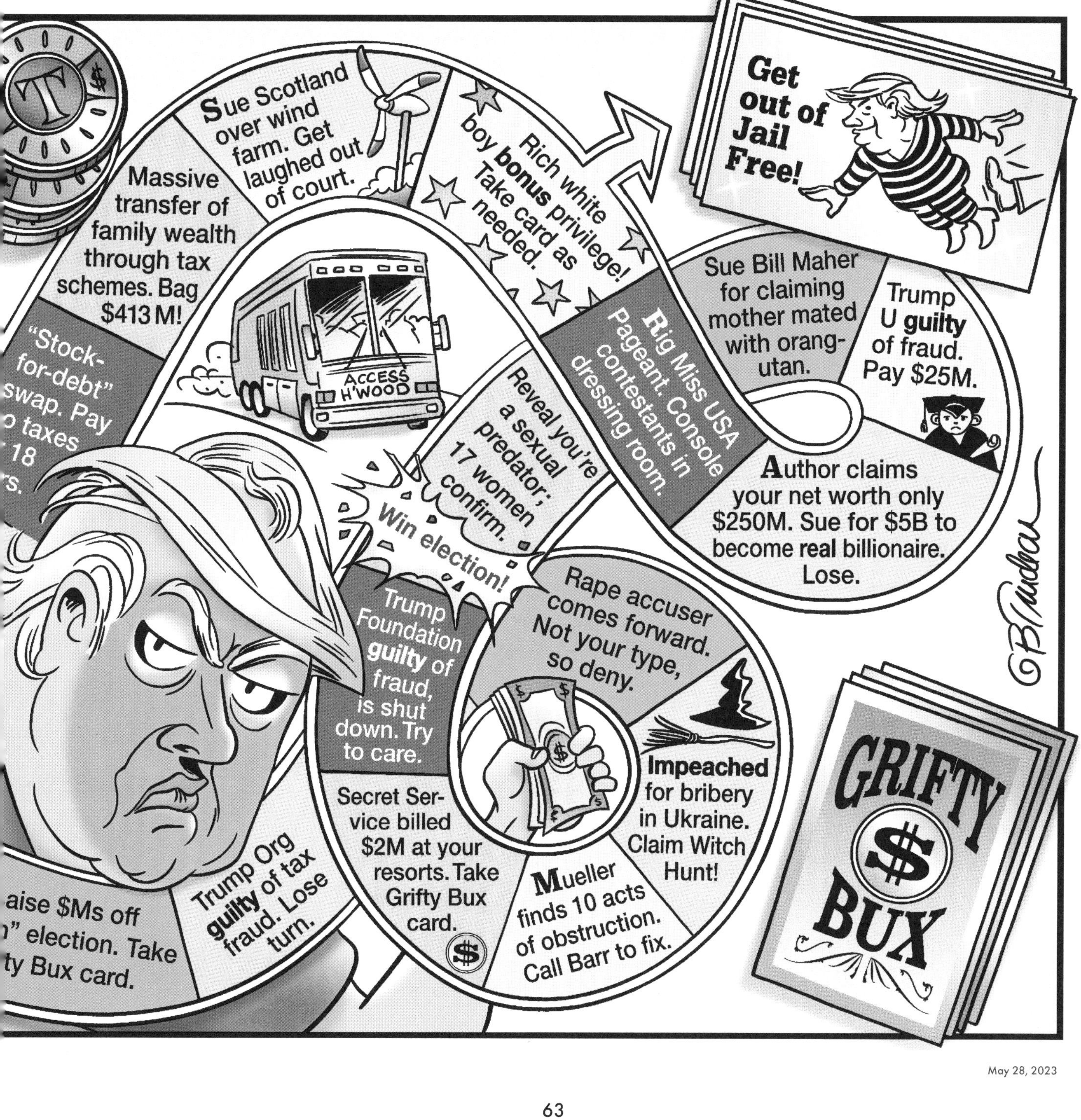

Sue Scotland over wind farm. Get laughed out of court.
Rich white boy bonus privilege! Take card as needed.
Get out of Jail Free!
Massive transfer of family wealth through tax schemes. Bag $413M!
"Stock-for-debt" swap. Pay o taxes 18 rs.
ACCESS H'WOOD
Sue Bill Maher for claiming mother mated with orang-utan.
Trump U guilty of fraud. Pay $25M.
Rig Miss USA Pageant. Console contestants in dressing room.
Reveal you're a sexual predator; 17 women confirm.
Author claims your net worth only $250M. Sue for $5B to become real billionaire. Lose.
Win election!
Trump Foundation guilty of fraud, is shut down. Try to care.
Rape accuser comes forward. Not your type, so deny.
Impeached for bribery in Ukraine. Claim Witch Hunt!
Secret Service billed $2M at your resorts. Take Grifty Bux card.
Mueller finds 10 acts of obstruction. Call Barr to fix.
Trump Org guilty of tax fraud. Lose turn.
aise $Ms off n" election. Take ty Bux card.
GRIFTY $ BUX

May 28, 2023

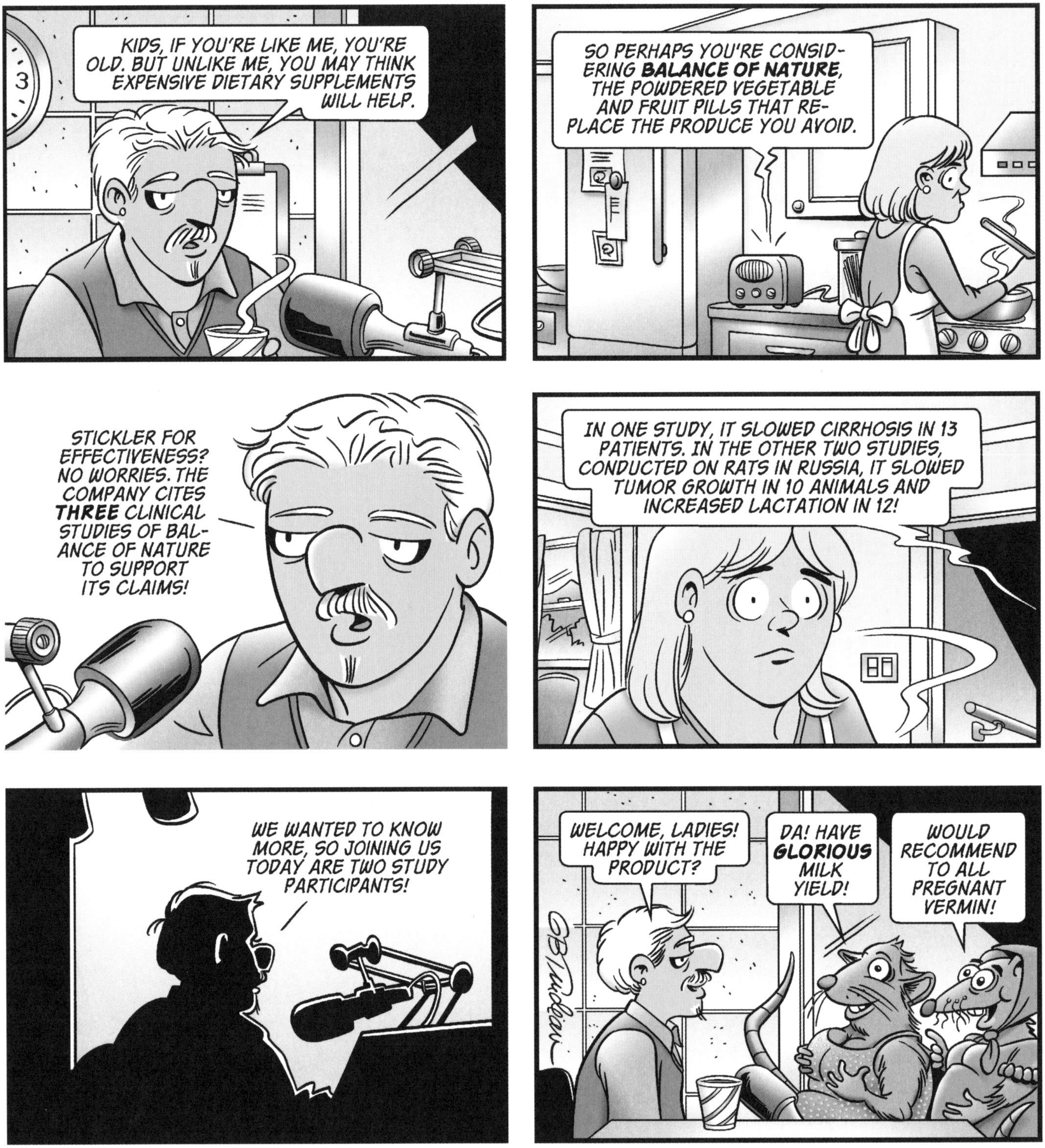
KIDS, IF YOU'RE LIKE ME, YOU'RE OLD. BUT UNLIKE ME, YOU MAY THINK EXPENSIVE DIETARY SUPPLEMENTS WILL HELP.
SO PERHAPS YOU'RE CONSIDERING **BALANCE OF NATURE**, THE POWDERED VEGETABLE AND FRUIT PILLS THAT REPLACE THE PRODUCE YOU AVOID.
STICKLER FOR EFFECTIVENESS? NO WORRIES. THE COMPANY CITES **THREE** CLINICAL STUDIES OF BALANCE OF NATURE TO SUPPORT ITS CLAIMS!
IN ONE STUDY, IT SLOWED CIRRHOSIS IN 13 PATIENTS. IN THE OTHER TWO STUDIES, CONDUCTED ON RATS IN RUSSIA, IT SLOWED TUMOR GROWTH IN 10 ANIMALS AND INCREASED LACTATION IN 12!
WE WANTED TO KNOW MORE, SO JOINING US TODAY ARE TWO STUDY PARTICIPANTS!
WELCOME, LADIES! HAPPY WITH THE PRODUCT?
DA! HAVE **GLORIOUS** MILK YIELD!
WOULD RECOMMEND TO ALL PREGNANT VERMIN!
GBTrudeau

June 4, 2023

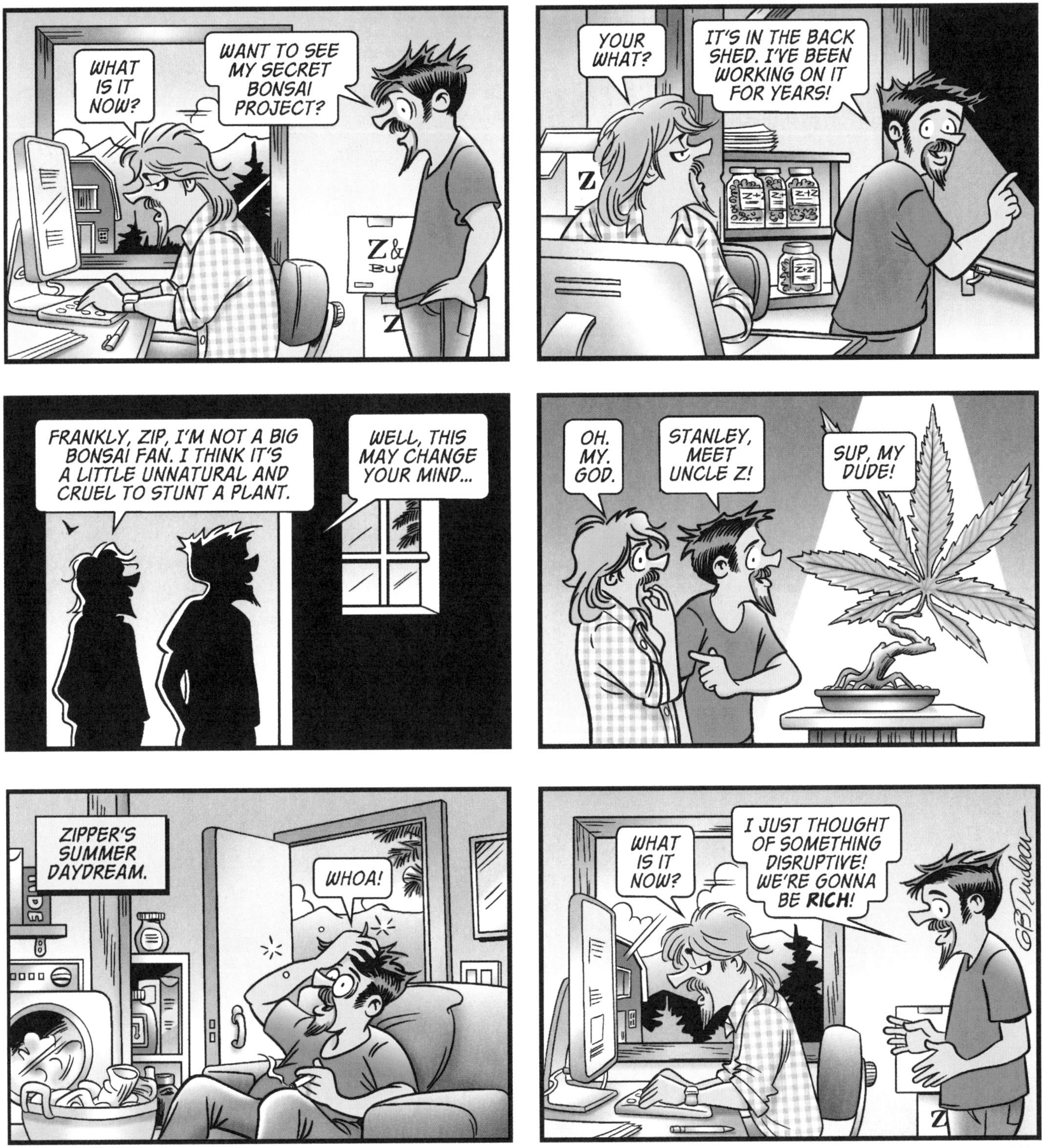
WHAT IS IT NOW?
WANT TO SEE MY SECRET BONSAI PROJECT?
YOUR WHAT?
IT'S IN THE BACK SHED. I'VE BEEN WORKING ON IT FOR YEARS!
FRANKLY, ZIP, I'M NOT A BIG BONSAI FAN. I THINK IT'S A LITTLE UNNATURAL AND CRUEL TO STUNT A PLANT.
WELL, THIS MAY CHANGE YOUR MIND...
OH. MY. GOD.
STANLEY, MEET UNCLE Z!
SUP, MY DUDE!
ZIPPER'S SUMMER DAYDREAM.
WHOA!
WHAT IS IT NOW?
I JUST THOUGHT OF SOMETHING DISRUPTIVE! WE'RE GONNA BE **RICH**!

June 11, 2023

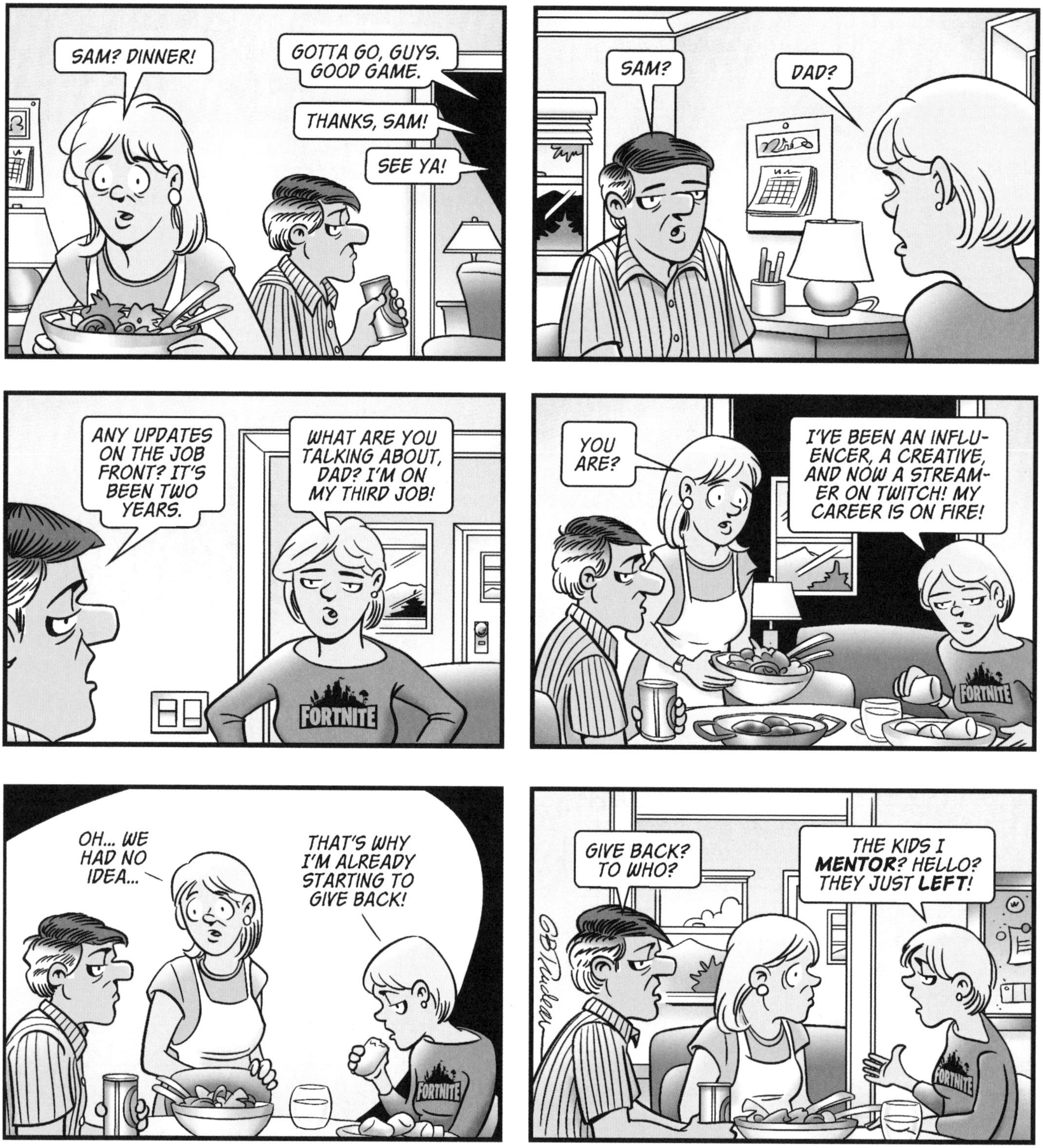
SAM? DINNER!
GOTTA GO, GUYS. GOOD GAME.
THANKS, SAM!
SEE YA!
SAM?
DAD?
ANY UPDATES ON THE JOB FRONT? IT'S BEEN TWO YEARS.
WHAT ARE YOU TALKING ABOUT, DAD? I'M ON MY THIRD JOB!
YOU ARE?
I'VE BEEN AN INFLUENCER, A CREATIVE, AND NOW A STREAMER ON TWITCH! MY CAREER IS ON FIRE!
OH... WE HAD NO IDEA...
THAT'S WHY I'M ALREADY STARTING TO GIVE BACK!
GIVE BACK? TO WHO?
THE KIDS I **MENTOR**? HELLO? THEY JUST **LEFT**!

June 18, 2023

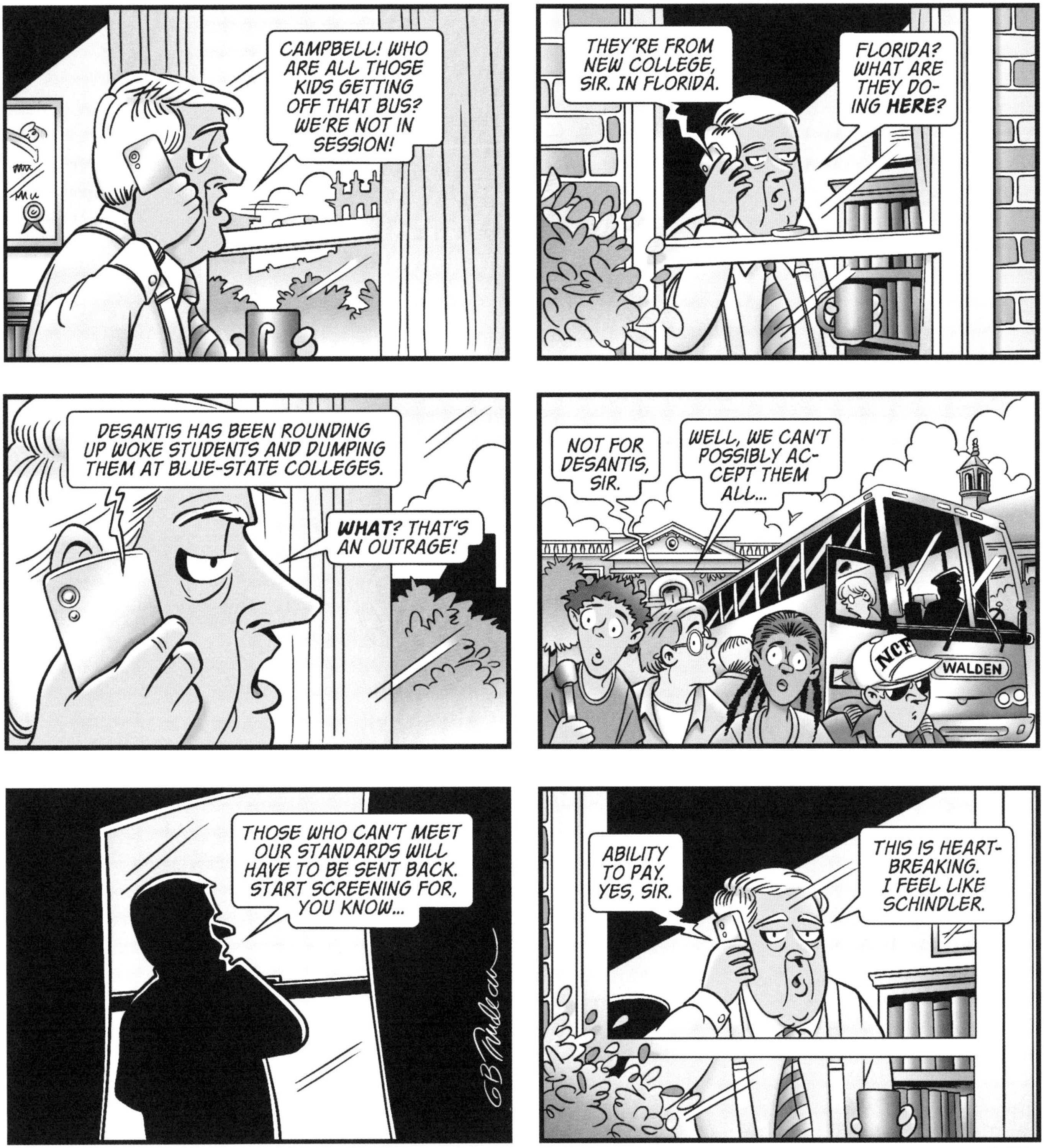

CAMPBELL! WHO ARE ALL THOSE KIDS GETTING OFF THAT BUS? WE'RE NOT IN SESSION!
THEY'RE FROM NEW COLLEGE, SIR. IN FLORIDA.
FLORIDA? WHAT ARE THEY DO-ING HERE?
DESANTIS HAS BEEN ROUNDING UP WOKE STUDENTS AND DUMPING THEM AT BLUE-STATE COLLEGES.
WHAT? THAT'S AN OUTRAGE!
NOT FOR DESANTIS, SIR.
WELL, WE CAN'T POSSIBLY AC-CEPT THEM ALL...
NCF
WALDEN
THOSE WHO CAN'T MEET OUR STANDARDS WILL HAVE TO BE SENT BACK. START SCREENING FOR, YOU KNOW...
GB Trudeau
ABILITY TO PAY. YES, SIR.
THIS IS HEART-BREAKING. I FEEL LIKE SCHINDLER.

June 25, 2023

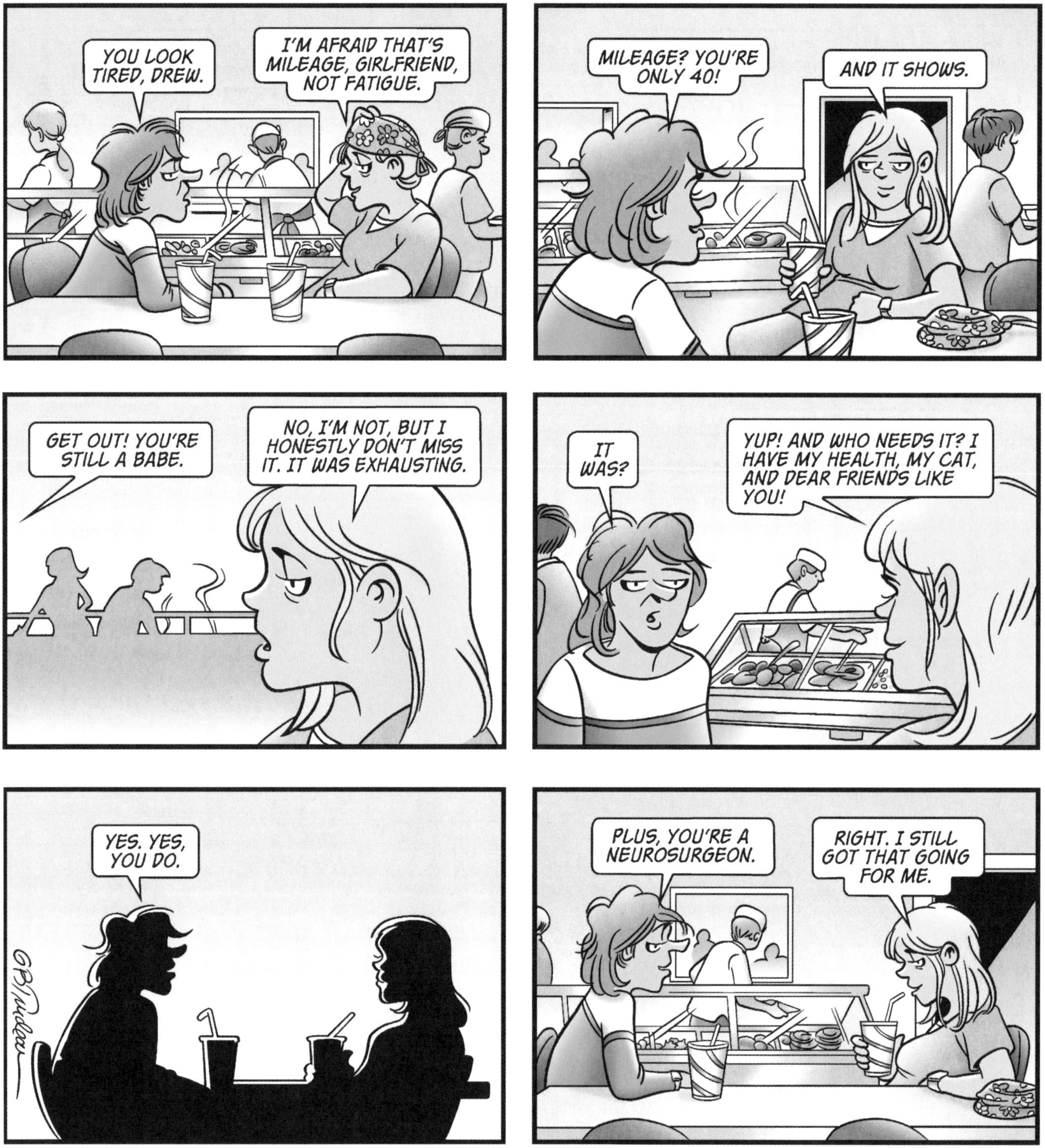
YOU LOOK TIRED, DREW.
I'M AFRAID THAT'S MILEAGE, GIRLFRIEND, NOT FATIGUE.
MILEAGE? YOU'RE ONLY 40!
AND IT SHOWS.
GET OUT! YOU'RE STILL A BABE.
NO, I'M NOT, BUT I HONESTLY DON'T MISS IT. IT WAS EXHAUSTING.
IT WAS?
YUP! AND WHO NEEDS IT? I HAVE MY HEALTH, MY CAT, AND DEAR FRIENDS LIKE YOU!
YES. YES, YOU DO.
PLUS, YOU'RE A NEUROSURGEON.
RIGHT. I STILL GOT THAT GOING FOR ME.

July 2, 2023

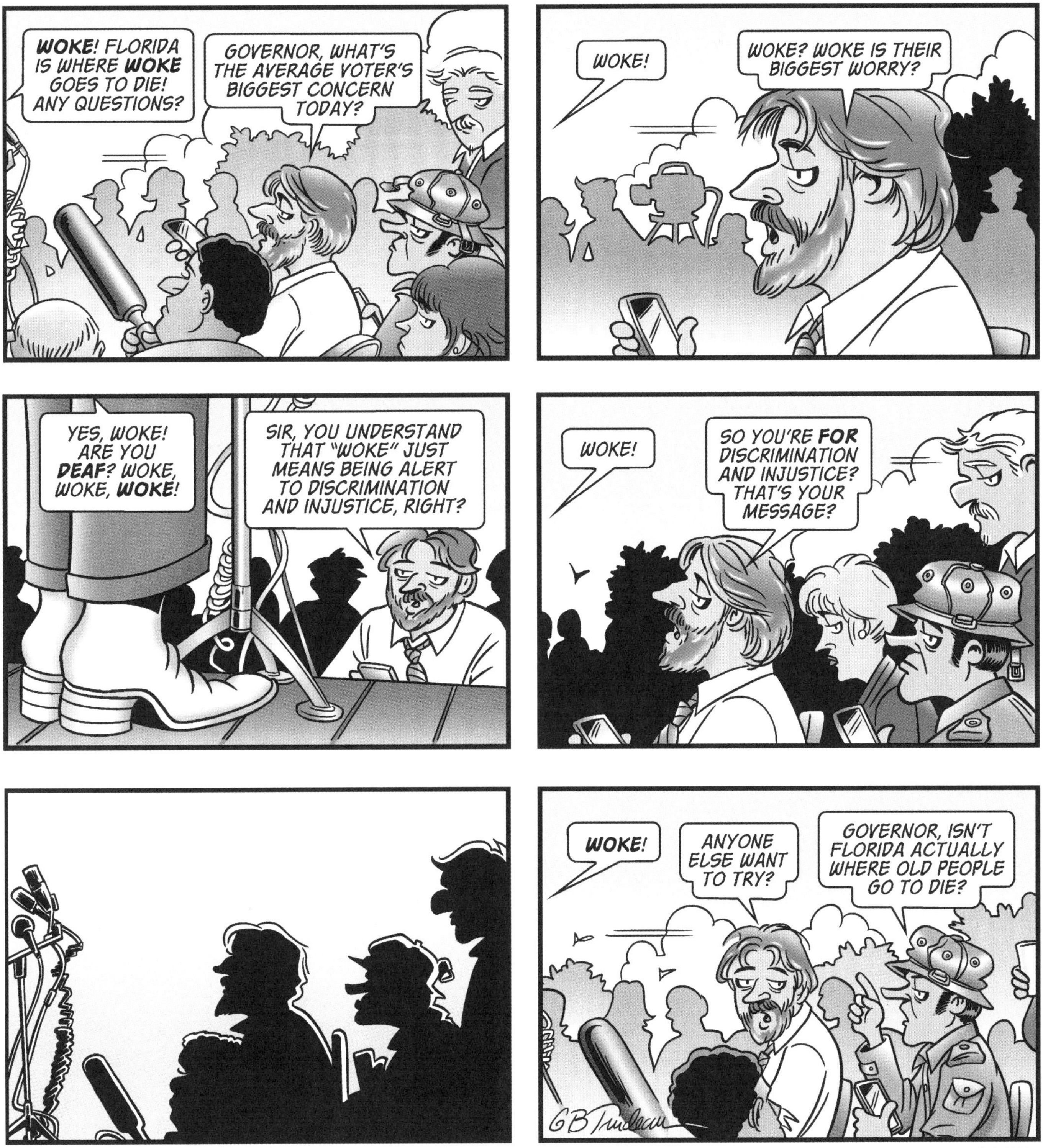
WOKE! FLORIDA IS WHERE WOKE GOES TO DIE! ANY QUESTIONS?
GOVERNOR, WHAT'S THE AVERAGE VOTER'S BIGGEST CONCERN TODAY?
WOKE!
WOKE? WOKE IS THEIR BIGGEST WORRY?
YES, WOKE! ARE YOU DEAF? WOKE, WOKE, WOKE!
SIR, YOU UNDERSTAND THAT "WOKE" JUST MEANS BEING ALERT TO DISCRIMINATION AND INJUSTICE, RIGHT?
WOKE!
SO YOU'RE FOR DISCRIMINATION AND INJUSTICE? THAT'S YOUR MESSAGE?
WOKE!
ANYONE ELSE WANT TO TRY?
GOVERNOR, ISN'T FLORIDA ACTUALLY WHERE OLD PEOPLE GO TO DIE?
GB Trudeau

July 9, 2023

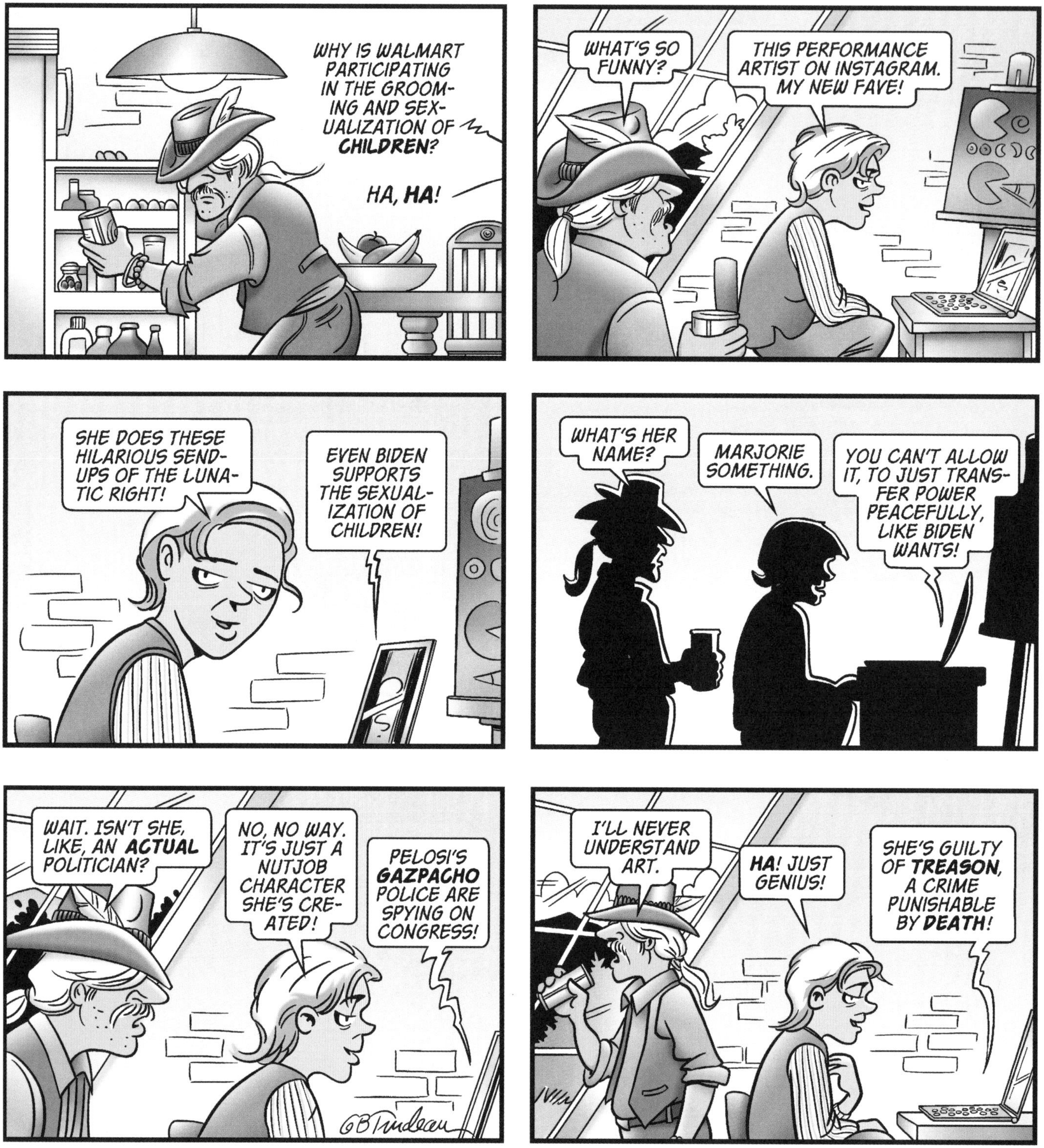
WHY IS WALMART PARTICIPATING IN THE GROOMING AND SEXUALIZATION OF **CHILDREN**?
HA, **HA**!
WHAT'S SO FUNNY?
THIS PERFORMANCE ARTIST ON INSTAGRAM. MY NEW FAVE!
SHE DOES THESE HILARIOUS SEND-UPS OF THE LUNATIC RIGHT!
EVEN BIDEN SUPPORTS THE SEXUALIZATION OF CHILDREN!
WHAT'S HER NAME?
MARJORIE SOMETHING.
YOU CAN'T ALLOW IT, TO JUST TRANSFER POWER PEACEFULLY, LIKE BIDEN WANTS!
WAIT. ISN'T SHE, LIKE, AN **ACTUAL** POLITICIAN?
NO, NO WAY. IT'S JUST A NUTJOB CHARACTER SHE'S CREATED!
PELOSI'S **GAZPACHO** POLICE ARE SPYING ON CONGRESS!
I'LL NEVER UNDERSTAND ART.
HA! JUST GENIUS!
SHE'S GUILTY OF **TREASON**, A CRIME PUNISHABLE BY **DEATH**!
GB Trudeau

July 16, 2023

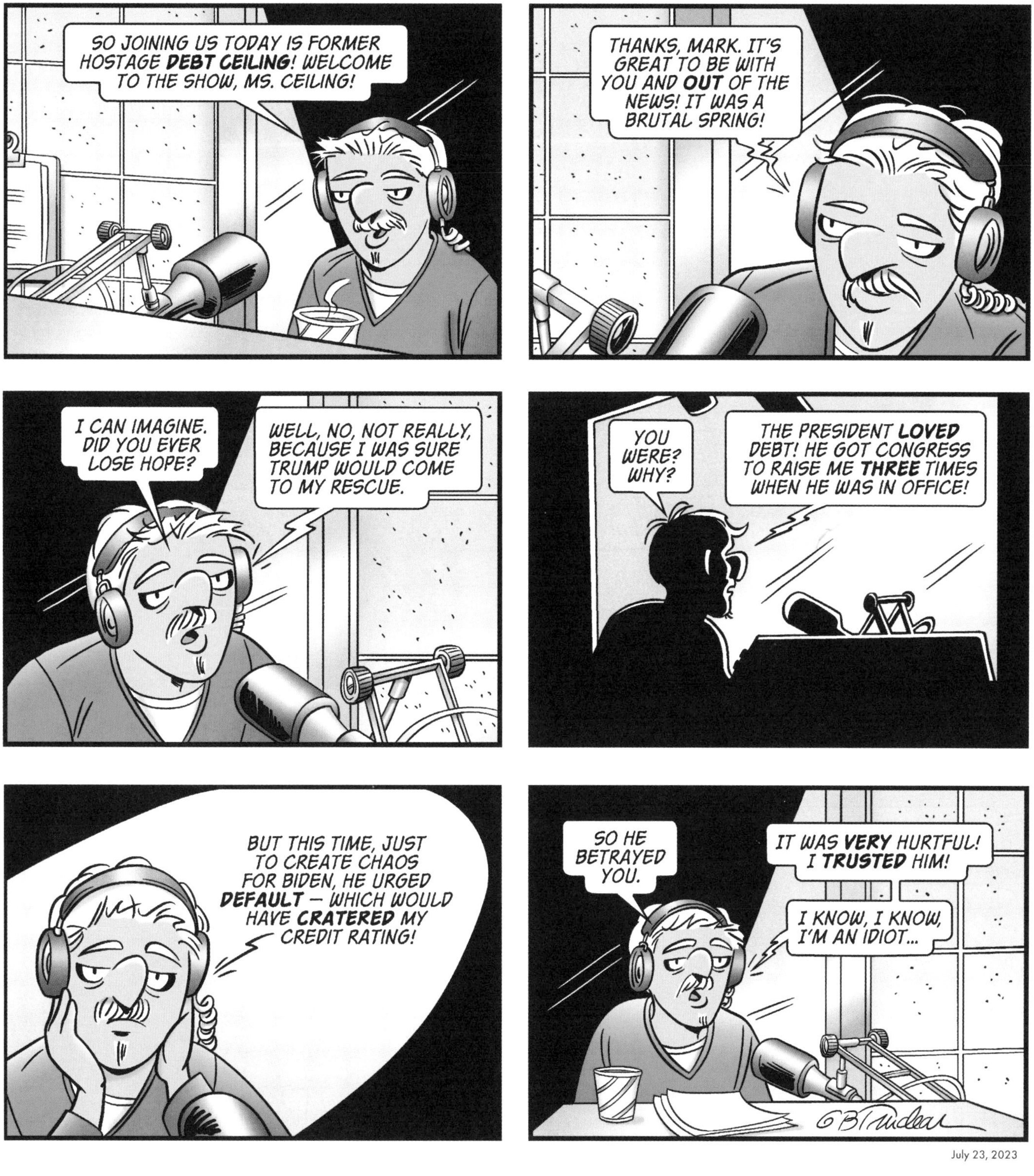
SO JOINING US TODAY IS FORMER HOSTAGE **DEBT CEILING**! WELCOME TO THE SHOW, MS. CEILING!
THANKS, MARK. IT'S GREAT TO BE WITH YOU AND **OUT** OF THE NEWS! IT WAS A BRUTAL SPRING!
I CAN IMAGINE. DID YOU EVER LOSE HOPE?
WELL, NO, NOT REALLY, BECAUSE I WAS SURE TRUMP WOULD COME TO MY RESCUE.
YOU WERE? WHY?
THE PRESIDENT **LOVED** DEBT! HE GOT CONGRESS TO RAISE ME **THREE** TIMES WHEN HE WAS IN OFFICE!
BUT THIS TIME, JUST TO CREATE CHAOS FOR BIDEN, HE URGED **DEFAULT** — WHICH WOULD HAVE **CRATERED** MY CREDIT RATING!
SO HE BETRAYED YOU.
IT WAS **VERY** HURTFUL! I **TRUSTED** HIM!
I KNOW, I KNOW, I'M AN IDIOT...
GBTrudeau

July 23, 2023

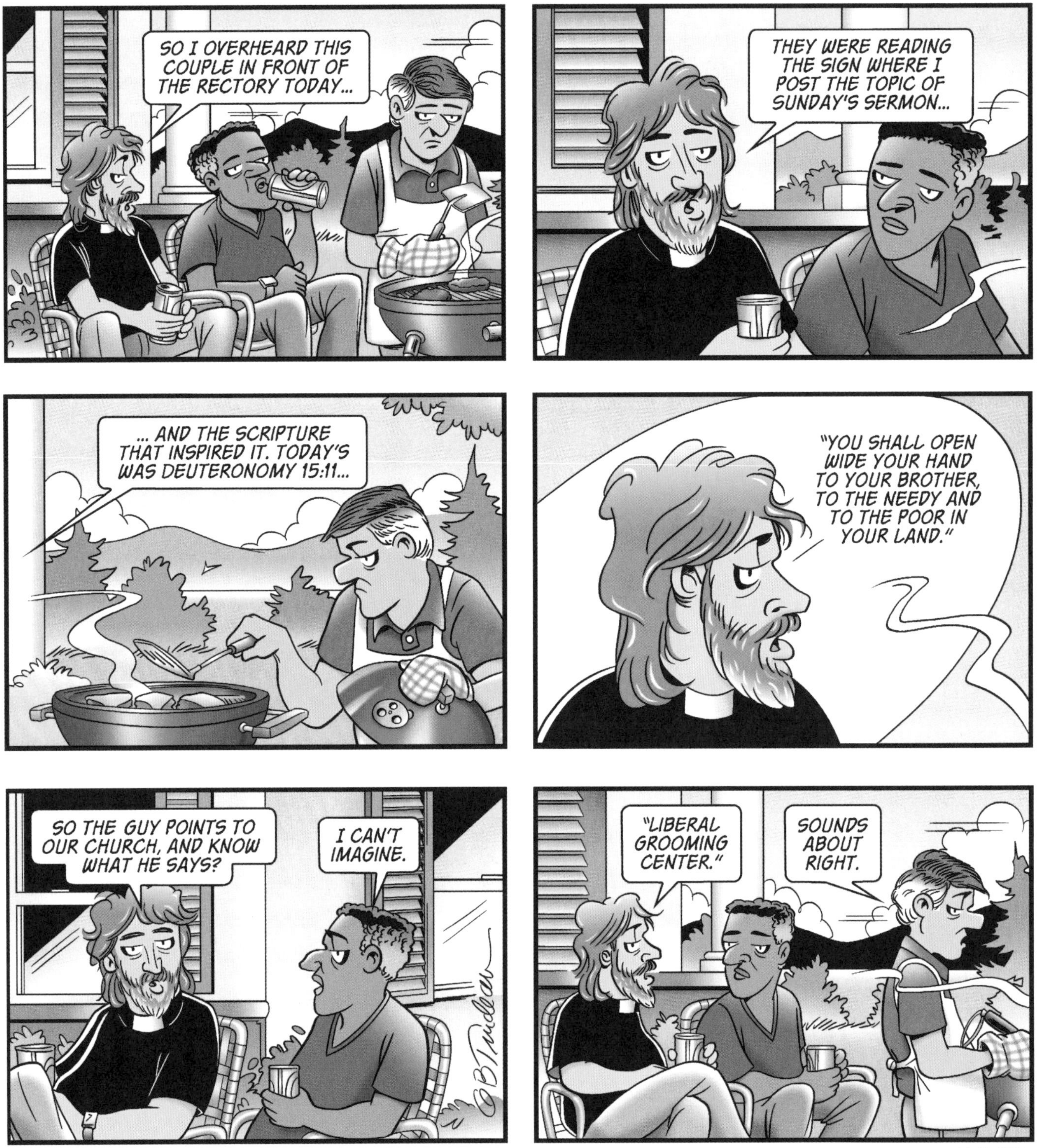
SO I OVERHEARD THIS COUPLE IN FRONT OF THE RECTORY TODAY...
THEY WERE READING THE SIGN WHERE I POST THE TOPIC OF SUNDAY'S SERMON...
... AND THE SCRIPTURE THAT INSPIRED IT. TODAY'S WAS DEUTERONOMY 15:11...
"YOU SHALL OPEN WIDE YOUR HAND TO YOUR BROTHER, TO THE NEEDY AND TO THE POOR IN YOUR LAND."
SO THE GUY POINTS TO OUR CHURCH, AND KNOW WHAT HE SAYS?
I CAN'T IMAGINE.
"LIBERAL GROOMING CENTER."
SOUNDS ABOUT RIGHT.

July 30, 2023

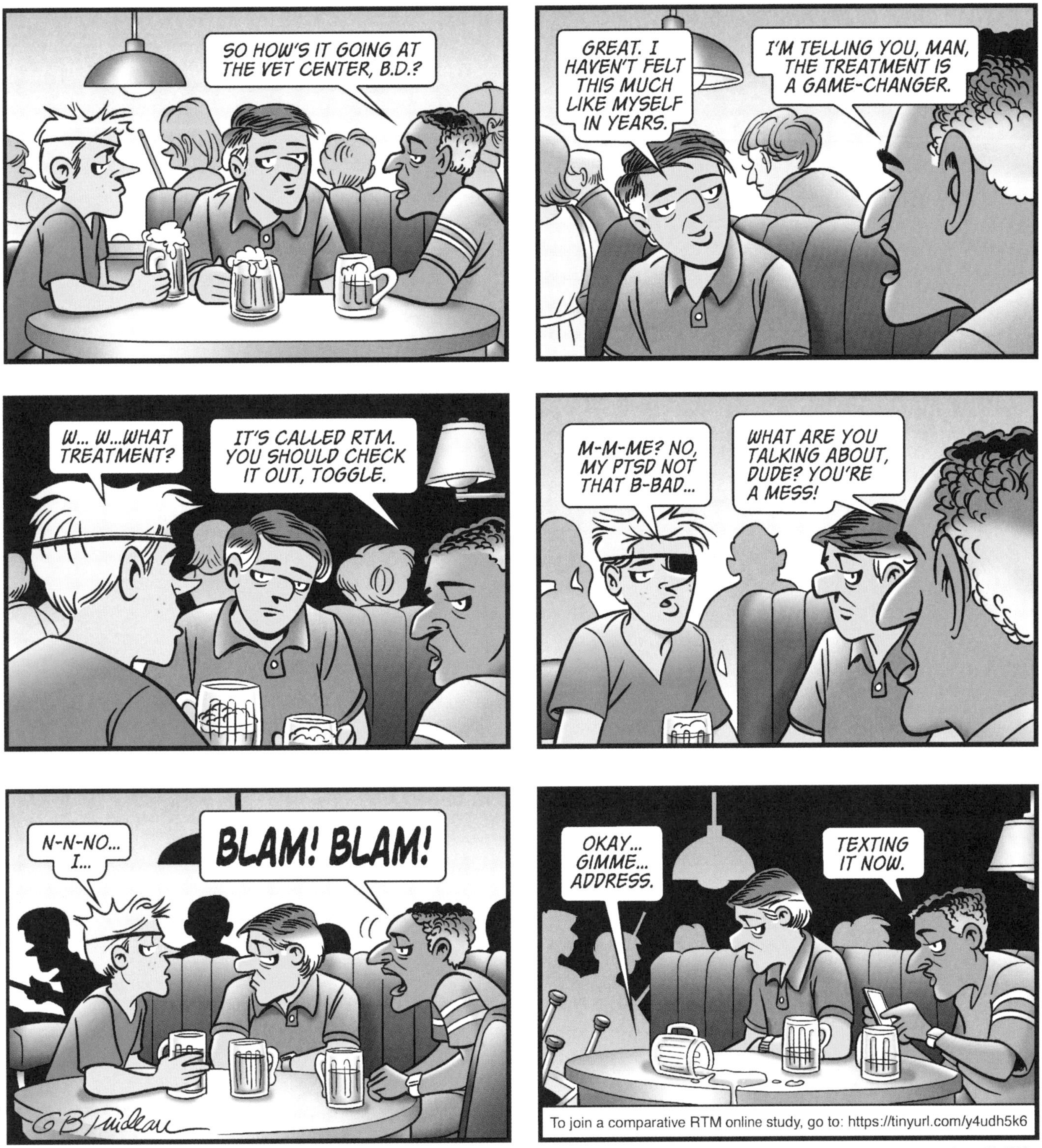
SO HOW'S IT GOING AT THE VET CENTER, B.D.?
GREAT. I HAVEN'T FELT THIS MUCH LIKE MYSELF IN YEARS.
I'M TELLING YOU, MAN, THE TREATMENT IS A GAME-CHANGER.
W... W...WHAT TREATMENT?
IT'S CALLED RTM. YOU SHOULD CHECK IT OUT, TOGGLE.
M-M-ME? NO, MY PTSD NOT THAT B-BAD...
WHAT ARE YOU TALKING ABOUT, DUDE? YOU'RE A MESS!
N-N-NO... I...
BLAM! BLAM!
OKAY... GIMME... ADDRESS.
TEXTING IT NOW.
GB Trudeau
To join a comparative RTM online study, go to: https://tinyurl.com/y4udh5k6

August 13, 2023

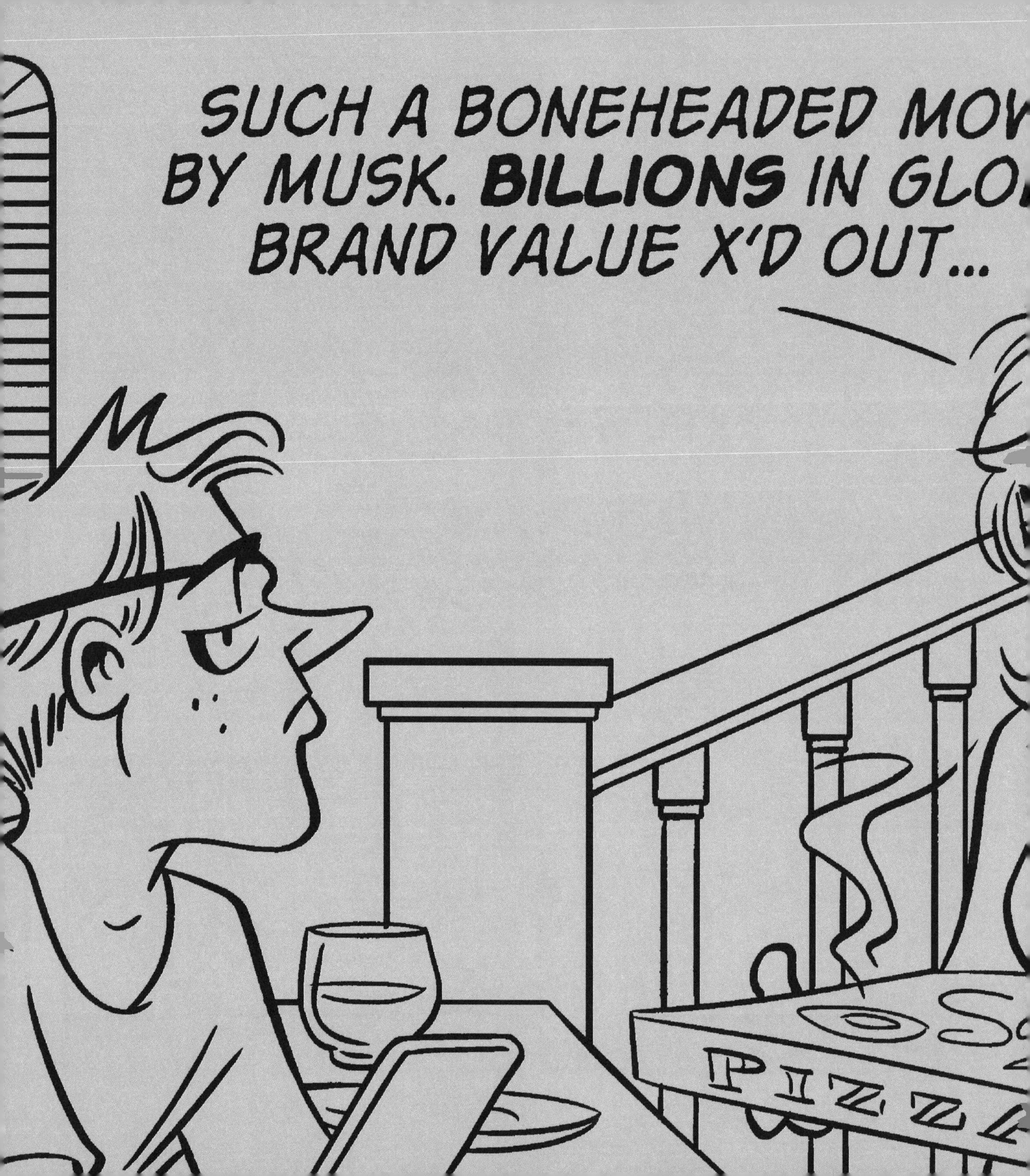
SUCH A BONEHEADED MOV
BY MUSK. **BILLIONS** IN GLO
BRAND VALUE X'D OUT...
PIZZ

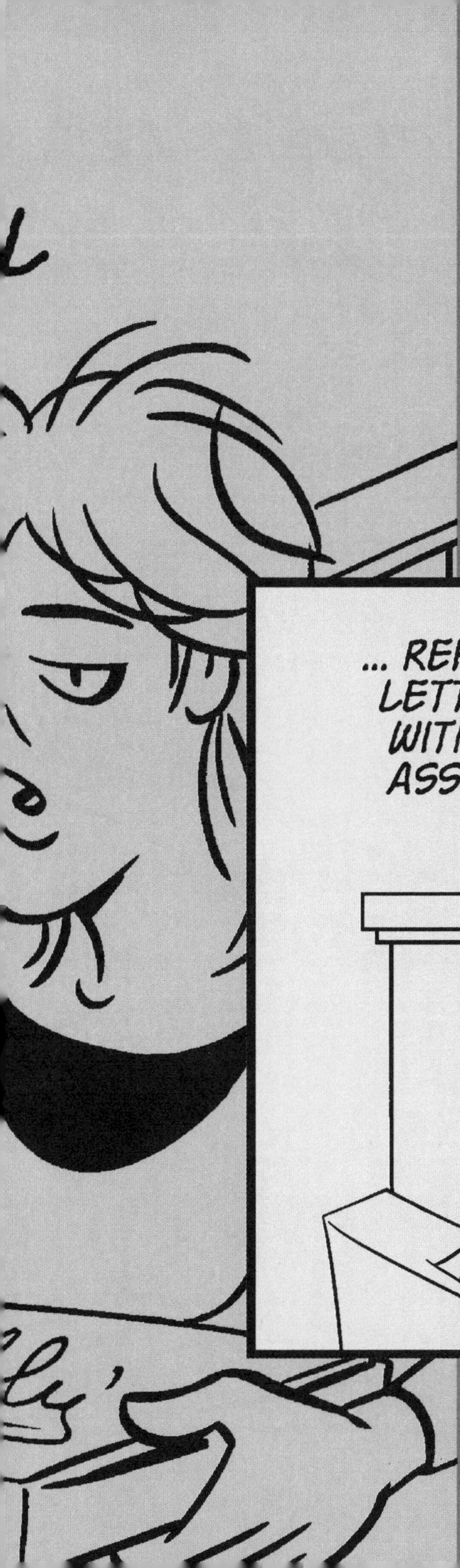

PART 3

The Age of X

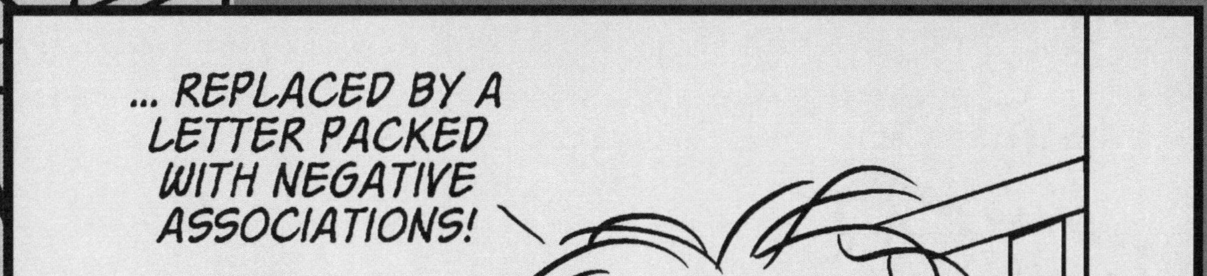
... REPLACED BY A LETTER PACKED WITH NEGATIVE ASSOCIATIONS!

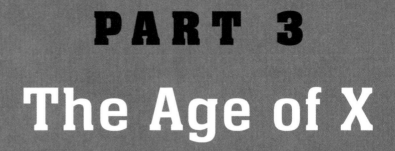

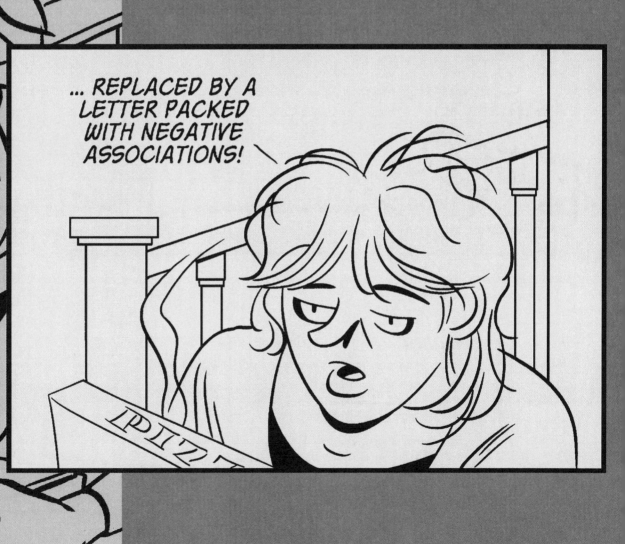

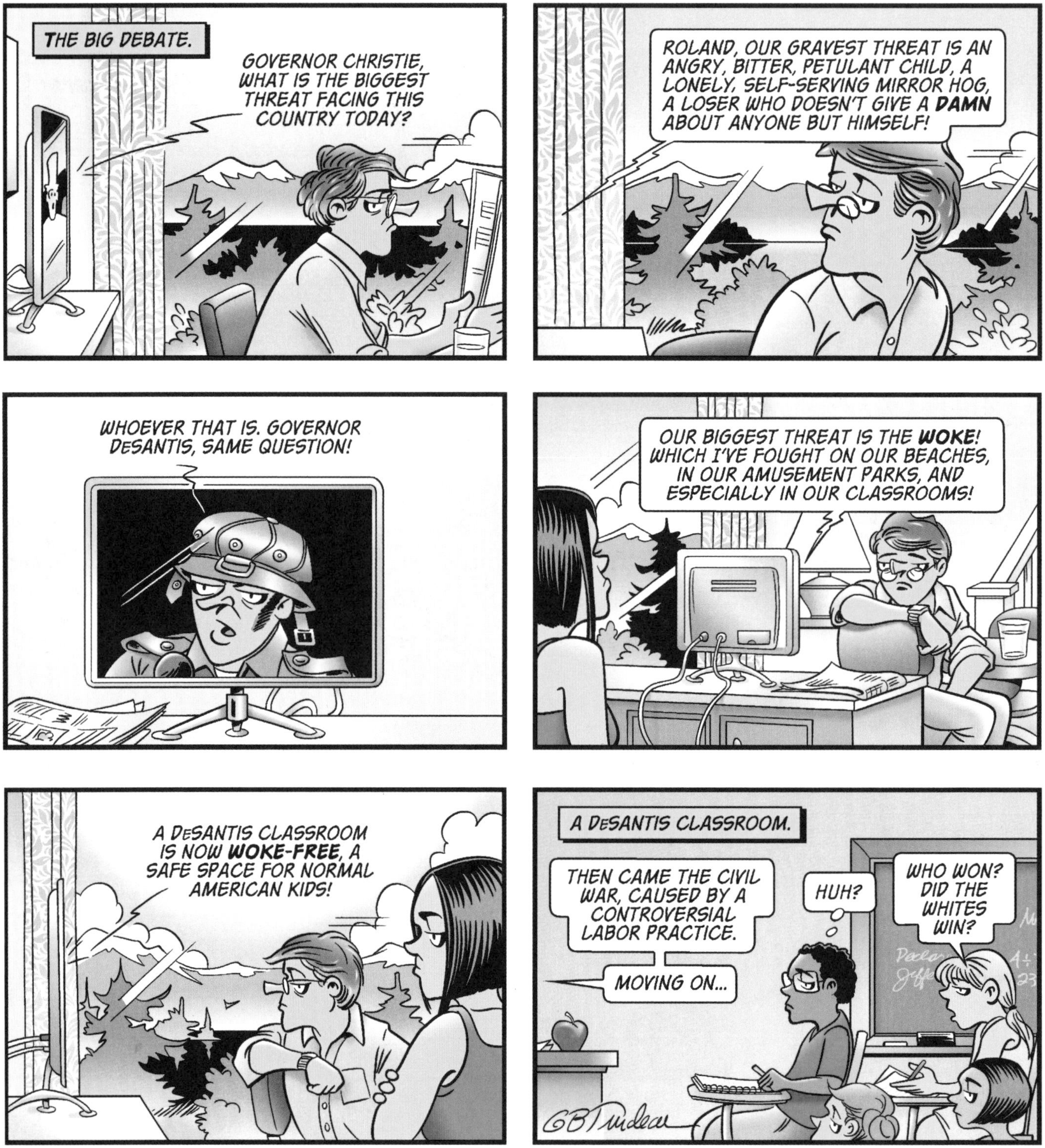
THE BIG DEBATE.
GOVERNOR CHRISTIE, WHAT IS THE BIGGEST THREAT FACING THIS COUNTRY TODAY?
ROLAND, OUR GRAVEST THREAT IS AN ANGRY, BITTER, PETULANT CHILD, A LONELY, SELF-SERVING MIRROR HOG, A LOSER WHO DOESN'T GIVE A **DAMN** ABOUT ANYONE BUT HIMSELF!
WHOEVER THAT IS. GOVERNOR DESANTIS, SAME QUESTION!
OUR BIGGEST THREAT IS THE **WOKE**! WHICH I'VE FOUGHT ON OUR BEACHES, IN OUR AMUSEMENT PARKS, AND ESPECIALLY IN OUR CLASSROOMS!
A DESANTIS CLASSROOM IS NOW **WOKE-FREE**, A SAFE SPACE FOR NORMAL AMERICAN KIDS!
A DESANTIS CLASSROOM.
THEN CAME THE CIVIL WAR, CAUSED BY A CONTROVERSIAL LABOR PRACTICE.
HUH?
WHO WON? DID THE WHITES WIN?
MOVING ON...
GBTrudeau

August 20, 2023

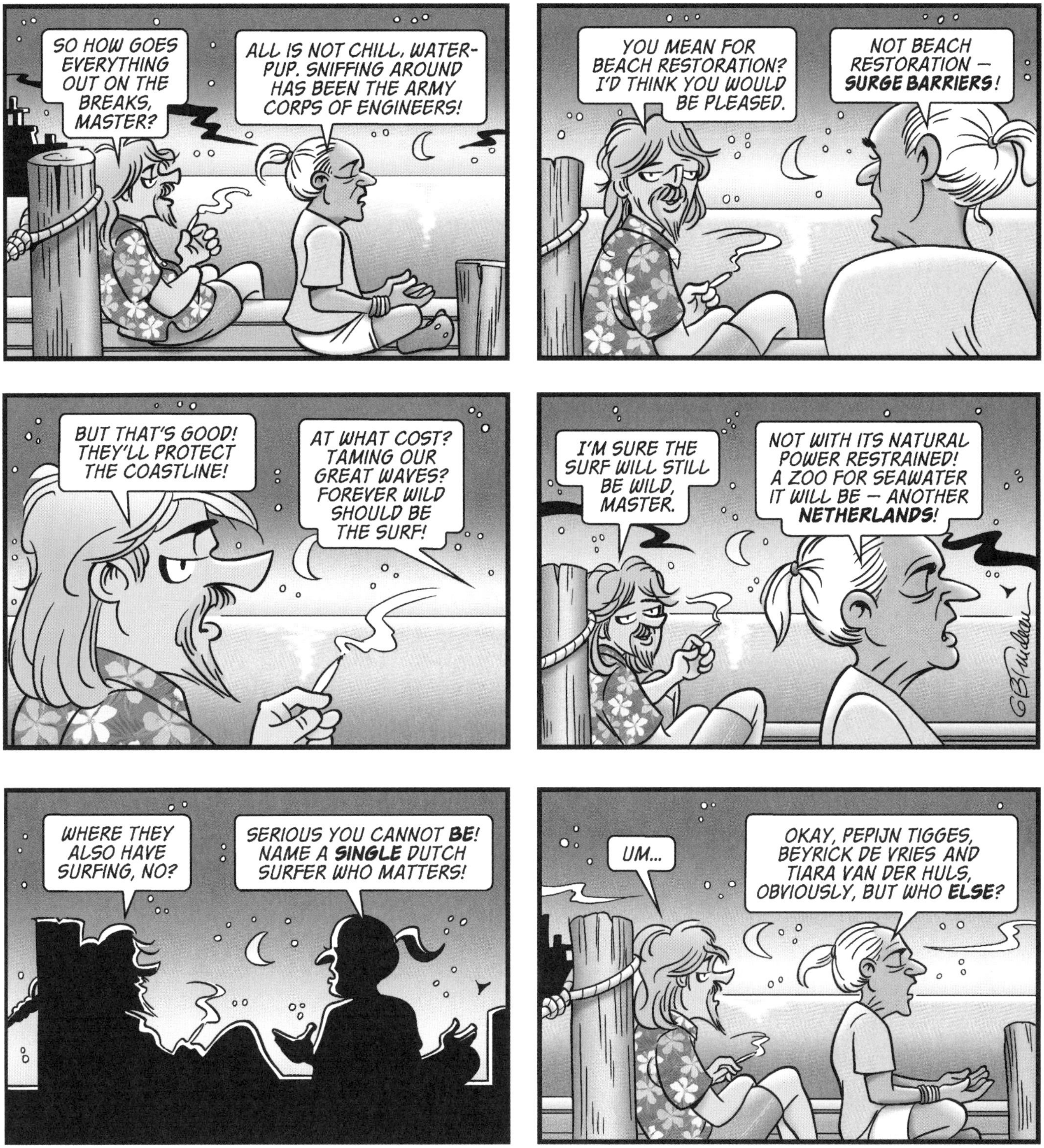
SO HOW GOES EVERYTHING OUT ON THE BREAKS, MASTER?
ALL IS NOT CHILL, WATER-PUP. SNIFFING AROUND HAS BEEN THE ARMY CORPS OF ENGINEERS!
YOU MEAN FOR BEACH RESTORATION? I'D THINK YOU WOULD BE PLEASED.
NOT BEACH RESTORATION — **SURGE BARRIERS**!
BUT THAT'S GOOD! THEY'LL PROTECT THE COASTLINE!
AT WHAT COST? TAMING OUR GREAT WAVES? FOREVER WILD SHOULD BE THE SURF!
I'M SURE THE SURF WILL STILL BE WILD, MASTER.
NOT WITH ITS NATURAL POWER RESTRAINED! A ZOO FOR SEAWATER IT WILL BE — ANOTHER **NETHERLANDS**!
WHERE THEY ALSO HAVE SURFING, NO?
SERIOUS YOU CANNOT **BE**! NAME A **SINGLE** DUTCH SURFER WHO MATTERS!
UM...
OKAY, PEPIJN TIGGES, BEYRICK DE VRIES AND TIARA VAN DER HULS, OBVIOUSLY, BUT WHO **ELSE**?

August 27, 2023

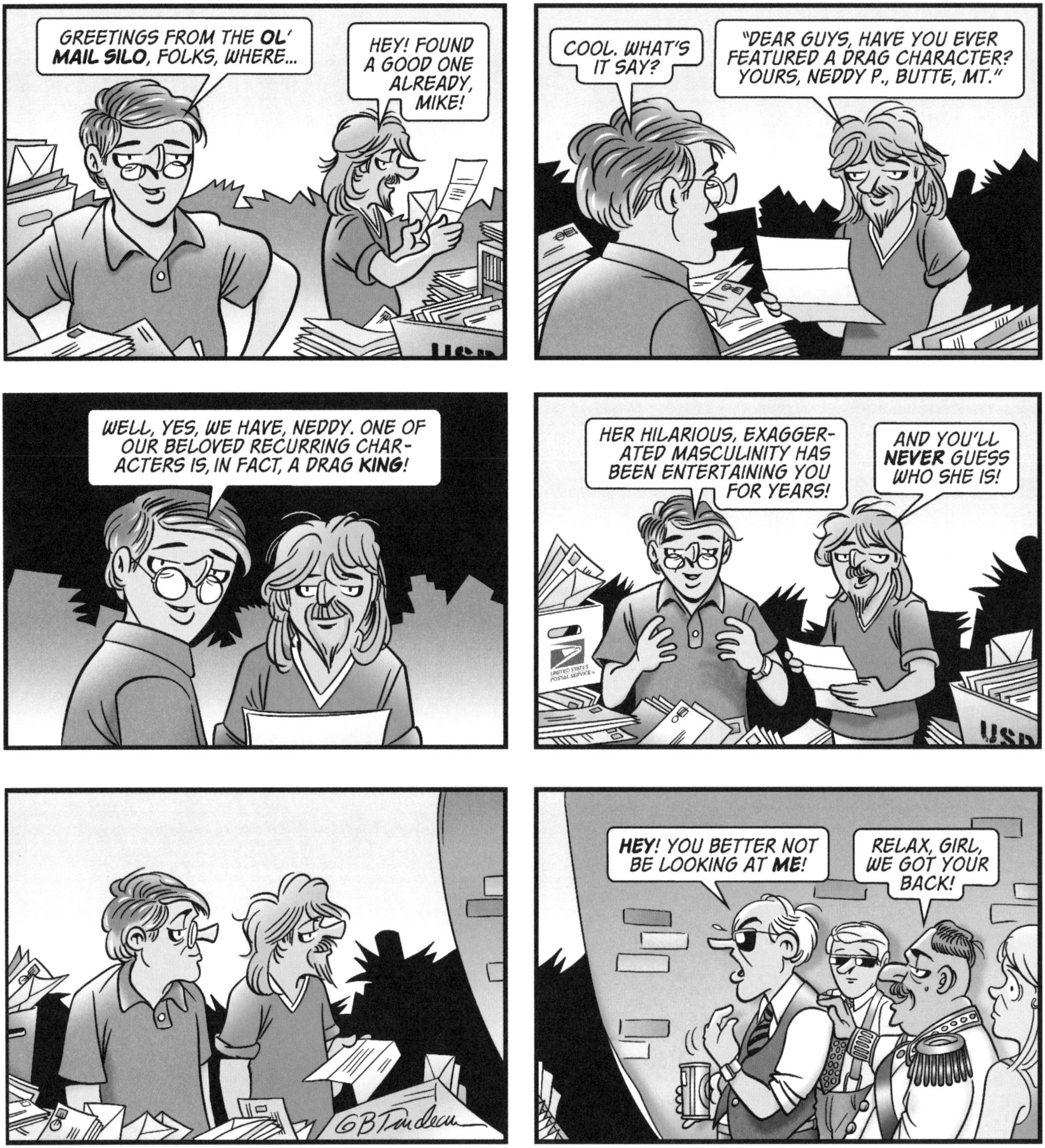
GREETINGS FROM THE **OL' MAIL SILO**, FOLKS, WHERE...
HEY! FOUND A GOOD ONE ALREADY, MIKE!
COOL. WHAT'S IT SAY?
"DEAR GUYS, HAVE YOU EVER FEATURED A DRAG CHARACTER? YOURS, NEDDY P., BUTTE, MT."
WELL, YES, WE HAVE, NEDDY. ONE OF OUR BELOVED RECURRING CHARACTERS IS, IN FACT, A DRAG **KING**!
HER HILARIOUS, EXAGGERATED MASCULINITY HAS BEEN ENTERTAINING YOU FOR YEARS!
AND YOU'LL **NEVER** GUESS WHO SHE IS!
HEY! YOU BETTER NOT BE LOOKING AT **ME**!
RELAX, GIRL, WE GOT YOUR BACK!
GBTrudeau

September 3, 2023

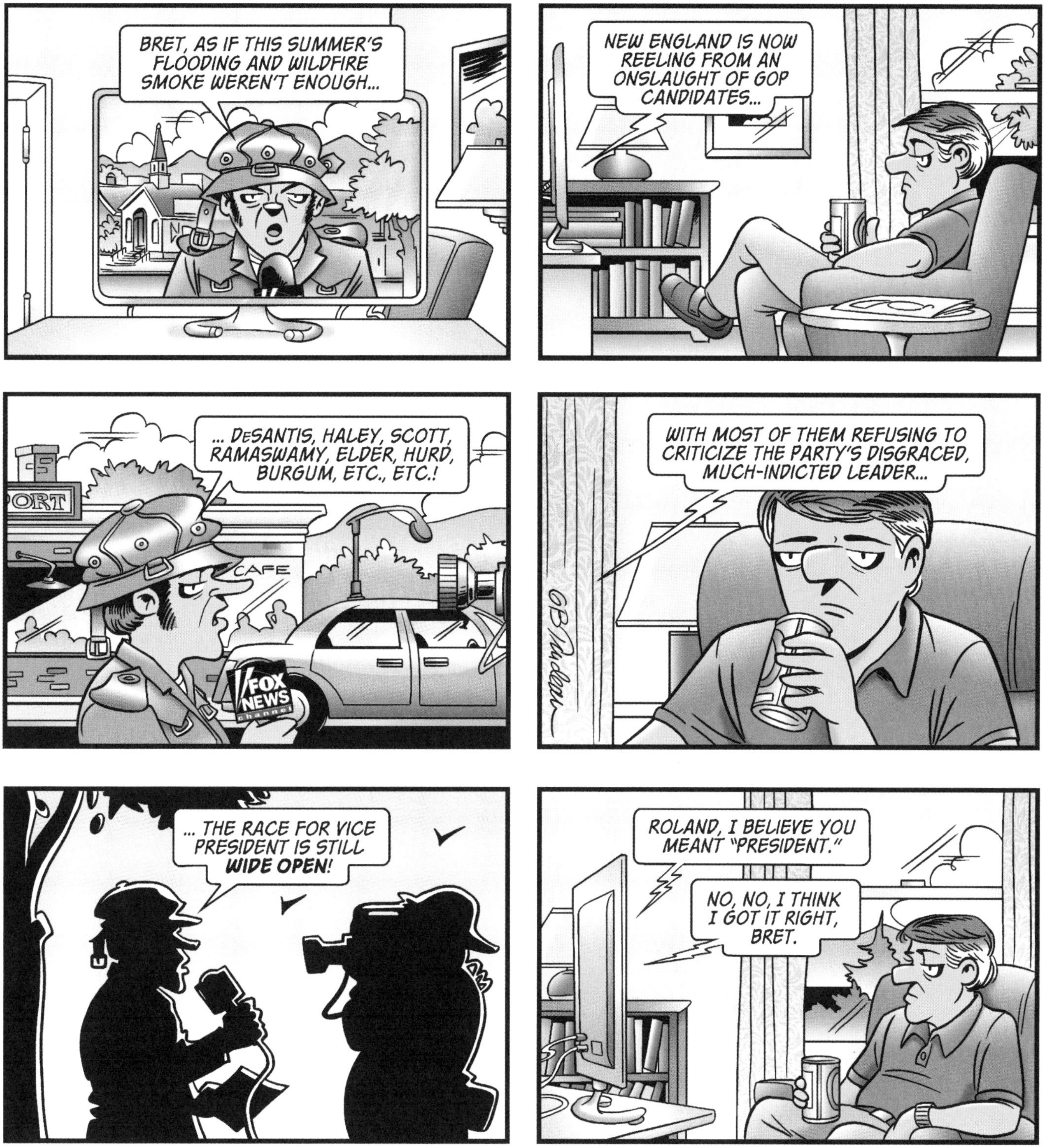
BRET, AS IF THIS SUMMER'S FLOODING AND WILDFIRE SMOKE WEREN'T ENOUGH...
NEW ENGLAND IS NOW REELING FROM AN ONSLAUGHT OF GOP CANDIDATES...
... DeSANTIS, HALEY, SCOTT, RAMASWAMY, ELDER, HURD, BURGUM, ETC., ETC.!
ORT
CAFE
FOX NEWS channel
WITH MOST OF THEM REFUSING TO CRITICIZE THE PARTY'S DISGRACED, MUCH-INDICTED LEADER...
GB Trudeau
... THE RACE FOR VICE PRESIDENT IS STILL **WIDE OPEN**!
ROLAND, I BELIEVE YOU MEANT "PRESIDENT."
NO, NO, I THINK I GOT IT RIGHT, BRET.

September 10, 2023

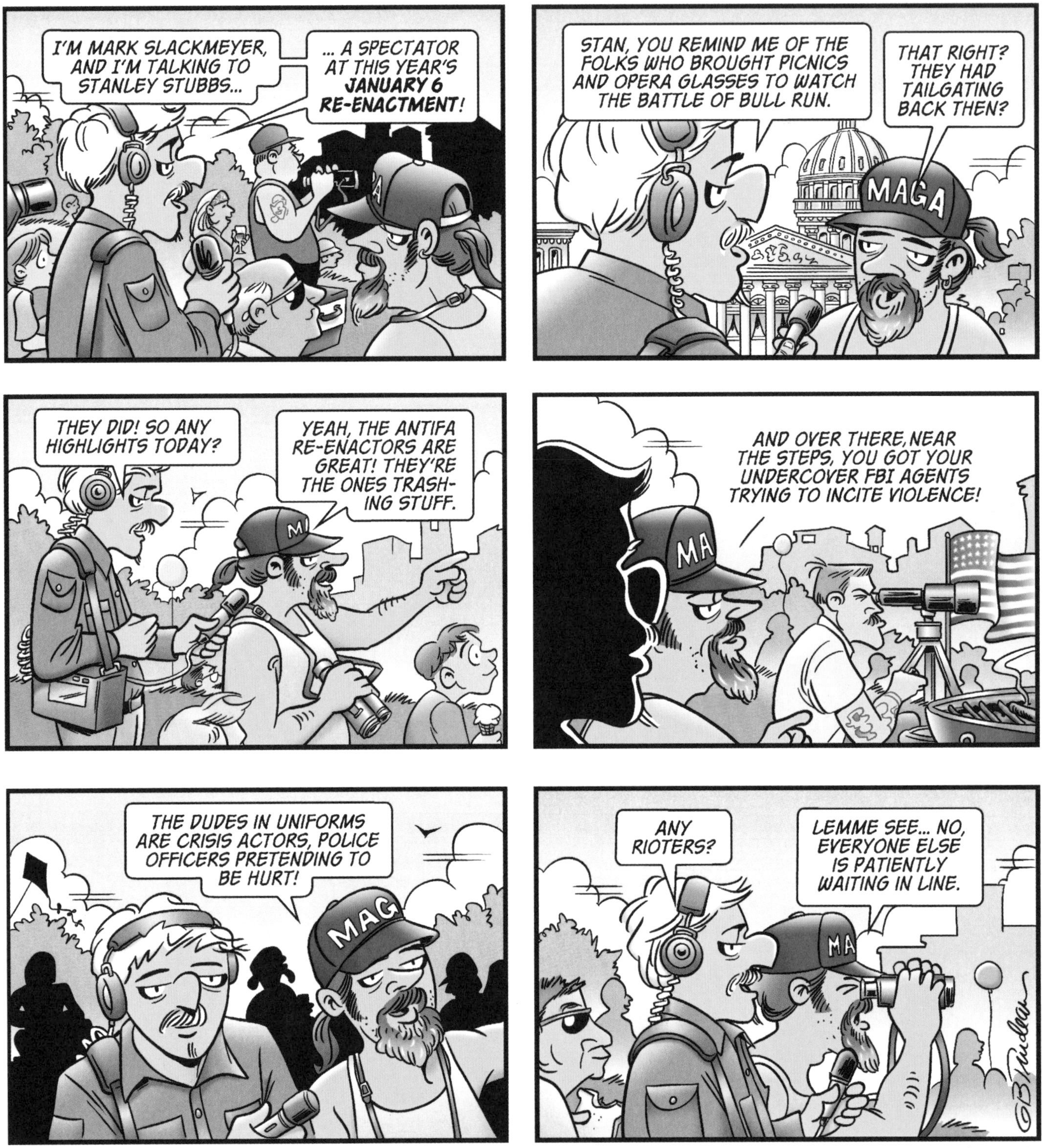
I'M MARK SLACKMEYER, AND I'M TALKING TO STANLEY STUBBS...
... A SPECTATOR AT THIS YEAR'S JANUARY 6 RE-ENACTMENT!
STAN, YOU REMIND ME OF THE FOLKS WHO BROUGHT PICNICS AND OPERA GLASSES TO WATCH THE BATTLE OF BULL RUN.
THAT RIGHT? THEY HAD TAILGATING BACK THEN?
MAGA
THEY DID! SO ANY HIGHLIGHTS TODAY?
YEAH, THE ANTIFA RE-ENACTORS ARE GREAT! THEY'RE THE ONES TRASHING STUFF.
AND OVER THERE, NEAR THE STEPS, YOU GOT YOUR UNDERCOVER FBI AGENTS TRYING TO INCITE VIOLENCE!
THE DUDES IN UNIFORMS ARE CRISIS ACTORS, POLICE OFFICERS PRETENDING TO BE HURT!
ANY RIOTERS?
LEMME SEE... NO, EVERYONE ELSE IS PATIENTLY WAITING IN LINE.

September 17, 2023

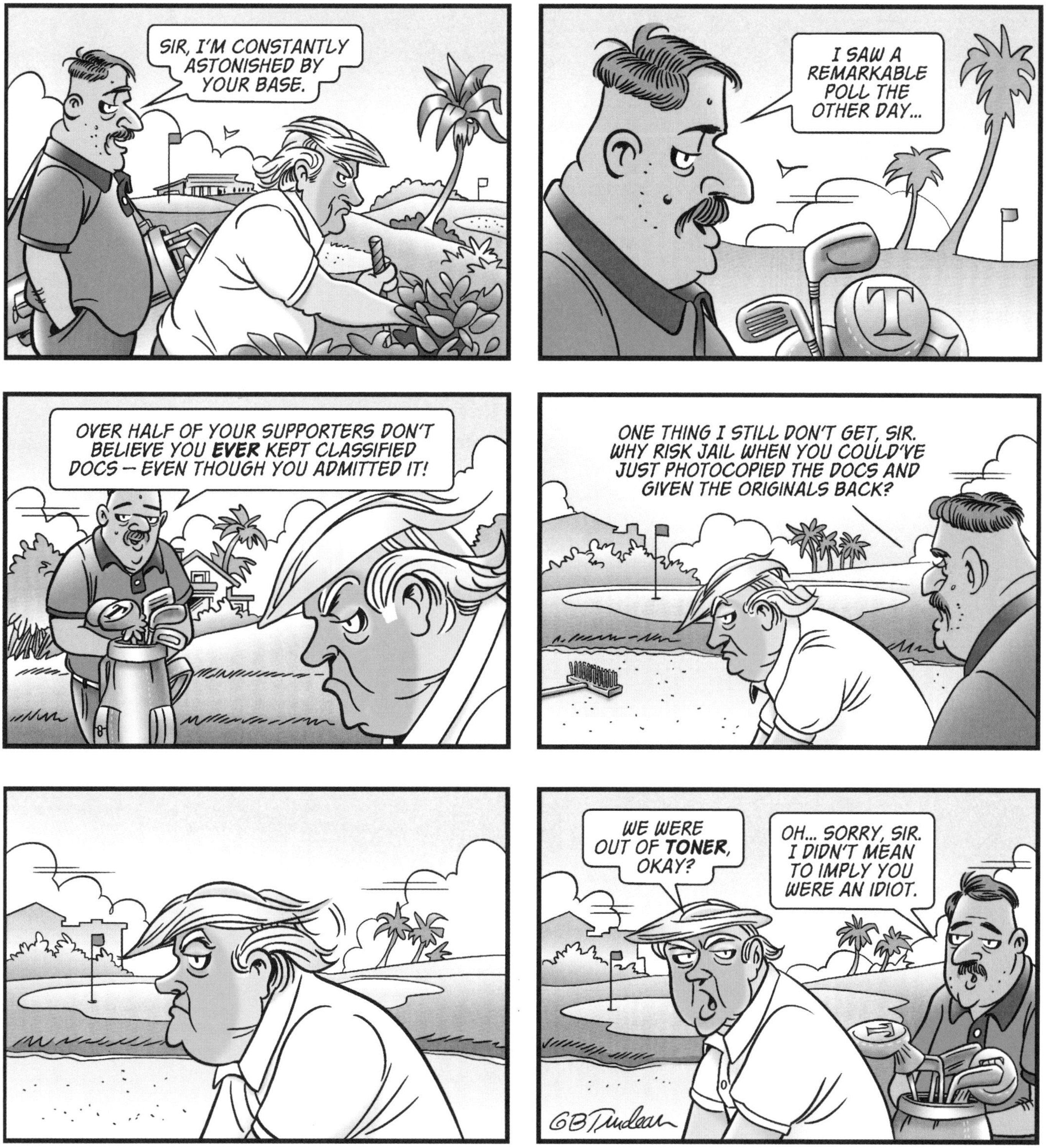
SIR, I'M CONSTANTLY ASTONISHED BY YOUR BASE.
I SAW A REMARKABLE POLL THE OTHER DAY...
OVER HALF OF YOUR SUPPORTERS DON'T BELIEVE YOU **EVER** KEPT CLASSIFIED DOCS — EVEN THOUGH YOU ADMITTED IT!
ONE THING I STILL DON'T GET, SIR. WHY RISK JAIL WHEN YOU COULD'VE JUST PHOTOCOPIED THE DOCS AND GIVEN THE ORIGINALS BACK?
WE WERE OUT OF **TONER**, OKAY?
OH... SORRY, SIR. I DIDN'T MEAN TO IMPLY YOU WERE AN IDIOT.
GBTrudeau

September 24, 2023

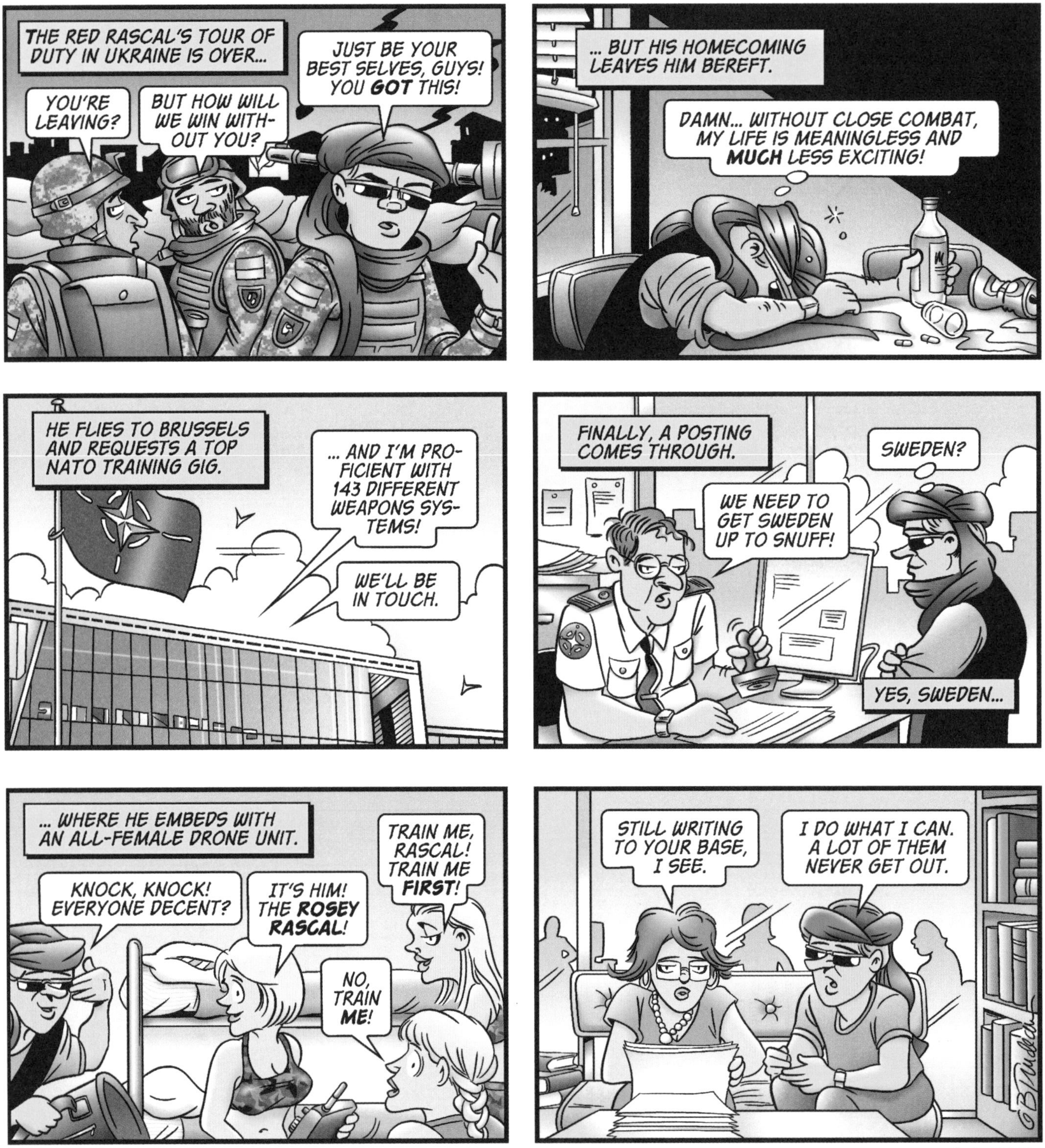
THE RED RASCAL'S TOUR OF DUTY IN UKRAINE IS OVER...
YOU'RE LEAVING?
BUT HOW WILL WE WIN WITH-OUT YOU?
JUST BE YOUR BEST SELVES, GUYS! YOU **GOT** THIS!
... BUT HIS HOMECOMING LEAVES HIM BEREFT.
DAMN... WITHOUT CLOSE COMBAT, MY LIFE IS MEANINGLESS AND **MUCH** LESS EXCITING!
HE FLIES TO BRUSSELS AND REQUESTS A TOP NATO TRAINING GIG.
... AND I'M PRO-FICIENT WITH 143 DIFFERENT WEAPONS SYS-TEMS!
WE'LL BE IN TOUCH.
FINALLY, A POSTING COMES THROUGH.
WE NEED TO GET SWEDEN UP TO SNUFF!
SWEDEN?
YES, SWEDEN...
... WHERE HE EMBEDS WITH AN ALL-FEMALE DRONE UNIT.
KNOCK, KNOCK! EVERYONE DECENT?
IT'S HIM! THE **ROSEY RASCAL**!
TRAIN ME, RASCAL! TRAIN ME **FIRST**!
NO, TRAIN **ME**!
STILL WRITING TO YOUR BASE, I SEE.
I DO WHAT I CAN. A LOT OF THEM NEVER GET OUT.

October 1, 2023

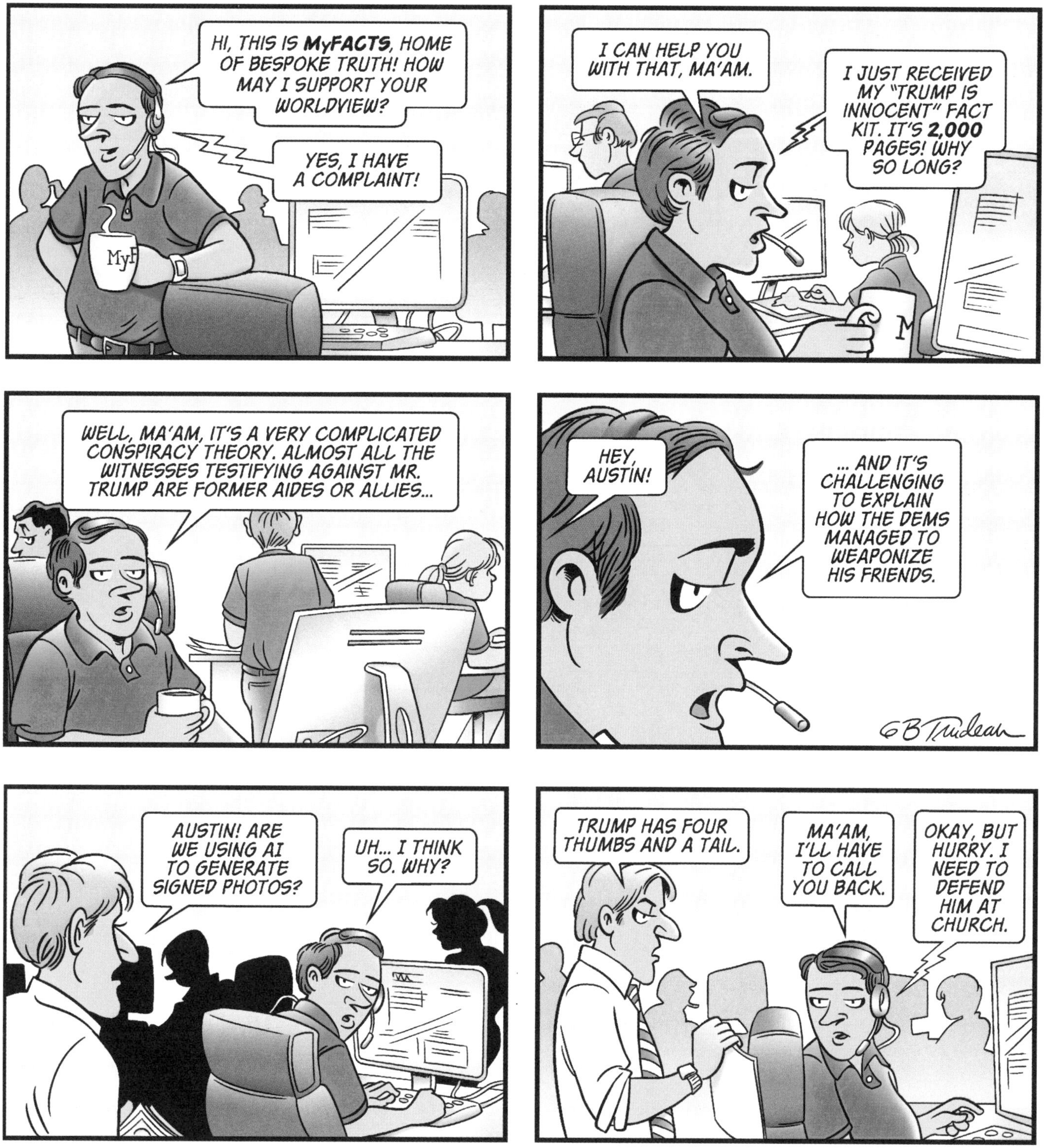
HI, THIS IS **MyFACTS**, HOME OF BESPOKE TRUTH! HOW MAY I SUPPORT YOUR WORLDVIEW?
YES, I HAVE A COMPLAINT!
I CAN HELP YOU WITH THAT, MA'AM.
I JUST RECEIVED MY "TRUMP IS INNOCENT" FACT KIT. IT'S **2,000** PAGES! WHY SO LONG?
WELL, MA'AM, IT'S A VERY COMPLICATED CONSPIRACY THEORY. ALMOST ALL THE WITNESSES TESTIFYING AGAINST MR. TRUMP ARE FORMER AIDES OR ALLIES...
HEY, AUSTIN!
... AND IT'S CHALLENGING TO EXPLAIN HOW THE DEMS MANAGED TO WEAPONIZE HIS FRIENDS.
GB Trudeau
AUSTIN! ARE WE USING AI TO GENERATE SIGNED PHOTOS?
UH... I THINK SO. WHY?
TRUMP HAS FOUR THUMBS AND A TAIL.
MA'AM, I'LL HAVE TO CALL YOU BACK.
OKAY, BUT HURRY. I NEED TO DEFEND HIM AT CHURCH.

October 8, 2023

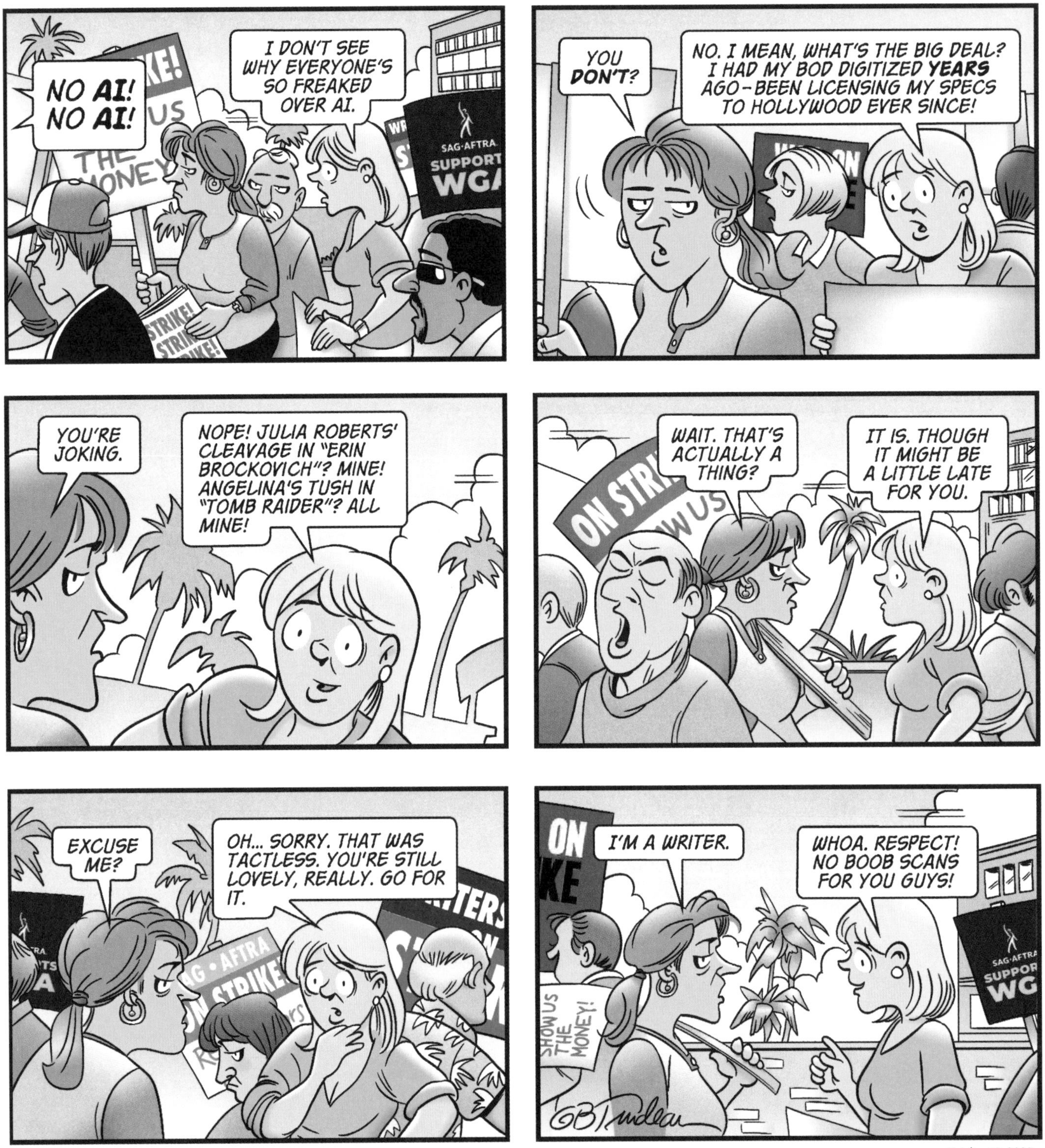
NO AI! NO AI!
I DON'T SEE WHY EVERYONE'S SO FREAKED OVER AI.
YOU DON'T?
NO. I MEAN, WHAT'S THE BIG DEAL? I HAD MY BOD DIGITIZED YEARS AGO–BEEN LICENSING MY SPECS TO HOLLYWOOD EVER SINCE!
YOU'RE JOKING.
NOPE! JULIA ROBERTS' CLEAVAGE IN "ERIN BROCKOVICH"? MINE! ANGELINA'S TUSH IN "TOMB RAIDER"? ALL MINE!
WAIT. THAT'S ACTUALLY A THING?
IT IS. THOUGH IT MIGHT BE A LITTLE LATE FOR YOU.
EXCUSE ME?
OH... SORRY. THAT WAS TACTLESS. YOU'RE STILL LOVELY, REALLY. GO FOR IT.
I'M A WRITER.
WHOA. RESPECT! NO BOOB SCANS FOR YOU GUYS!

October 15, 2023

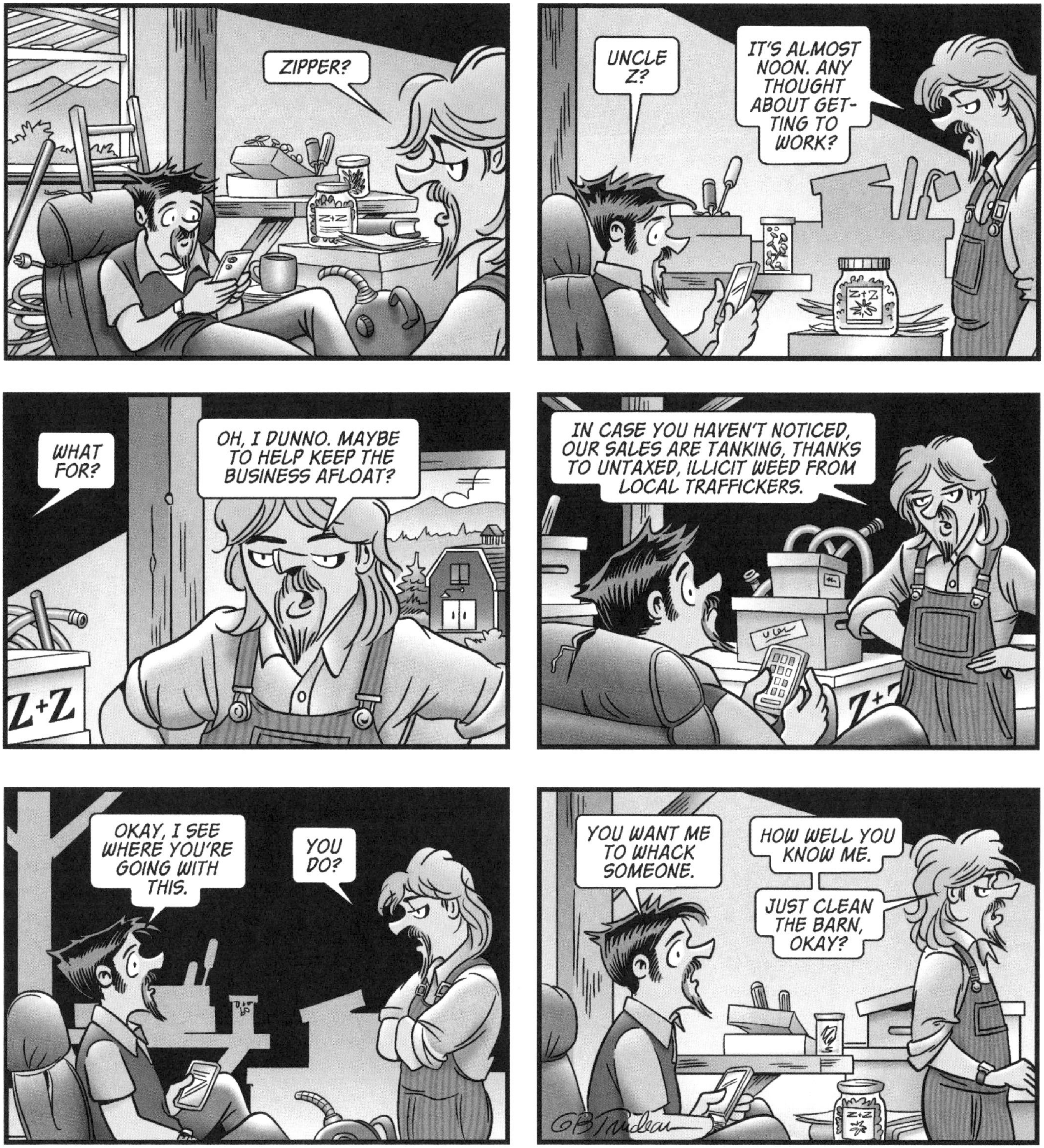
ZIPPER?
UNCLE Z?
IT'S ALMOST NOON. ANY THOUGHT ABOUT GET-TING TO WORK?
WHAT FOR?
OH, I DUNNO. MAYBE TO HELP KEEP THE BUSINESS AFLOAT?
IN CASE YOU HAVEN'T NOTICED, OUR SALES ARE TANKING, THANKS TO UNTAXED, ILLICIT WEED FROM LOCAL TRAFFICKERS.
OKAY, I SEE WHERE YOU'RE GOING WITH THIS.
YOU DO?
YOU WANT ME TO WHACK SOMEONE.
HOW WELL YOU KNOW ME.
JUST CLEAN THE BARN, OKAY?
GB Trudeau

October 22, 2023

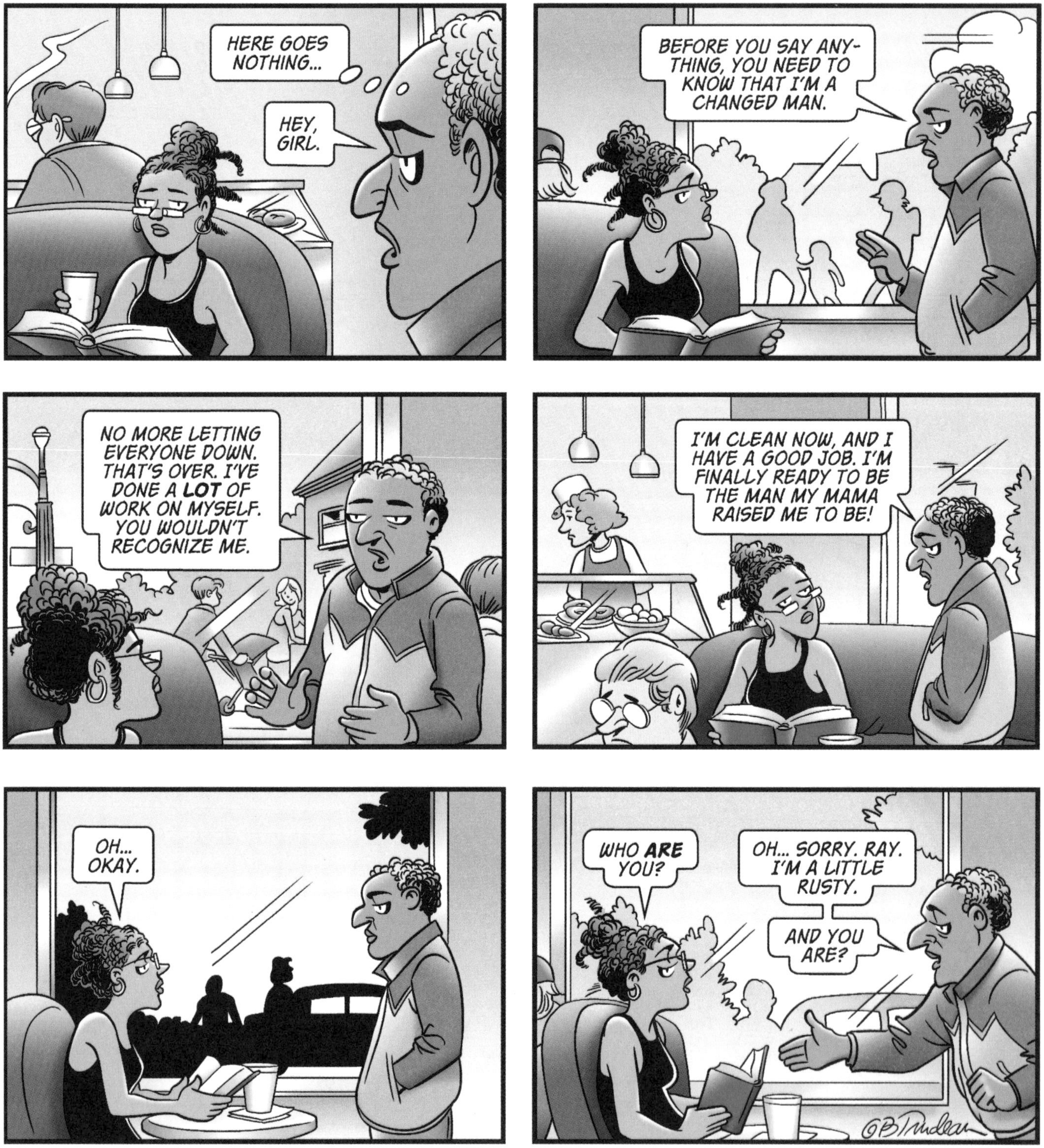
HERE GOES NOTHING...
HEY, GIRL.
BEFORE YOU SAY ANY-THING, YOU NEED TO KNOW THAT I'M A CHANGED MAN.
NO MORE LETTING EVERYONE DOWN. THAT'S OVER. I'VE DONE A **LOT** OF WORK ON MYSELF. YOU WOULDN'T RECOGNIZE ME.
I'M CLEAN NOW, AND I HAVE A GOOD JOB. I'M FINALLY READY TO BE THE MAN MY MAMA RAISED ME TO BE!
OH... OKAY.
WHO **ARE** YOU?
OH... SORRY. RAY. I'M A LITTLE RUSTY.
AND YOU ARE?
©B Trudeau

October 29, 2023

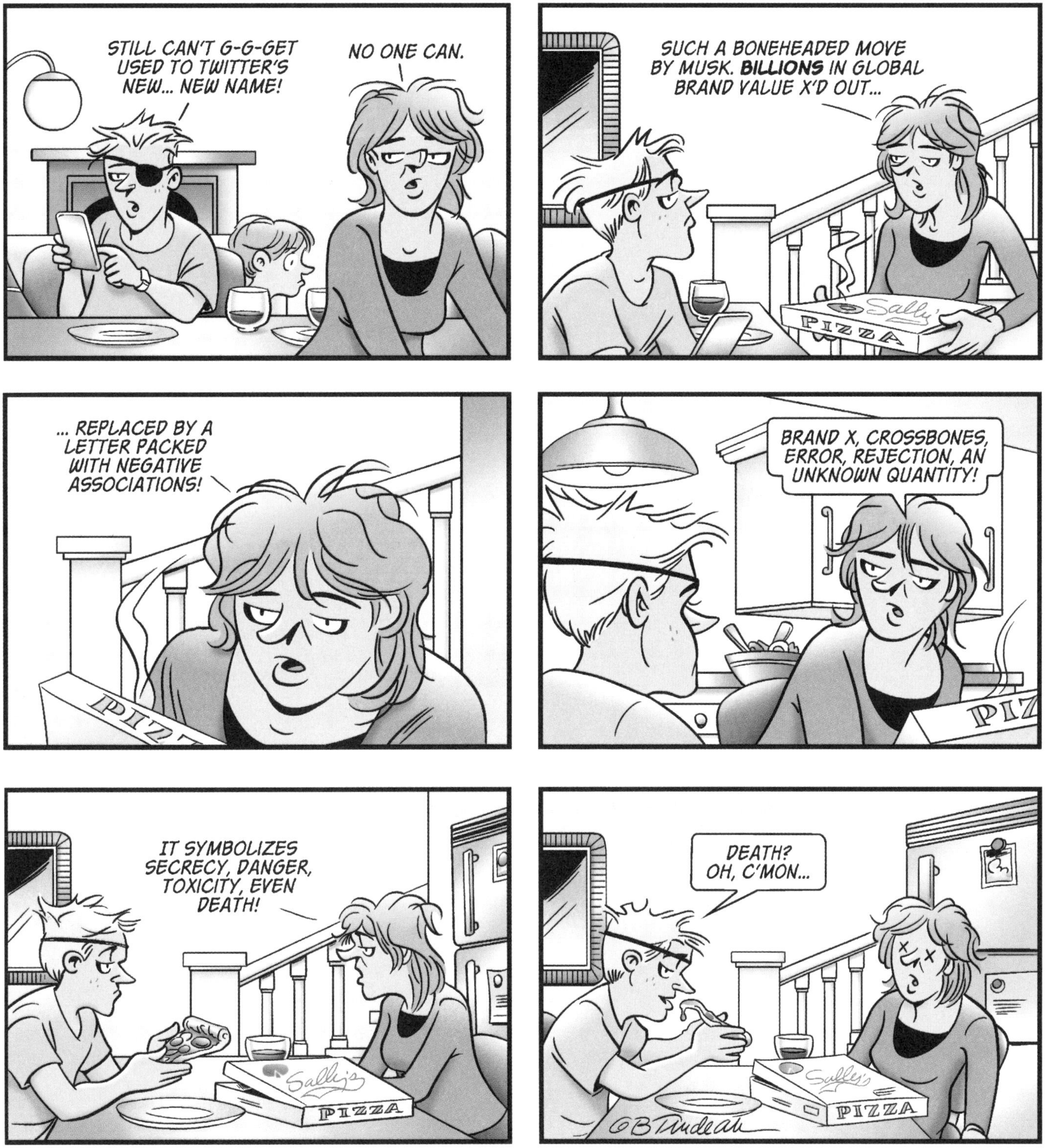
STILL CAN'T G-G-GET USED TO TWITTER'S NEW... NEW NAME!
NO ONE CAN.
SUCH A BONEHEADED MOVE BY MUSK. **BILLIONS** IN GLOBAL BRAND VALUE X'D OUT...
Sally's
PIZZA
... REPLACED BY A LETTER PACKED WITH NEGATIVE ASSOCIATIONS!
BRAND X, CROSSBONES, ERROR, REJECTION, AN UNKNOWN QUANTITY!
IT SYMBOLIZES SECRECY, DANGER, TOXICITY, EVEN DEATH!
DEATH? OH, C'MON...
©B Trudeau

November 5, 2023

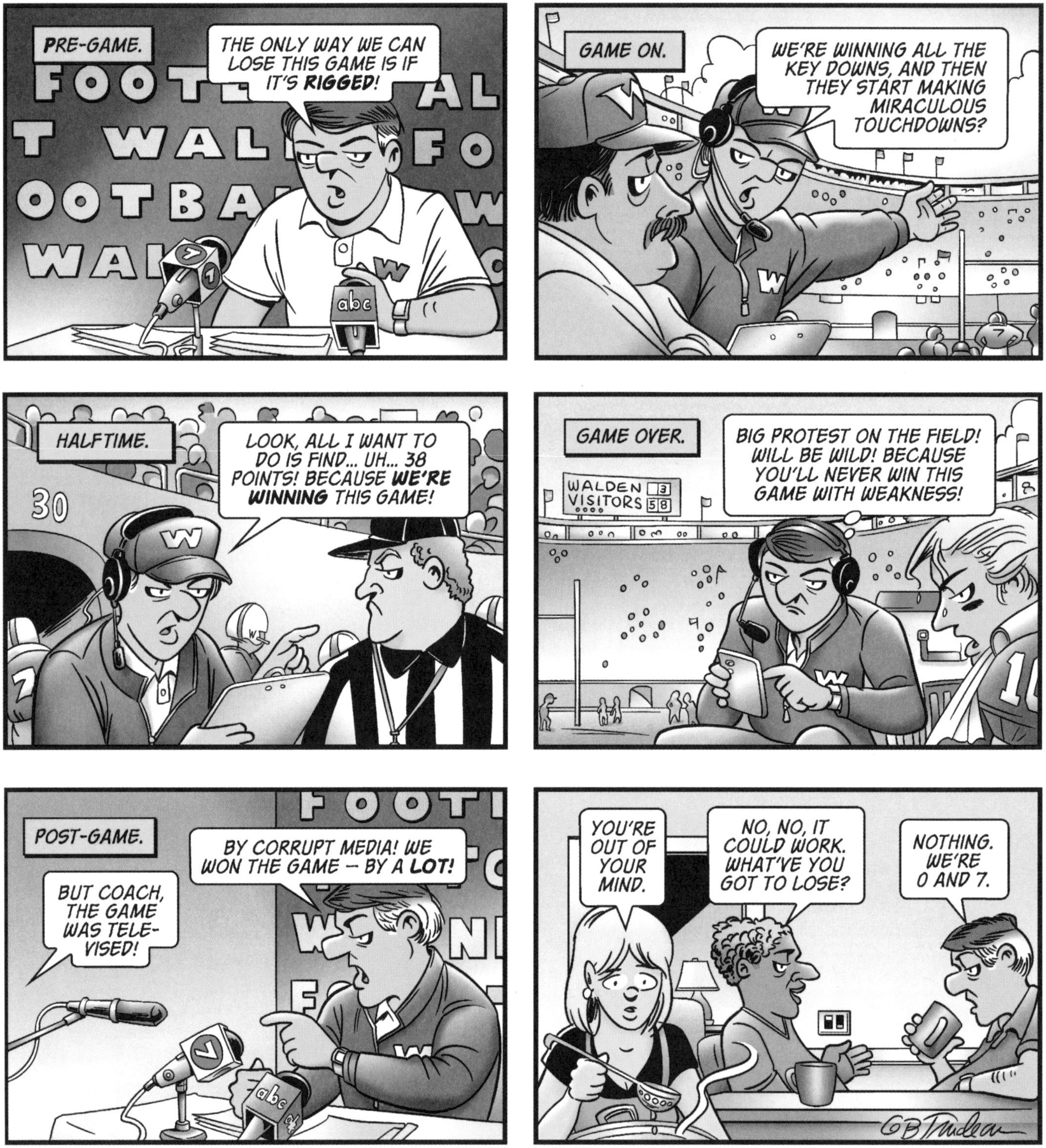
PRE-GAME.
THE ONLY WAY WE CAN LOSE THIS GAME IS IF IT'S **RIGGED**!
GAME ON.
WE'RE WINNING ALL THE KEY DOWNS, AND THEN THEY START MAKING MIRACULOUS TOUCHDOWNS?
HALFTIME.
LOOK, ALL I WANT TO DO IS FIND... UH... 38 POINTS! BECAUSE **WE'RE WINNING** THIS GAME!
GAME OVER.
WALDEN 3
VISITORS 58
BIG PROTEST ON THE FIELD! WILL BE WILD! BECAUSE YOU'LL NEVER WIN THIS GAME WITH WEAKNESS!
POST-GAME.
BUT COACH, THE GAME WAS TELE-VISED!
BY CORRUPT MEDIA! WE WON THE GAME — BY A **LOT**!
YOU'RE OUT OF YOUR MIND.
NO, NO, IT COULD WORK. WHAT'VE YOU GOT TO LOSE?
NOTHING. WE'RE 0 AND 7.
GB Trudeau

November 12, 2023

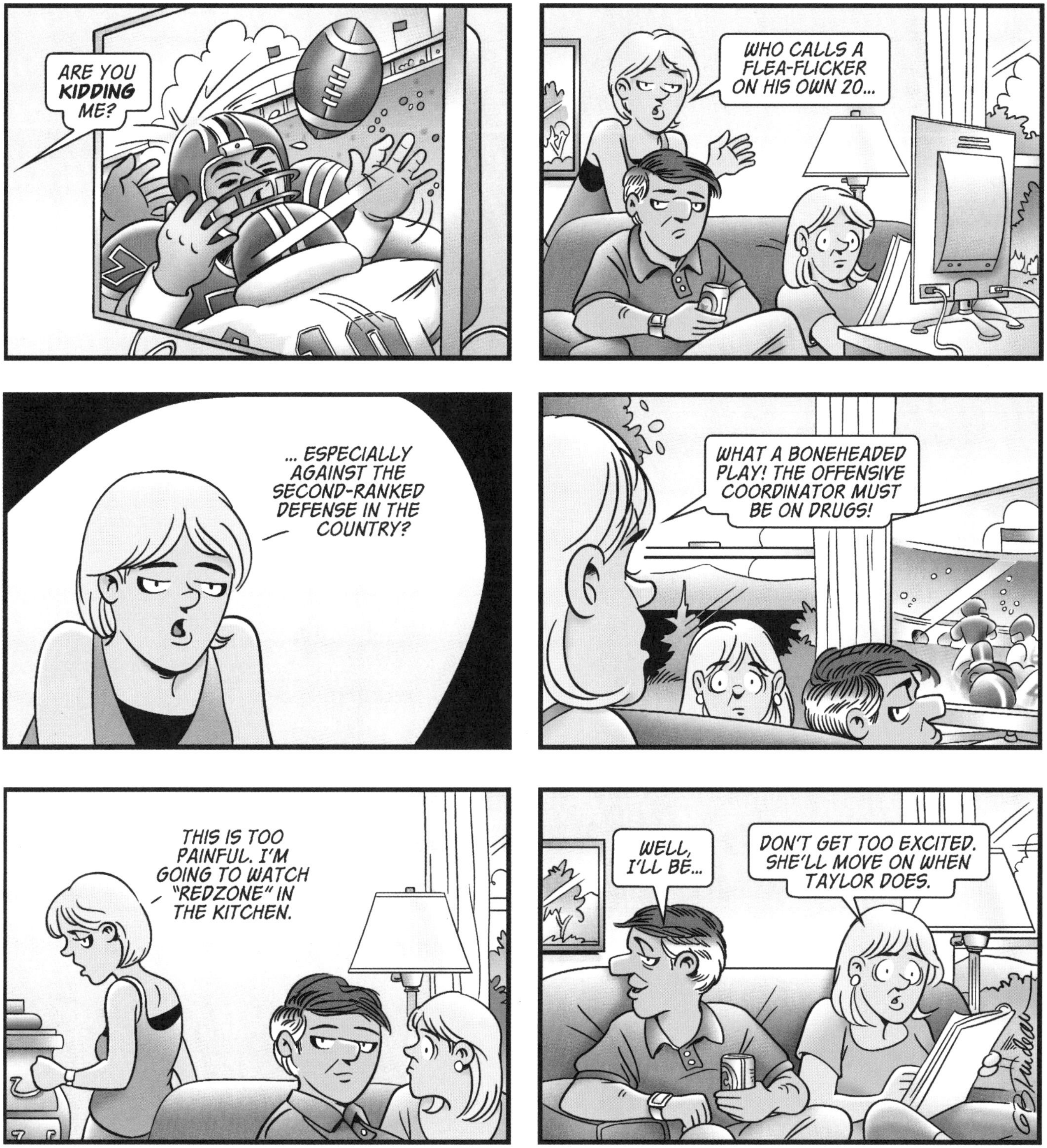
ARE YOU KIDDING ME?
WHO CALLS A FLEA-FLICKER ON HIS OWN 20...
... ESPECIALLY AGAINST THE SECOND-RANKED DEFENSE IN THE COUNTRY?
WHAT A BONEHEADED PLAY! THE OFFENSIVE COORDINATOR MUST BE ON DRUGS!
THIS IS TOO PAINFUL. I'M GOING TO WATCH "REDZONE" IN THE KITCHEN.
WELL, I'LL BE...
DON'T GET TOO EXCITED. SHE'LL MOVE ON WHEN TAYLOR DOES.

November 19, 2023

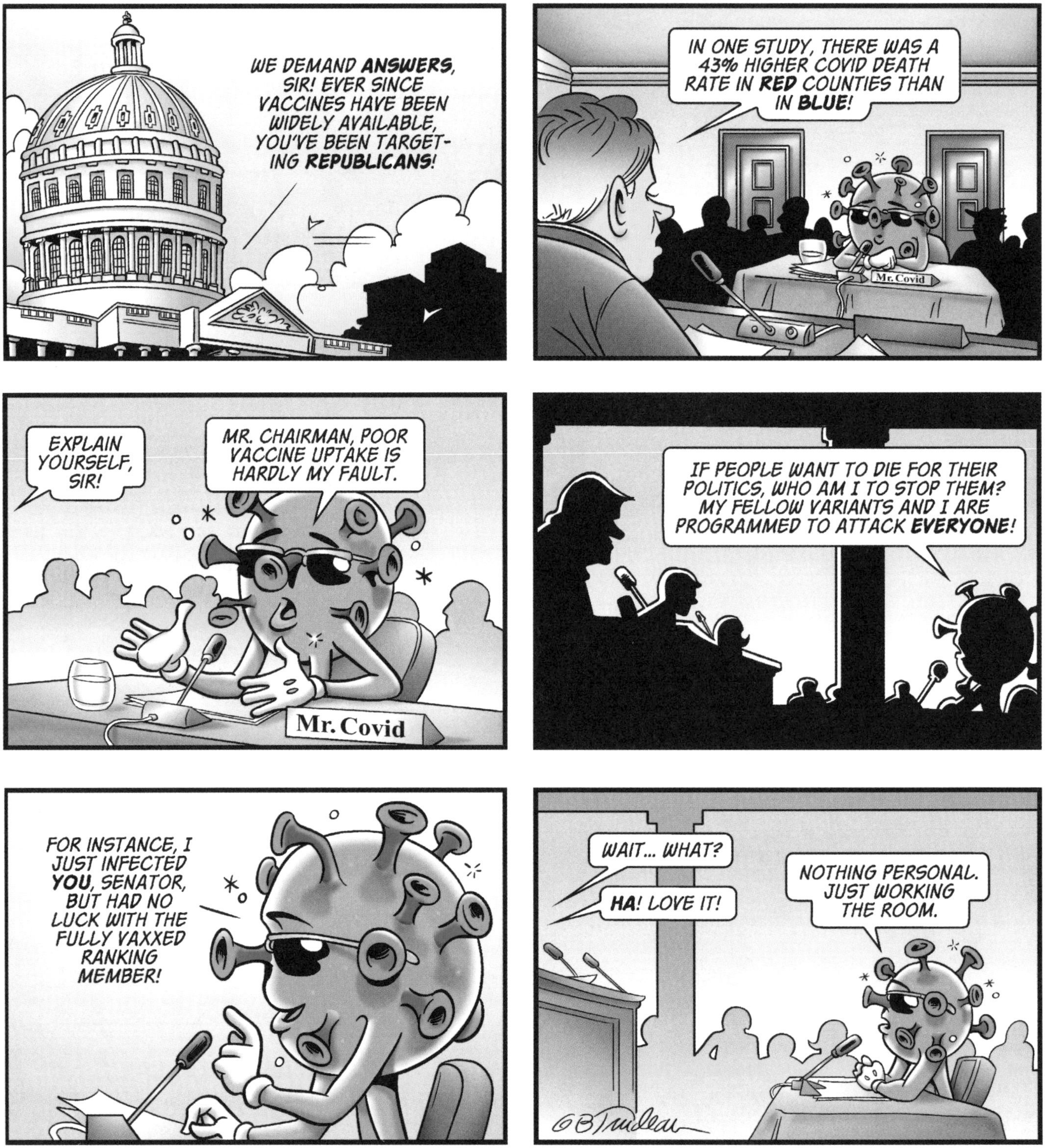
WE DEMAND **ANSWERS**, SIR! EVER SINCE VACCINES HAVE BEEN WIDELY AVAILABLE, YOU'VE BEEN TARGETING **REPUBLICANS**!
IN ONE STUDY, THERE WAS A 43% HIGHER COVID DEATH RATE IN **RED** COUNTIES THAN IN **BLUE**!
Mr. Covid
EXPLAIN YOURSELF, SIR!
MR. CHAIRMAN, POOR VACCINE UPTAKE IS HARDLY MY FAULT.
Mr. Covid
IF PEOPLE WANT TO DIE FOR THEIR POLITICS, WHO AM I TO STOP THEM? MY FELLOW VARIANTS AND I ARE PROGRAMMED TO ATTACK **EVERYONE**!
FOR INSTANCE, I JUST INFECTED **YOU**, SENATOR, BUT HAD NO LUCK WITH THE FULLY VAXXED RANKING MEMBER!
WAIT... WHAT?
HA! LOVE IT!
NOTHING PERSONAL. JUST WORKING THE ROOM.

November 26, 2023

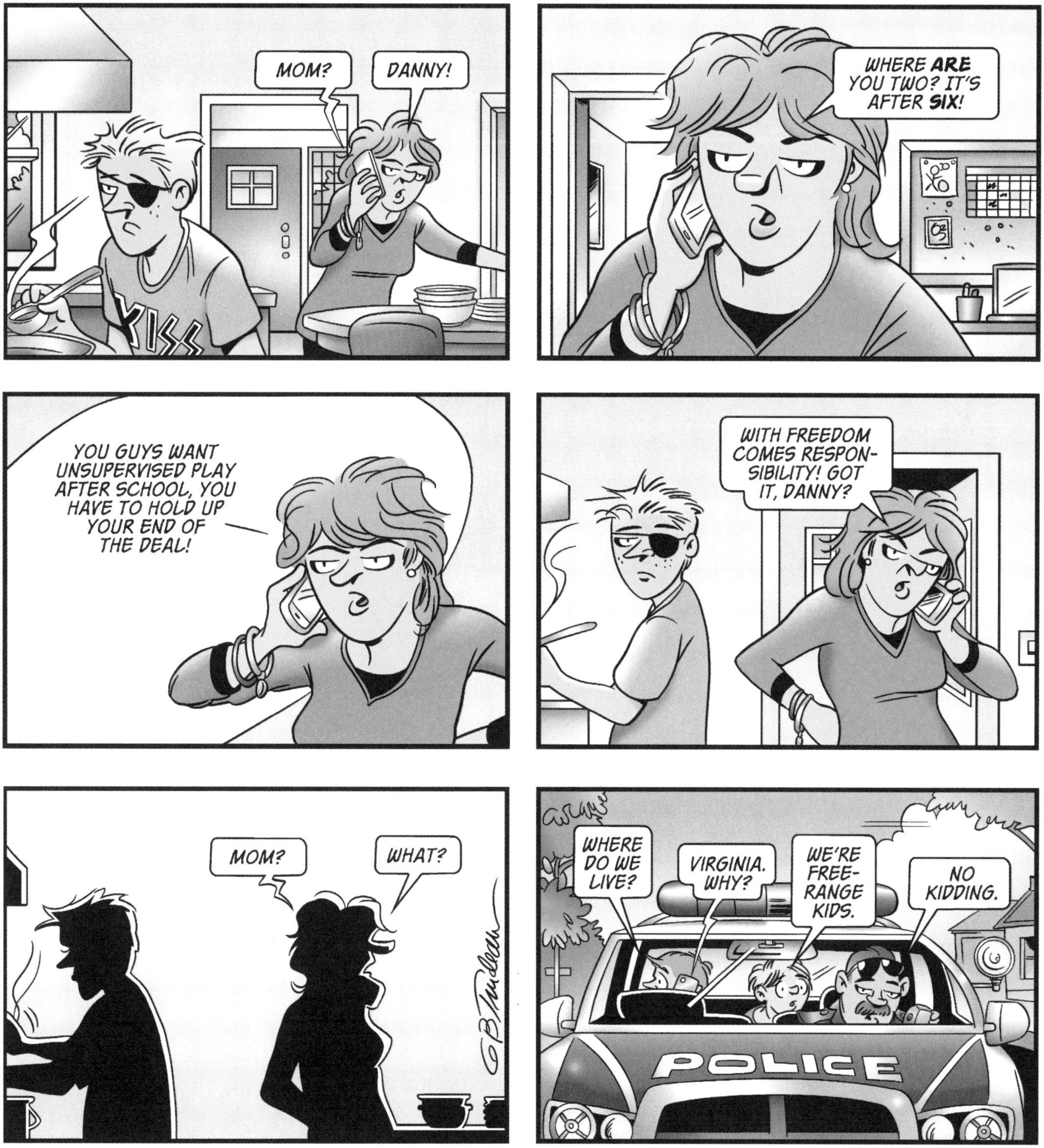
MOM?
DANNY!
WHERE **ARE** YOU TWO? IT'S AFTER **SIX**!
YOU GUYS WANT UNSUPERVISED PLAY AFTER SCHOOL, YOU HAVE TO HOLD UP YOUR END OF THE DEAL!
WITH FREEDOM COMES RESPON-SIBILITY! GOT IT, DANNY?
MOM?
WHAT?
WHERE DO WE LIVE?
VIRGINIA. WHY?
WE'RE FREE-RANGE KIDS.
NO KIDDING.
POLICE
GB Trudeau

December 3, 2023

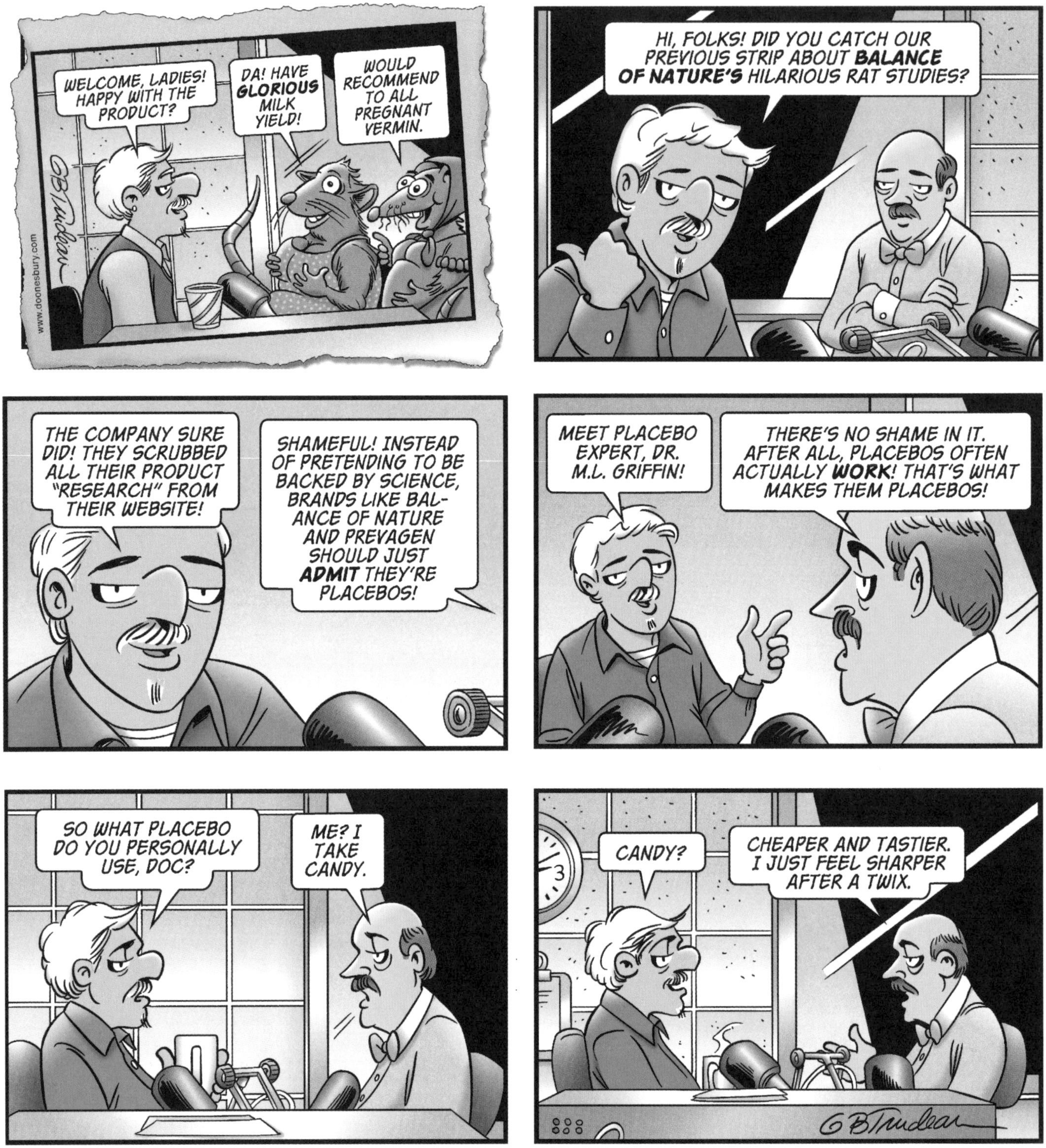
WELCOME, LADIES! HAPPY WITH THE PRODUCT?
DA! HAVE **GLORIOUS** MILK YIELD!
WOULD RECOMMEND TO ALL PREGNANT VERMIN.
www.doonesbury.com
HI, FOLKS! DID YOU CATCH OUR PREVIOUS STRIP ABOUT **BALANCE OF NATURE'S** HILARIOUS RAT STUDIES?
THE COMPANY SURE DID! THEY SCRUBBED ALL THEIR PRODUCT "RESEARCH" FROM THEIR WEBSITE!
SHAMEFUL! INSTEAD OF PRETENDING TO BE BACKED BY SCIENCE, BRANDS LIKE BALANCE OF NATURE AND PREVAGEN SHOULD JUST **ADMIT** THEY'RE PLACEBOS!
MEET PLACEBO EXPERT, DR. M.L. GRIFFIN!
THERE'S NO SHAME IN IT. AFTER ALL, PLACEBOS OFTEN ACTUALLY **WORK**! THAT'S WHAT MAKES THEM PLACEBOS!
SO WHAT PLACEBO DO YOU PERSONALLY USE, DOC?
ME? I TAKE CANDY.
CANDY?
CHEAPER AND TASTIER. I JUST FEEL SHARPER AFTER A TWIX.

December 10, 2023

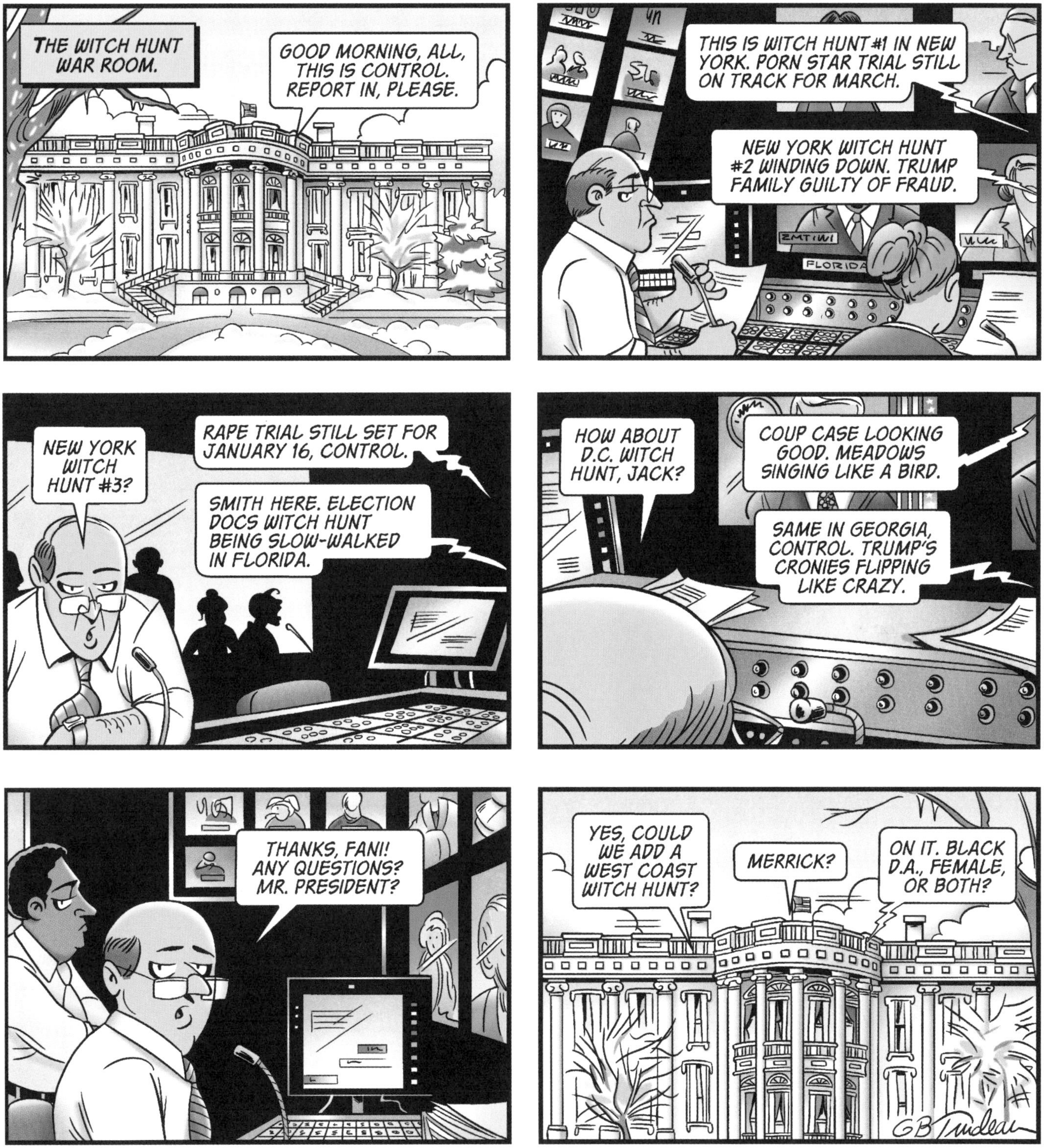
THE WITCH HUNT WAR ROOM.
GOOD MORNING, ALL, THIS IS CONTROL. REPORT IN, PLEASE.
THIS IS WITCH HUNT #1 IN NEW YORK. PORN STAR TRIAL STILL ON TRACK FOR MARCH.
NEW YORK WITCH HUNT #2 WINDING DOWN. TRUMP FAMILY GUILTY OF FRAUD.
NEW YORK WITCH HUNT #3?
RAPE TRIAL STILL SET FOR JANUARY 16, CONTROL.
SMITH HERE. ELECTION DOCS WITCH HUNT BEING SLOW-WALKED IN FLORIDA.
HOW ABOUT D.C. WITCH HUNT, JACK?
COUP CASE LOOKING GOOD. MEADOWS SINGING LIKE A BIRD.
SAME IN GEORGIA, CONTROL. TRUMP'S CRONIES FLIPPING LIKE CRAZY.
THANKS, FANI! ANY QUESTIONS? MR. PRESIDENT?
YES, COULD WE ADD A WEST COAST WITCH HUNT?
MERRICK?
ON IT. BLACK D.A., FEMALE, OR BOTH?
GB Trudeau

December 17, 2023

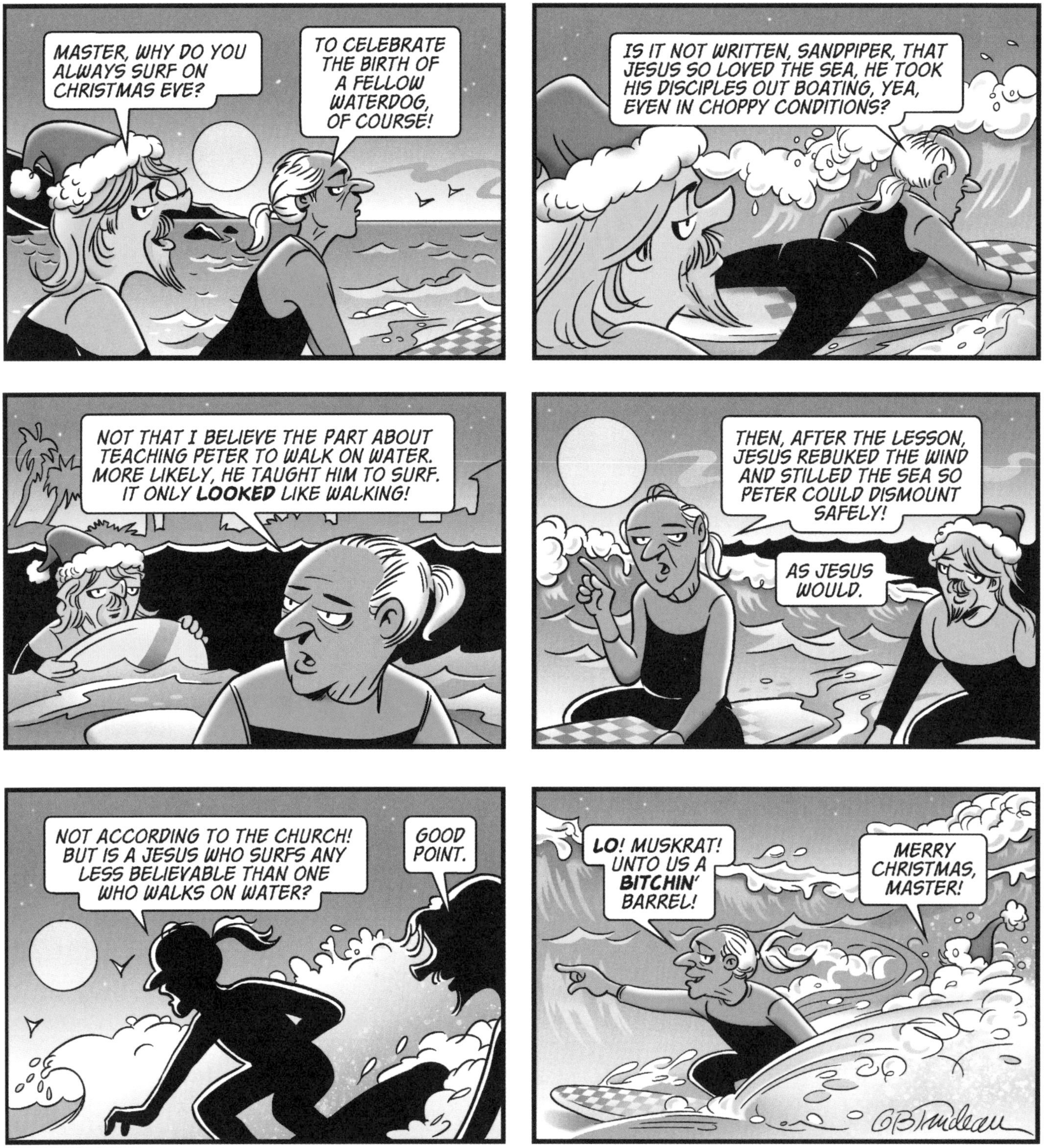
MASTER, WHY DO YOU ALWAYS SURF ON CHRISTMAS EVE?
TO CELEBRATE THE BIRTH OF A FELLOW WATERDOG, OF COURSE!
IS IT NOT WRITTEN, SANDPIPER, THAT JESUS SO LOVED THE SEA, HE TOOK HIS DISCIPLES OUT BOATING, YEA, EVEN IN CHOPPY CONDITIONS?
NOT THAT I BELIEVE THE PART ABOUT TEACHING PETER TO WALK ON WATER. MORE LIKELY, HE TAUGHT HIM TO SURF. IT ONLY **LOOKED** LIKE WALKING!
THEN, AFTER THE LESSON, JESUS REBUKED THE WIND AND STILLED THE SEA SO PETER COULD DISMOUNT SAFELY!
AS JESUS WOULD.
NOT ACCORDING TO THE CHURCH! BUT IS A JESUS WHO SURFS ANY LESS BELIEVABLE THAN ONE WHO WALKS ON WATER?
GOOD POINT.
LO! MUSKRAT! UNTO US A **BITCHIN'** BARREL!
MERRY CHRISTMAS, MASTER!
GBTrudeau

December 24, 2023

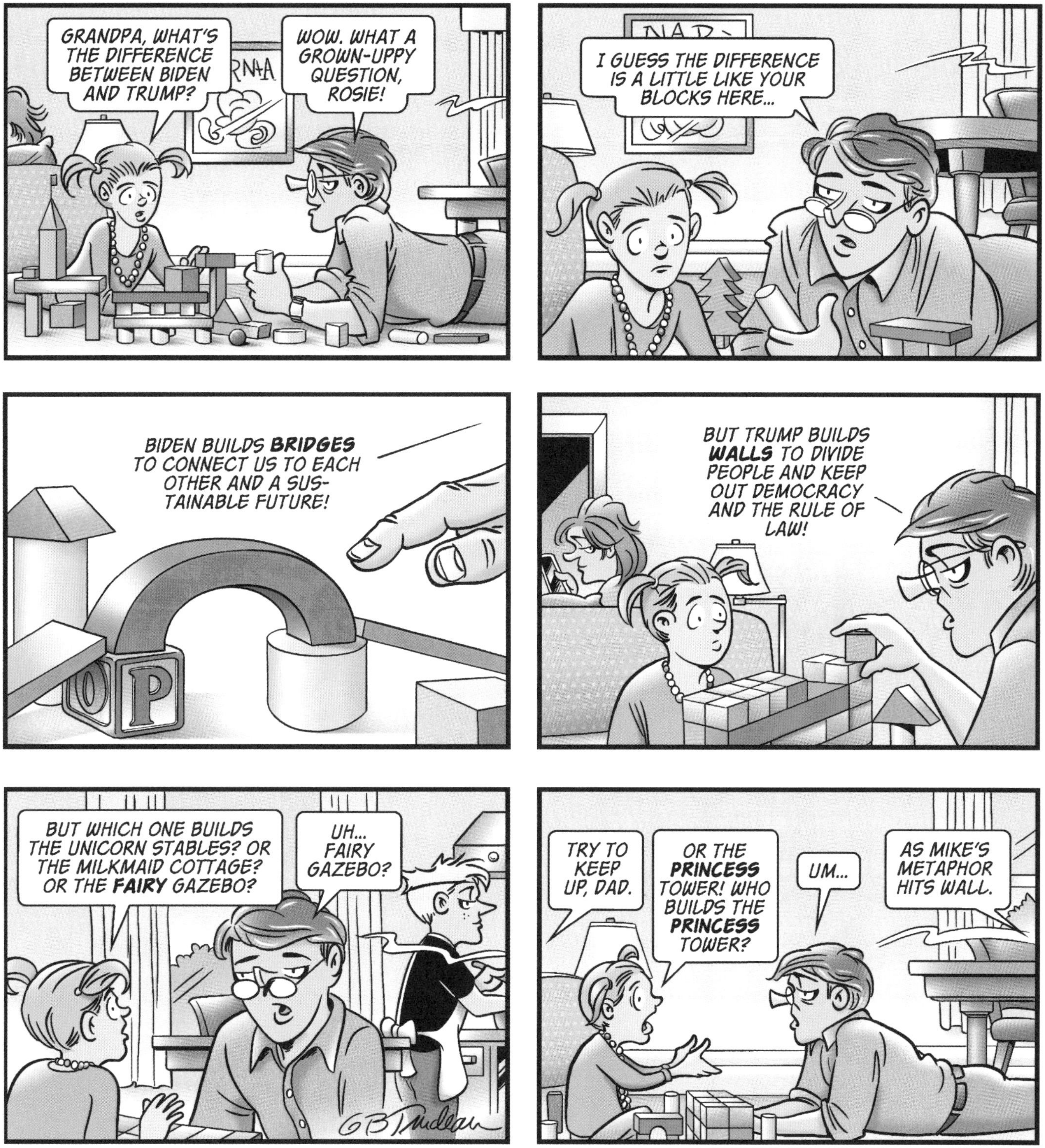
GRANDPA, WHAT'S THE DIFFERENCE BETWEEN BIDEN AND TRUMP?
WOW. WHAT A GROWN-UPPY QUESTION, ROSIE!
I GUESS THE DIFFERENCE IS A LITTLE LIKE YOUR BLOCKS HERE...
BIDEN BUILDS **BRIDGES** TO CONNECT US TO EACH OTHER AND A SUSTAINABLE FUTURE!
BUT TRUMP BUILDS **WALLS** TO DIVIDE PEOPLE AND KEEP OUT DEMOCRACY AND THE RULE OF LAW!
BUT WHICH ONE BUILDS THE UNICORN STABLES? OR THE MILKMAID COTTAGE? OR THE **FAIRY** GAZEBO?
UH... FAIRY GAZEBO?
GB Trudeau
TRY TO KEEP UP, DAD.
OR THE **PRINCESS** TOWER! WHO BUILDS THE **PRINCESS** TOWER?
UM...
AS MIKE'S METAPHOR HITS WALL.

December 31, 2023

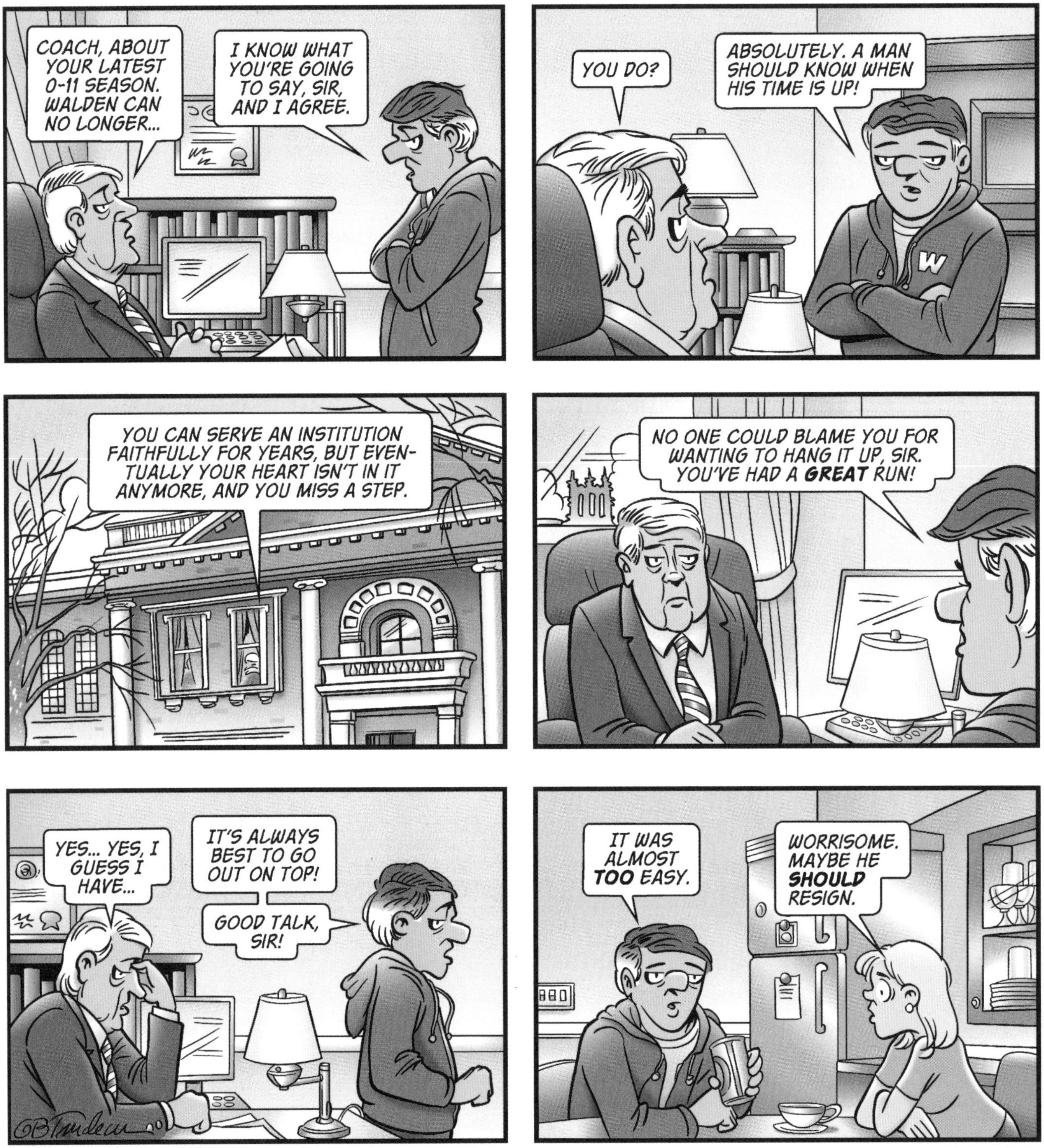
COACH, ABOUT YOUR LATEST 0-11 SEASON. WALDEN CAN NO LONGER...
I KNOW WHAT YOU'RE GOING TO SAY, SIR, AND I AGREE.
YOU DO?
ABSOLUTELY. A MAN SHOULD KNOW WHEN HIS TIME IS UP!
YOU CAN SERVE AN INSTITUTION FAITHFULLY FOR YEARS, BUT EVEN-TUALLY YOUR HEART ISN'T IN IT ANYMORE, AND YOU MISS A STEP.
NO ONE COULD BLAME YOU FOR WANTING TO HANG IT UP, SIR. YOU'VE HAD A GREAT RUN!
YES... YES, I GUESS I HAVE...
IT'S ALWAYS BEST TO GO OUT ON TOP!
GOOD TALK, SIR!
IT WAS ALMOST TOO EASY.
WORRISOME. MAYBE HE SHOULD RESIGN.

January 7, 2024

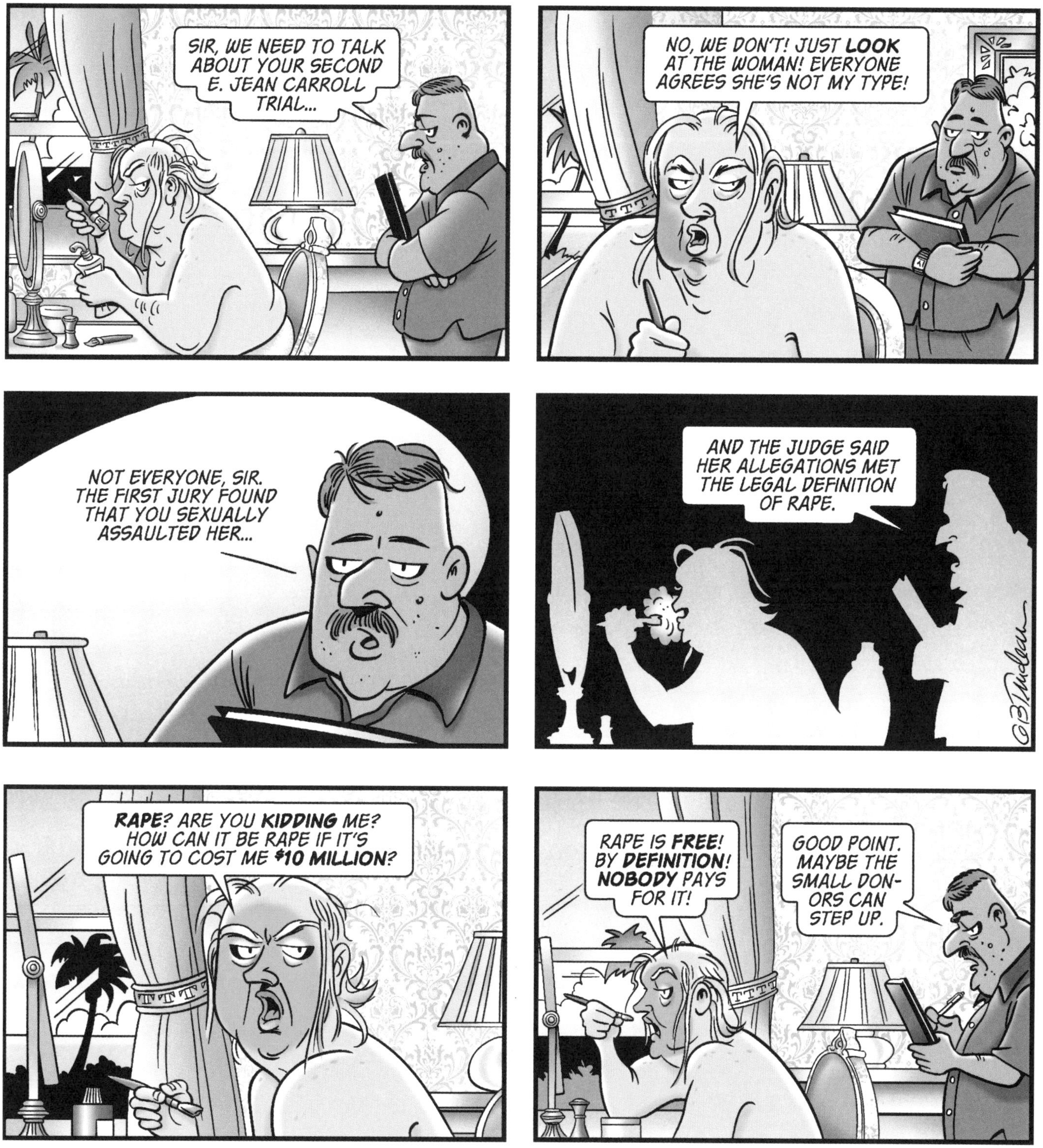
SIR, WE NEED TO TALK ABOUT YOUR SECOND E. JEAN CARROLL TRIAL...
NO, WE DON'T! JUST **LOOK** AT THE WOMAN! EVERYONE AGREES SHE'S NOT MY TYPE!
NOT EVERYONE, SIR. THE FIRST JURY FOUND THAT YOU SEXUALLY ASSAULTED HER...
AND THE JUDGE SAID HER ALLEGATIONS MET THE LEGAL DEFINITION OF RAPE.
RAPE? ARE YOU **KIDDING** ME? HOW CAN IT BE RAPE IF IT'S GOING TO COST ME **$10 MILLION**?
RAPE IS **FREE**! BY **DEFINITION**! **NOBODY** PAYS FOR IT!
GOOD POINT. MAYBE THE SMALL DON-ORS CAN STEP UP.

January 14, 2024

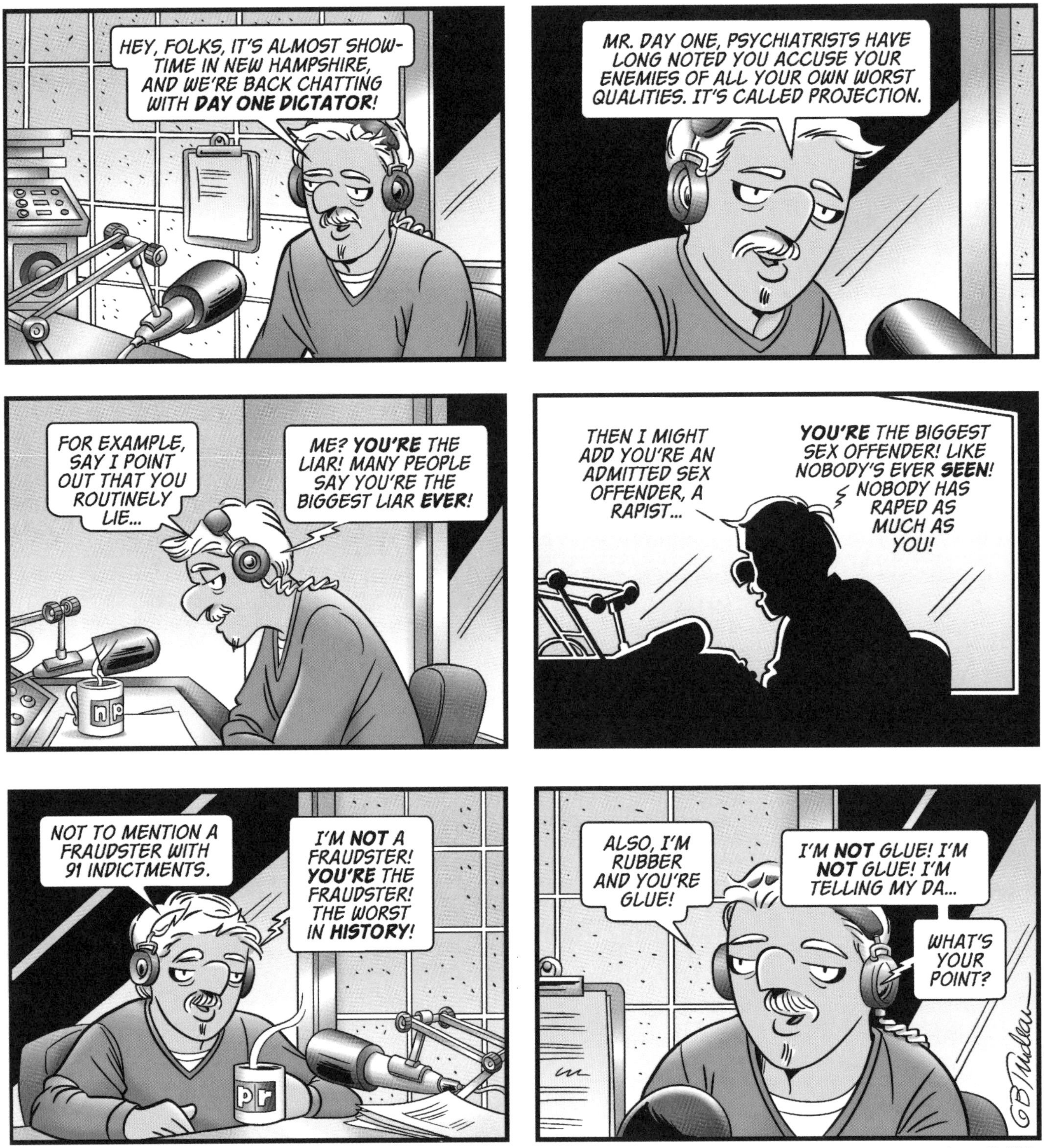
HEY, FOLKS, IT'S ALMOST SHOW-TIME IN NEW HAMPSHIRE, AND WE'RE BACK CHATTING WITH **DAY ONE DICTATOR**!
MR. DAY ONE, PSYCHIATRISTS HAVE LONG NOTED YOU ACCUSE YOUR ENEMIES OF ALL YOUR OWN WORST QUALITIES. IT'S CALLED PROJECTION.
FOR EXAMPLE, SAY I POINT OUT THAT YOU ROUTINELY LIE...
ME? **YOU'RE** THE LIAR! MANY PEOPLE SAY YOU'RE THE BIGGEST LIAR **EVER**!
THEN I MIGHT ADD YOU'RE AN ADMITTED SEX OFFENDER, A RAPIST...
YOU'RE THE BIGGEST SEX OFFENDER! LIKE NOBODY'S EVER **SEEN**! NOBODY HAS RAPED AS MUCH AS YOU!
NOT TO MENTION A FRAUDSTER WITH 91 INDICTMENTS.
I'M **NOT** A FRAUDSTER! **YOU'RE** THE FRAUDSTER! THE WORST IN **HISTORY**!
ALSO, I'M RUBBER AND YOU'RE GLUE!
I'M **NOT** GLUE! I'M **NOT** GLUE! I'M TELLING MY DA...
WHAT'S YOUR POINT?
GBTrudeau

January 21, 2024

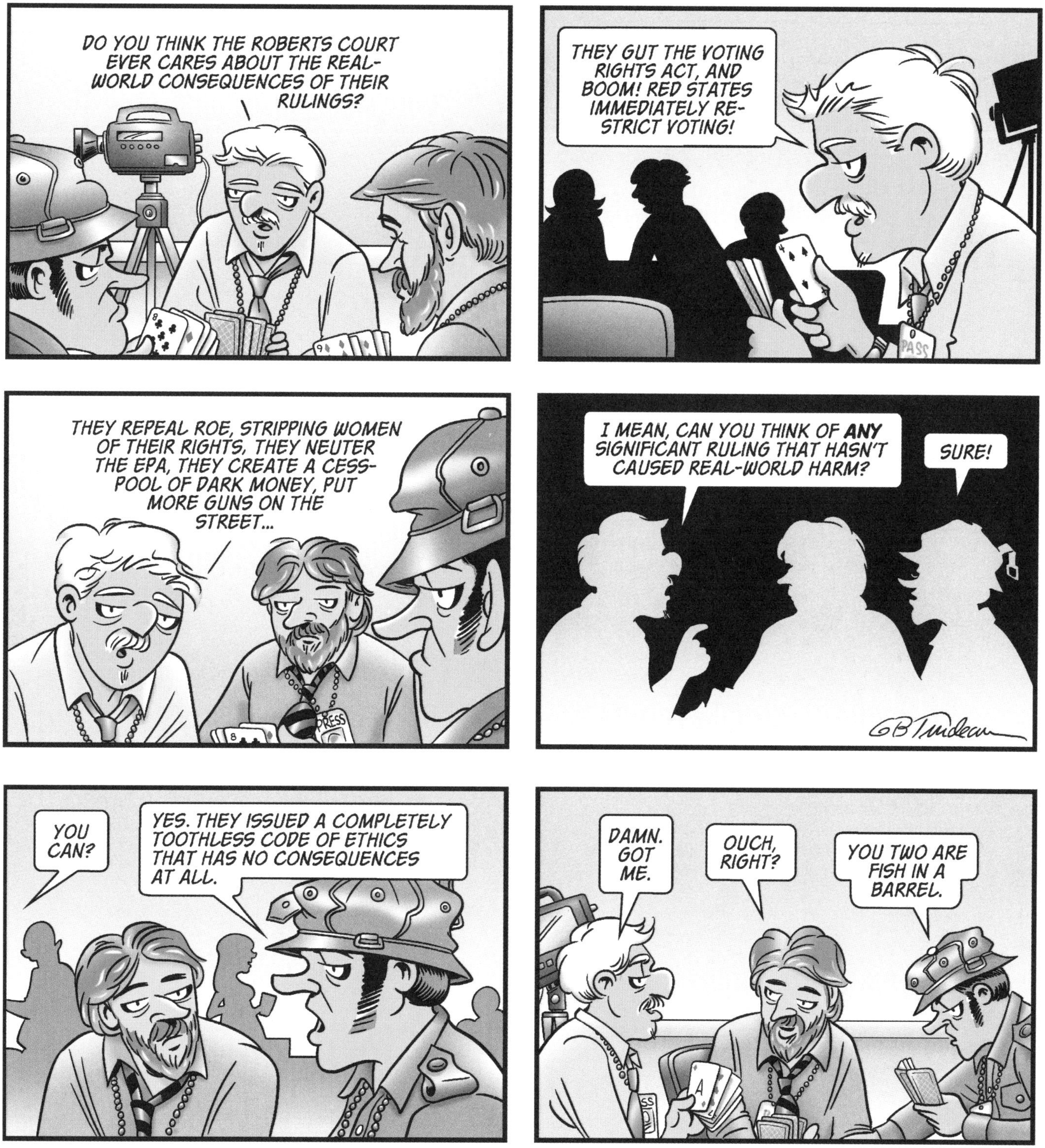
DO YOU THINK THE ROBERTS COURT EVER CARES ABOUT THE REAL-WORLD CONSEQUENCES OF THEIR RULINGS?
THEY GUT THE VOTING RIGHTS ACT, AND BOOM! RED STATES IMMEDIATELY RE-STRICT VOTING!
PASS
THEY REPEAL ROE, STRIPPING WOMEN OF THEIR RIGHTS, THEY NEUTER THE EPA, THEY CREATE A CESS-POOL OF DARK MONEY, PUT MORE GUNS ON THE STREET...
PRESS
I MEAN, CAN YOU THINK OF **ANY** SIGNIFICANT RULING THAT HASN'T CAUSED REAL-WORLD HARM?
SURE!
GB Trudeau
YOU CAN?
YES. THEY ISSUED A COMPLETELY TOOTHLESS CODE OF ETHICS THAT HAS NO CONSEQUENCES AT ALL.
DAMN. GOT ME.
OUCH, RIGHT?
YOU TWO ARE FISH IN A BARREL.

January 28, 2024

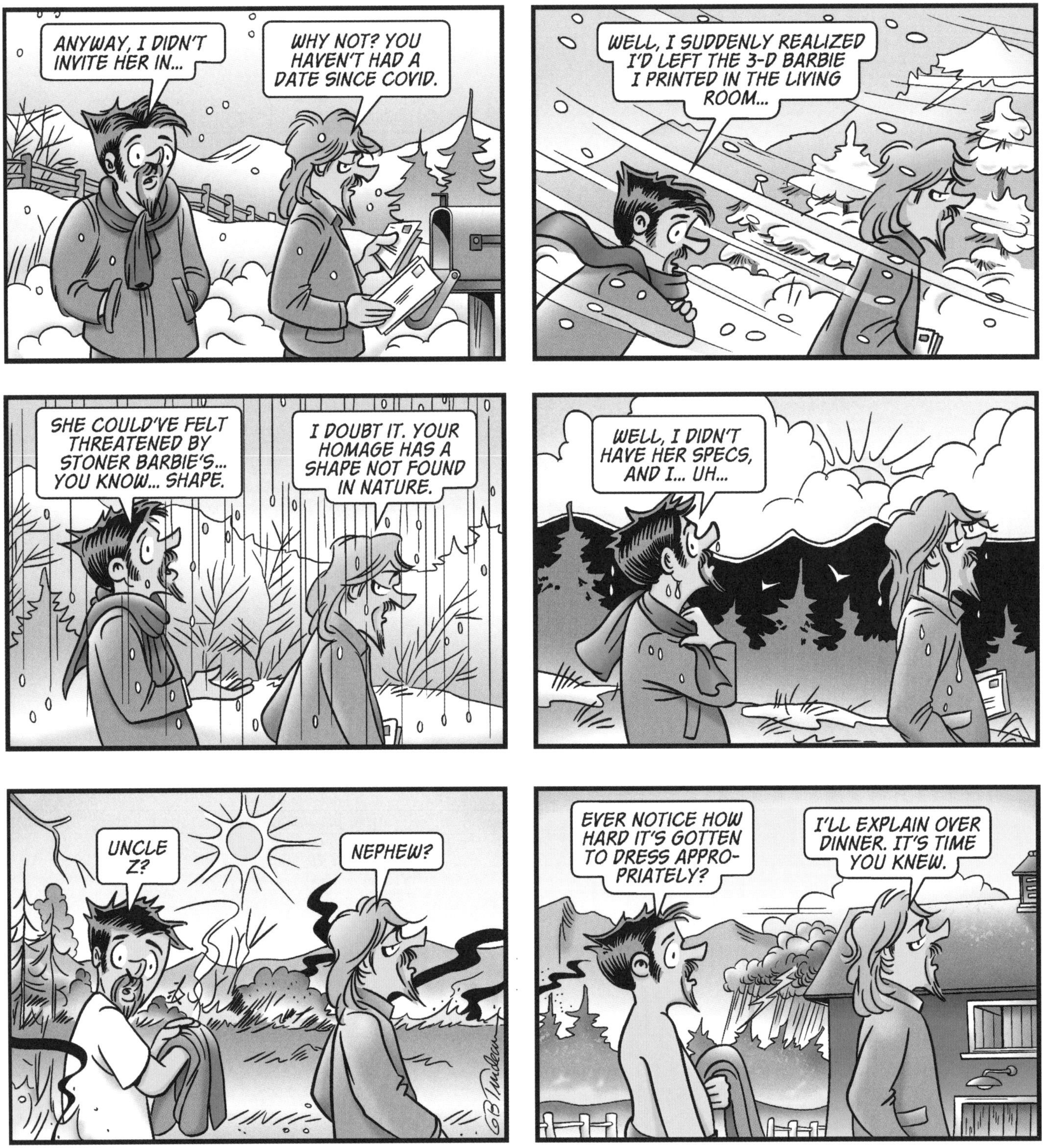
ANYWAY, I DIDN'T INVITE HER IN...
WHY NOT? YOU HAVEN'T HAD A DATE SINCE COVID.
WELL, I SUDDENLY REALIZED I'D LEFT THE 3-D BARBIE I PRINTED IN THE LIVING ROOM...
SHE COULD'VE FELT THREATENED BY STONER BARBIE'S... YOU KNOW... SHAPE.
I DOUBT IT. YOUR HOMAGE HAS A SHAPE NOT FOUND IN NATURE.
WELL, I DIDN'T HAVE HER SPECS, AND I... UH...
UNCLE Z?
NEPHEW?
EVER NOTICE HOW HARD IT'S GOTTEN TO DRESS APPRO-PRIATELY?
I'LL EXPLAIN OVER DINNER. IT'S TIME YOU KNEW.
GBTrudeau

February 4, 2024

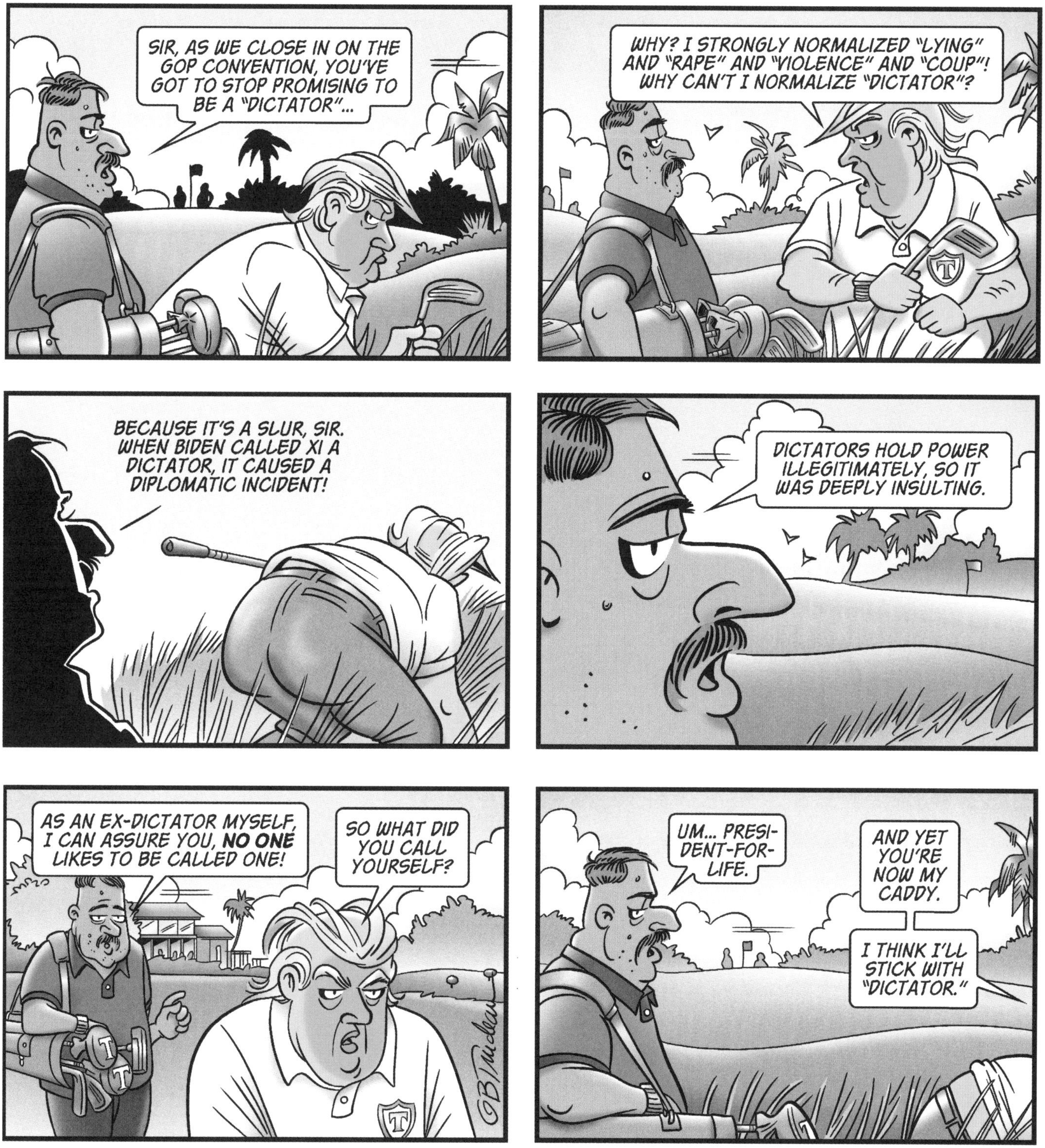
SIR, AS WE CLOSE IN ON THE GOP CONVENTION, YOU'VE GOT TO STOP PROMISING TO BE A "DICTATOR"...
WHY? I STRONGLY NORMALIZED "LYING" AND "RAPE" AND "VIOLENCE" AND "COUP"! WHY CAN'T I NORMALIZE "DICTATOR"?
BECAUSE IT'S A SLUR, SIR. WHEN BIDEN CALLED XI A DICTATOR, IT CAUSED A DIPLOMATIC INCIDENT!
DICTATORS HOLD POWER ILLEGITIMATELY, SO IT WAS DEEPLY INSULTING.
AS AN EX-DICTATOR MYSELF, I CAN ASSURE YOU, **NO ONE** LIKES TO BE CALLED ONE!
SO WHAT DID YOU CALL YOURSELF?
UM... PRESI-DENT-FOR-LIFE.
AND YET YOU'RE NOW MY CADDY.
I THINK I'LL STICK WITH "DICTATOR."
GBTrudeau

February 11, 2024

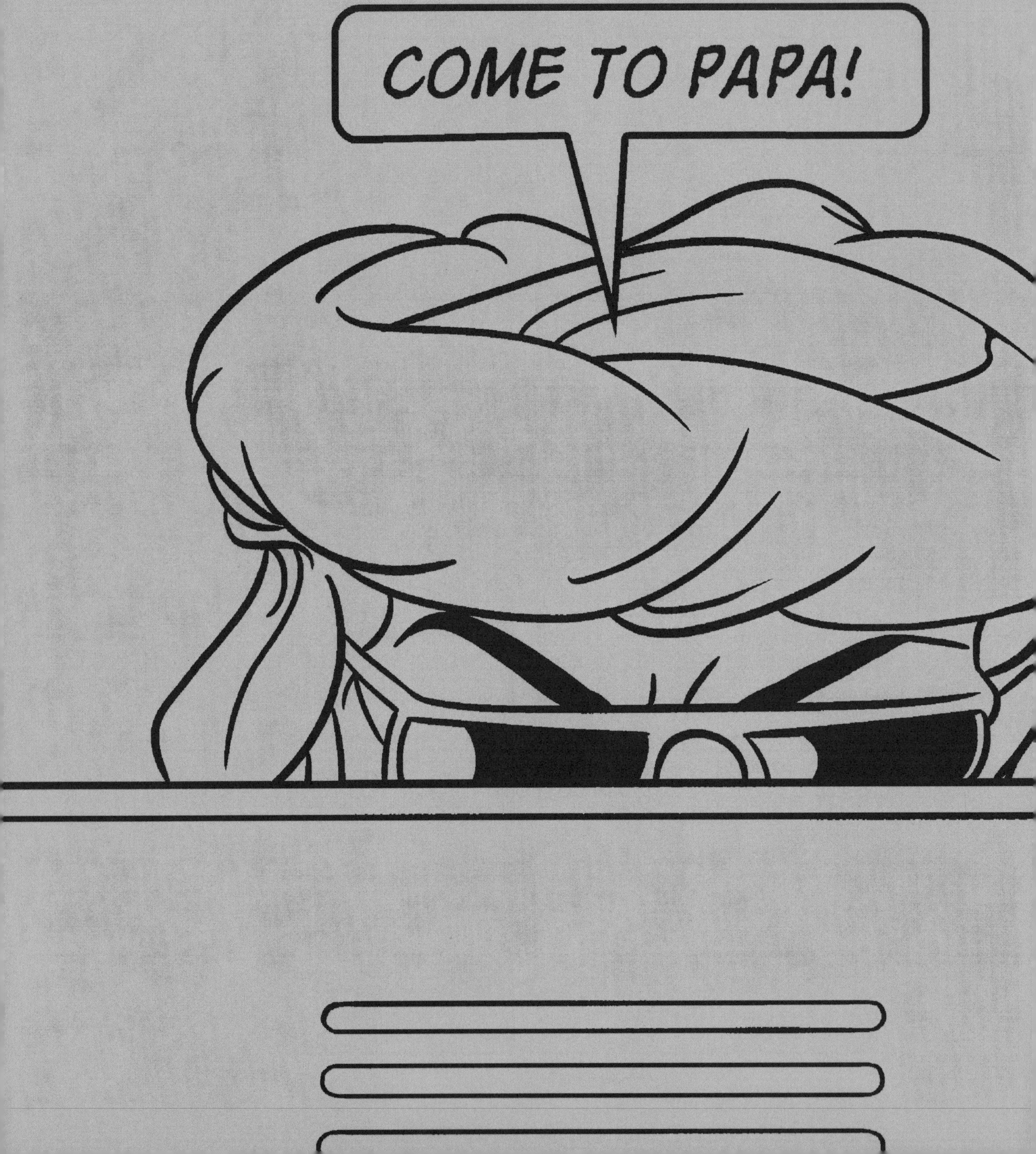
COME TO PAPA!

PART 4

Sedition Hunting

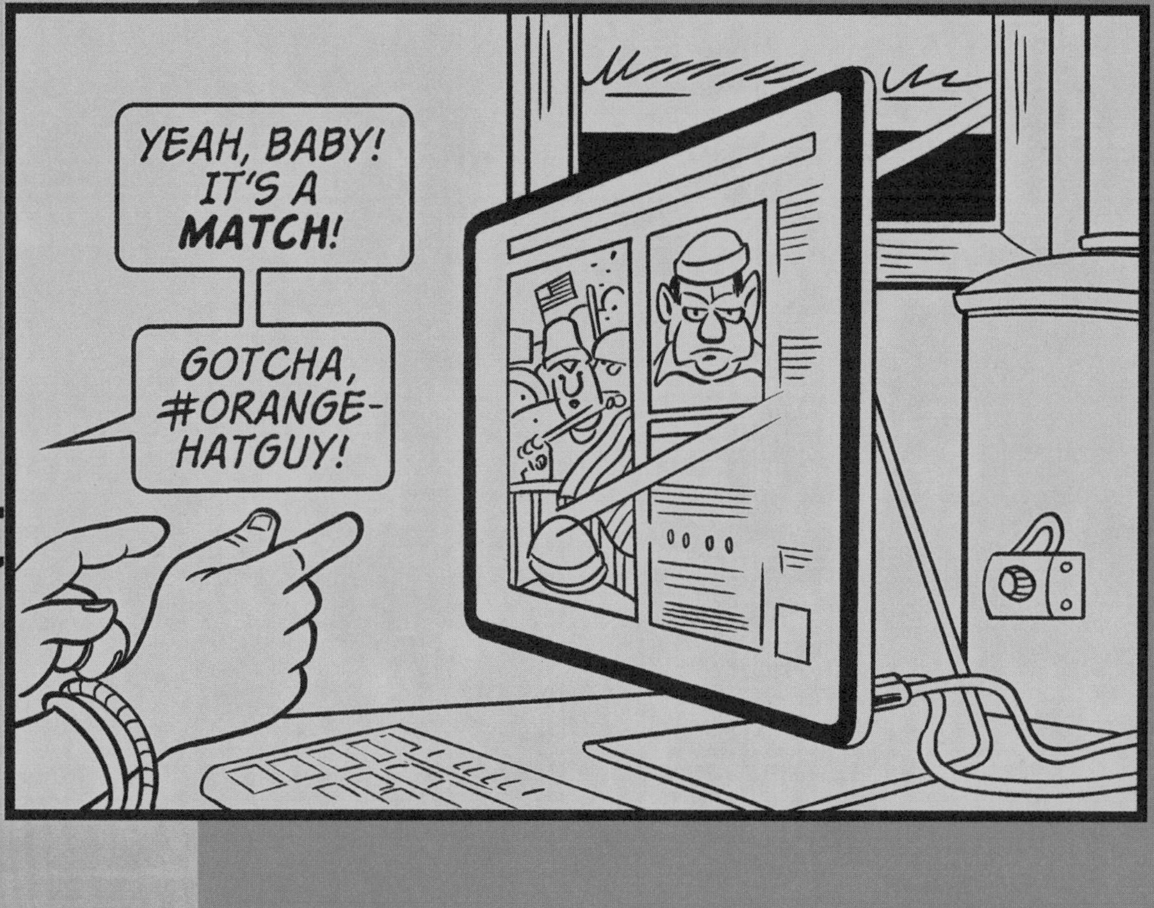

YEAH, BABY! IT'S A **MATCH**!
GOTCHA, #ORANGE-HATGUY!

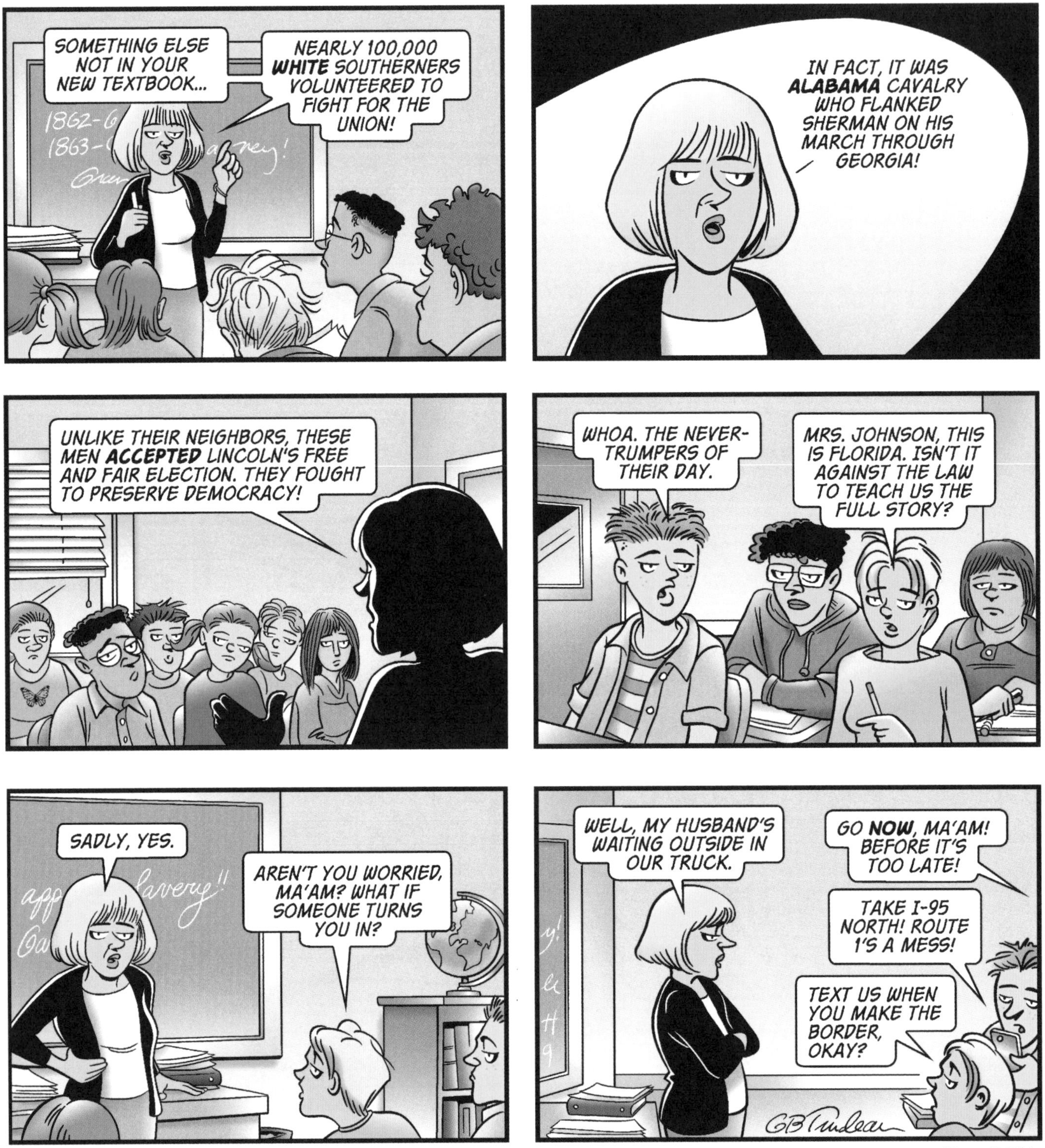
SOMETHING ELSE NOT IN YOUR NEW TEXTBOOK...
NEARLY 100,000 **WHITE** SOUTHERNERS VOLUNTEERED TO FIGHT FOR THE UNION!
IN FACT, IT WAS **ALABAMA** CAVALRY WHO FLANKED SHERMAN ON HIS MARCH THROUGH GEORGIA!
UNLIKE THEIR NEIGHBORS, THESE MEN **ACCEPTED** LINCOLN'S FREE AND FAIR ELECTION. THEY FOUGHT TO PRESERVE DEMOCRACY!
WHOA. THE NEVER-TRUMPERS OF THEIR DAY.
MRS. JOHNSON, THIS IS FLORIDA. ISN'T IT AGAINST THE LAW TO TEACH US THE FULL STORY?
SADLY, YES.
AREN'T YOU WORRIED, MA'AM? WHAT IF SOMEONE TURNS YOU IN?
WELL, MY HUSBAND'S WAITING OUTSIDE IN OUR TRUCK.
GO **NOW**, MA'AM! BEFORE IT'S TOO LATE!
TAKE I-95 NORTH! ROUTE 1'S A MESS!
TEXT US WHEN YOU MAKE THE BORDER, OKAY?
GBTrudeau

February 18, 2024

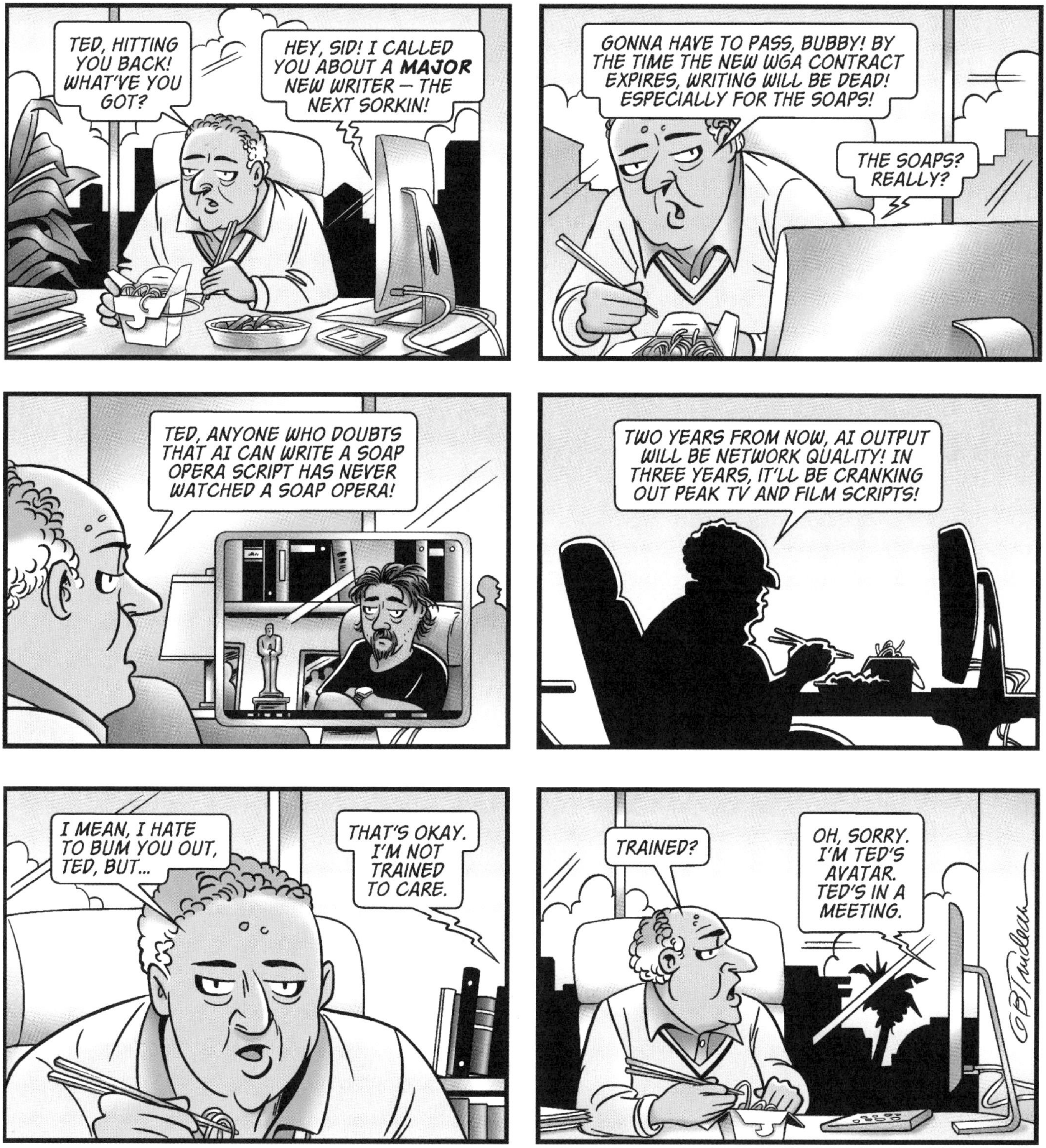
TED, HITTING YOU BACK! WHAT'VE YOU GOT?
HEY, SID! I CALLED YOU ABOUT A **MAJOR** NEW WRITER — THE NEXT SORKIN!
GONNA HAVE TO PASS, BUBBY! BY THE TIME THE NEW WGA CONTRACT EXPIRES, WRITING WILL BE DEAD! ESPECIALLY FOR THE SOAPS!
THE SOAPS? REALLY?
TED, ANYONE WHO DOUBTS THAT AI CAN WRITE A SOAP OPERA SCRIPT HAS NEVER WATCHED A SOAP OPERA!
TWO YEARS FROM NOW, AI OUTPUT WILL BE NETWORK QUALITY! IN THREE YEARS, IT'LL BE CRANKING OUT PEAK TV AND FILM SCRIPTS!
I MEAN, I HATE TO BUM YOU OUT, TED, BUT...
THAT'S OKAY. I'M NOT TRAINED TO CARE.
TRAINED?
OH, SORRY. I'M TED'S AVATAR. TED'S IN A MEETING.
© BTrudeau

February 25, 2024

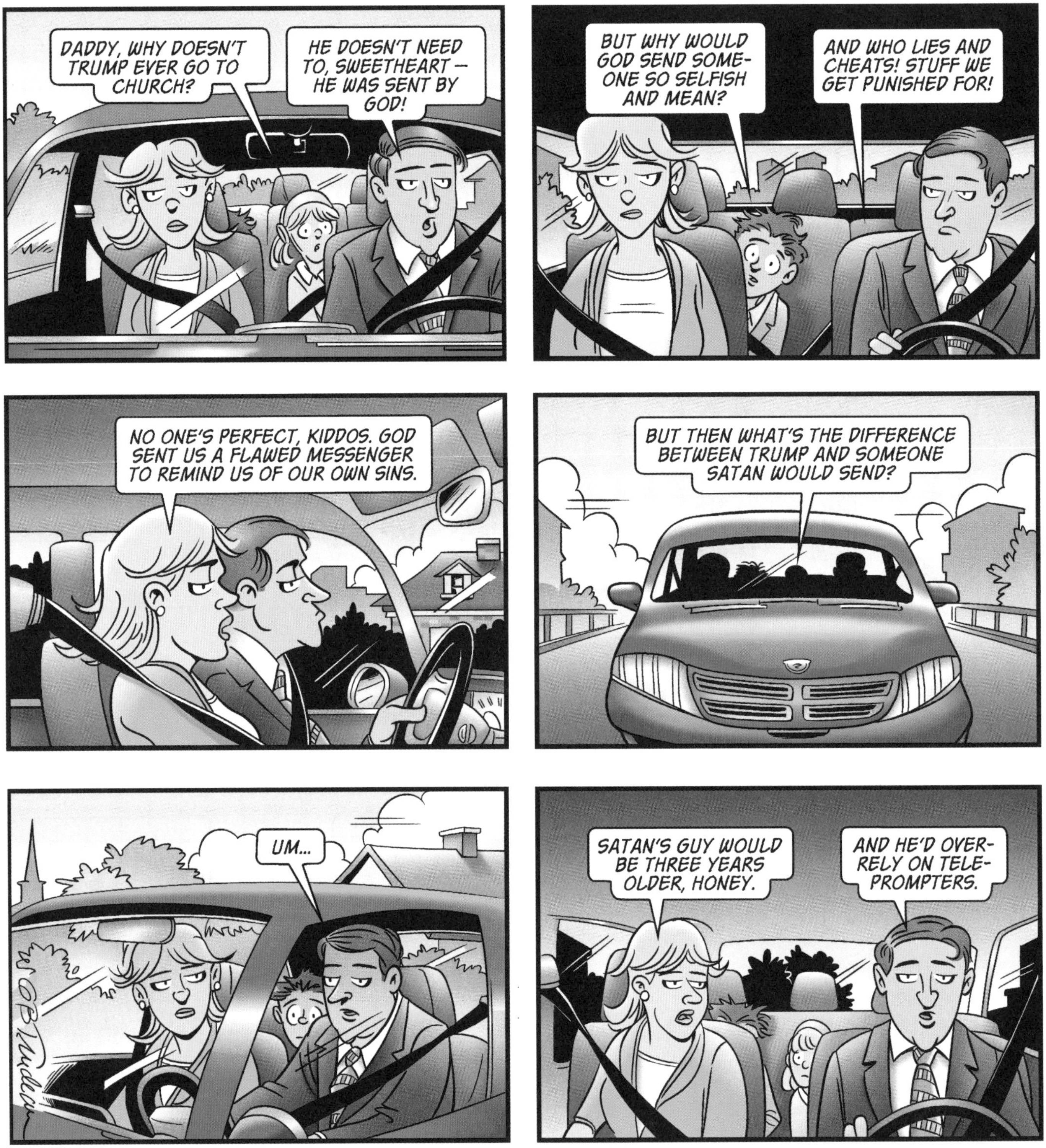
DADDY, WHY DOESN'T TRUMP EVER GO TO CHURCH?
HE DOESN'T NEED TO, SWEETHEART -- HE WAS SENT BY GOD!
BUT WHY WOULD GOD SEND SOME-ONE SO SELFISH AND MEAN?
AND WHO LIES AND CHEATS! STUFF WE GET PUNISHED FOR!
NO ONE'S PERFECT, KIDDOS. GOD SENT US A FLAWED MESSENGER TO REMIND US OF OUR OWN SINS.
BUT THEN WHAT'S THE DIFFERENCE BETWEEN TRUMP AND SOMEONE SATAN WOULD SEND?
UM...
SATAN'S GUY WOULD BE THREE YEARS OLDER, HONEY.
AND HE'D OVER-RELY ON TELE-PROMPTERS.

March 3, 2024

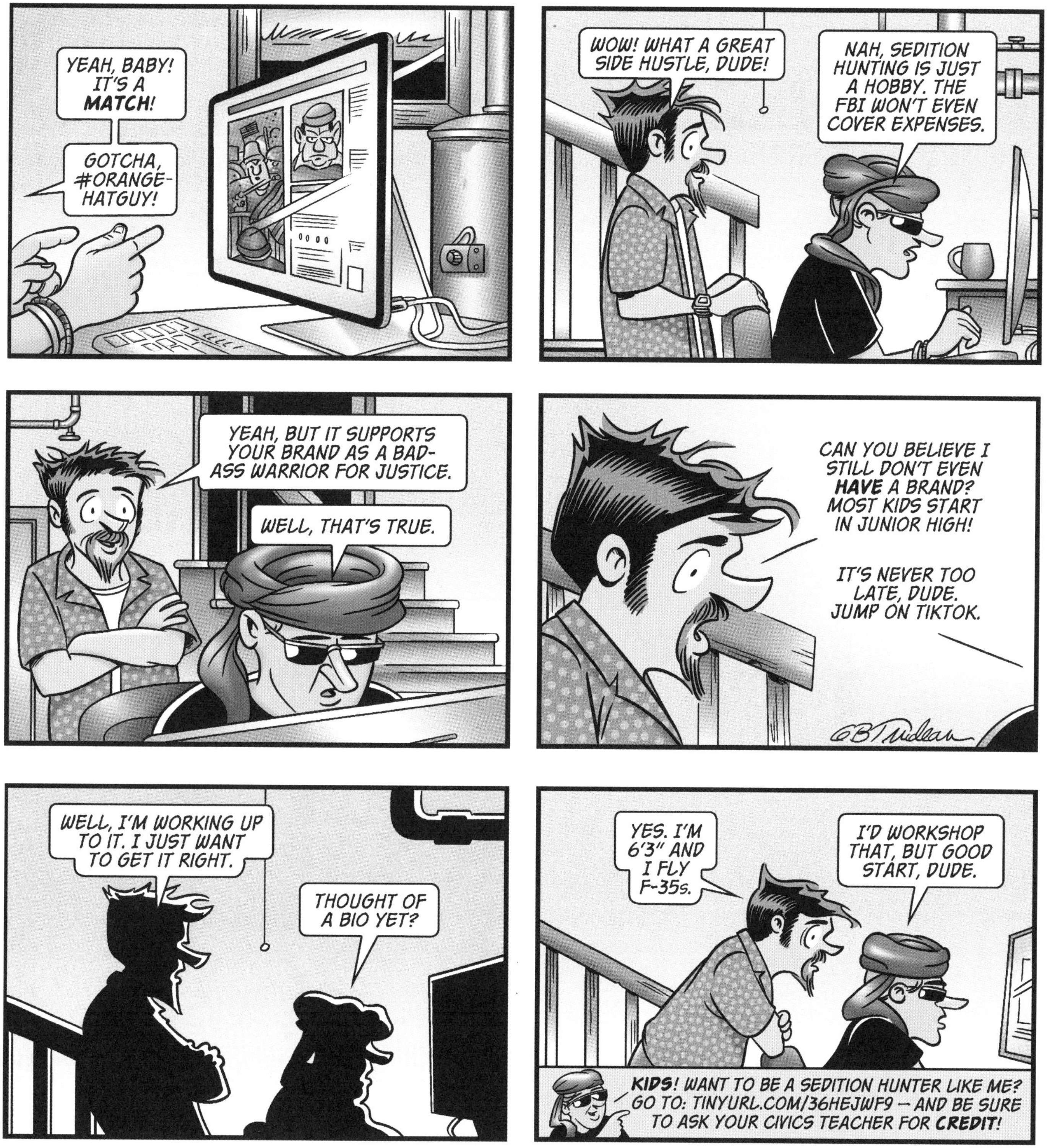
YEAH, BABY! IT'S A **MATCH**!
GOTCHA, #ORANGE-HATGUY!
WOW! WHAT A GREAT SIDE HUSTLE, DUDE!
NAH, SEDITION HUNTING IS JUST A HOBBY. THE FBI WON'T EVEN COVER EXPENSES.
YEAH, BUT IT SUPPORTS YOUR BRAND AS A BAD-ASS WARRIOR FOR JUSTICE.
WELL, THAT'S TRUE.
CAN YOU BELIEVE I STILL DON'T EVEN **HAVE** A BRAND? MOST KIDS START IN JUNIOR HIGH!
IT'S NEVER TOO LATE, DUDE. JUMP ON TIKTOK.
GBTrudeau
WELL, I'M WORKING UP TO IT. I JUST WANT TO GET IT RIGHT.
THOUGHT OF A BIO YET?
YES. I'M 6'3" AND I FLY F-35s.
I'D WORKSHOP THAT, BUT GOOD START, DUDE.
KIDS! WANT TO BE A SEDITION HUNTER LIKE ME? GO TO: TINYURL.COM/36HEJWF9 — AND BE SURE TO ASK YOUR CIVICS TEACHER FOR **CREDIT**!

March 10, 2024

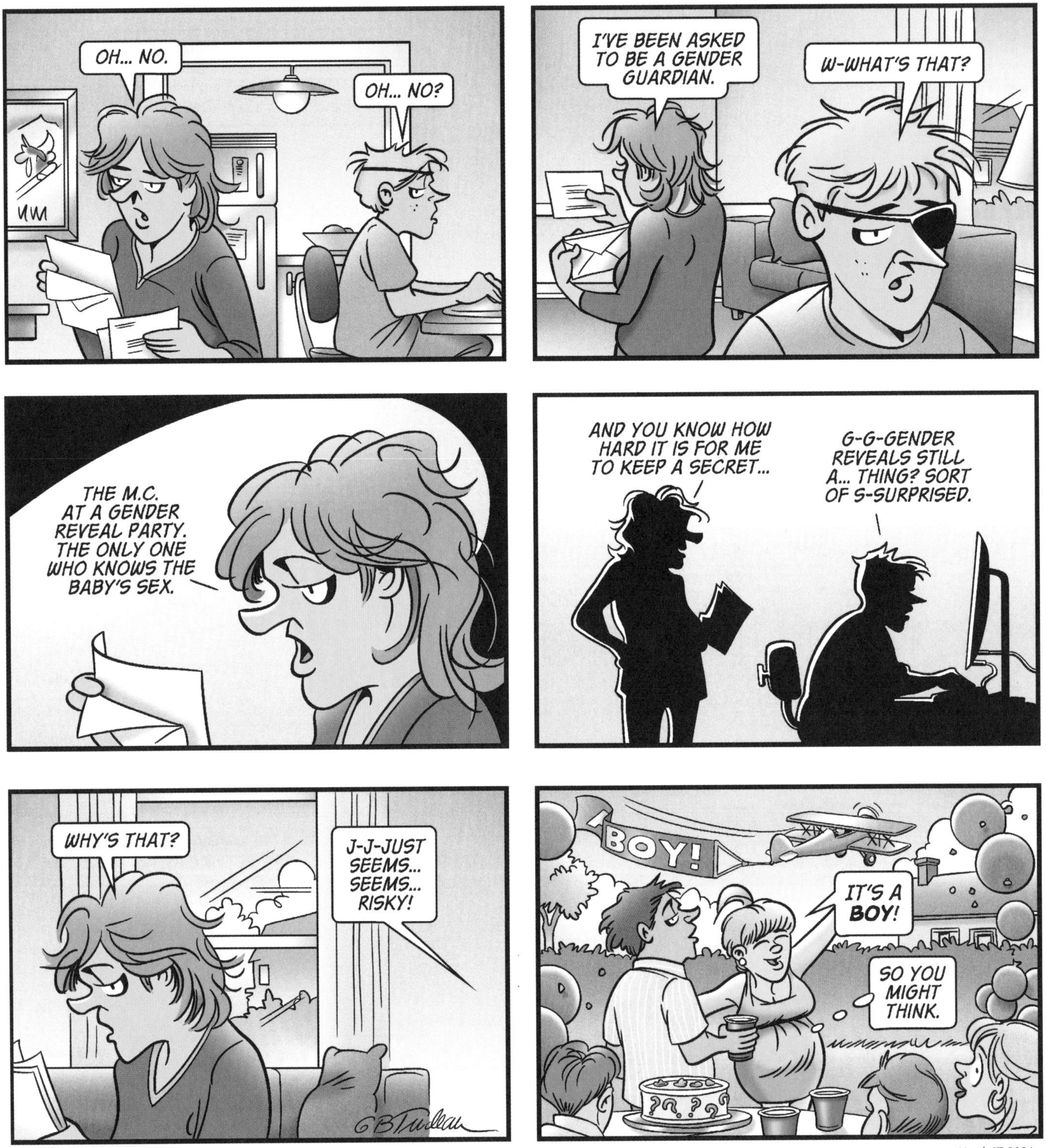
OH... NO.
OH... NO?
I'VE BEEN ASKED TO BE A GENDER GUARDIAN.
W-WHAT'S THAT?
THE M.C. AT A GENDER REVEAL PARTY. THE ONLY ONE WHO KNOWS THE BABY'S SEX.
AND YOU KNOW HOW HARD IT IS FOR ME TO KEEP A SECRET...
G-G-GENDER REVEALS STILL A... THING? SORT OF S-SURPRISED.
WHY'S THAT?
J-J-JUST SEEMS... SEEMS... RISKY!
BOY!
IT'S A BOY!
SO YOU MIGHT THINK.
GBTrudeau

March 17, 2024

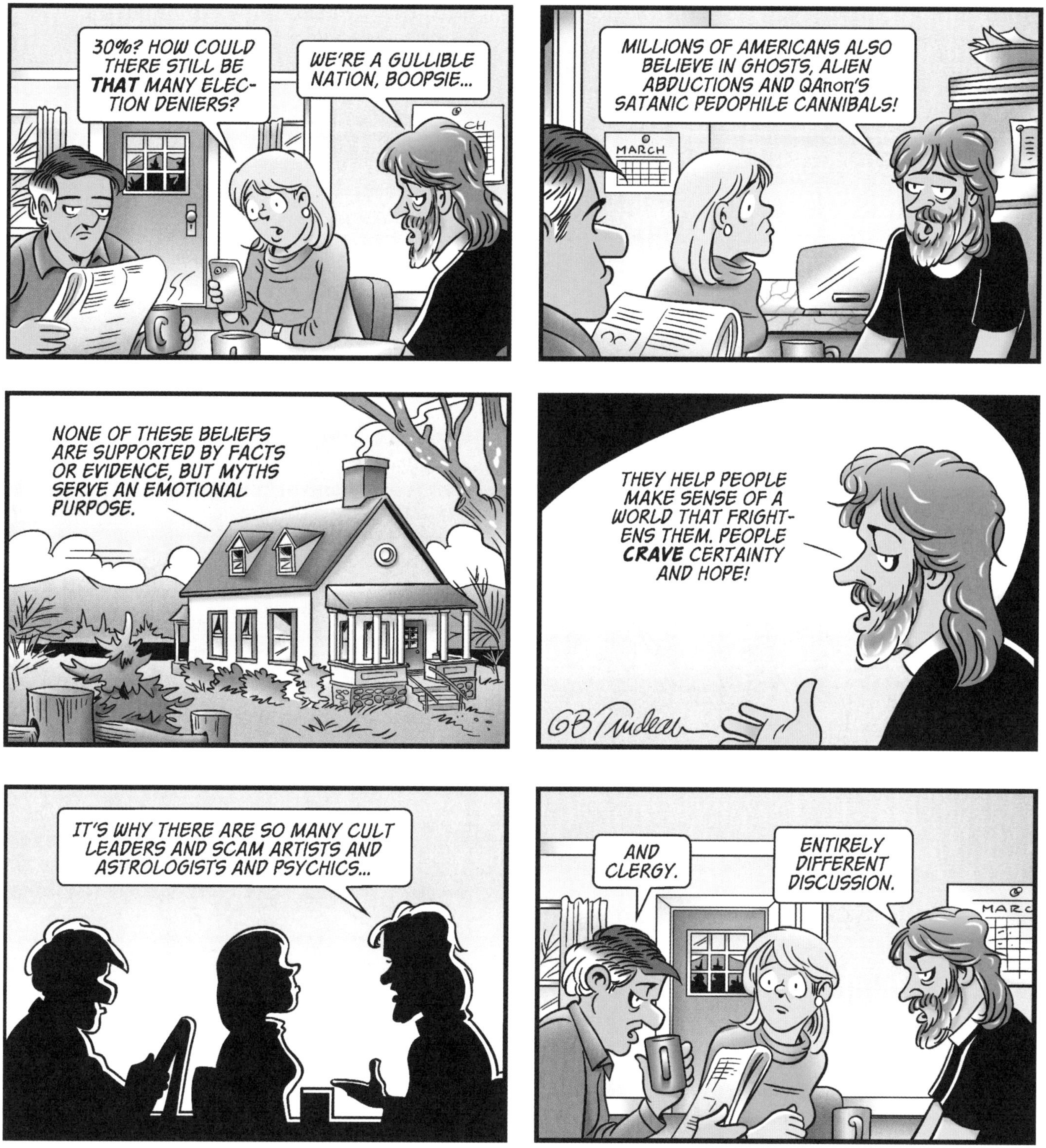
30%? HOW COULD THERE STILL BE **THAT** MANY ELECTION DENIERS?
WE'RE A GULLIBLE NATION, BOOPSIE...
MARCH
MILLIONS OF AMERICANS ALSO BELIEVE IN GHOSTS, ALIEN ABDUCTIONS AND QAnon'S SATANIC PEDOPHILE CANNIBALS!
NONE OF THESE BELIEFS ARE SUPPORTED BY FACTS OR EVIDENCE, BUT MYTHS SERVE AN EMOTIONAL PURPOSE.
THEY HELP PEOPLE MAKE SENSE OF A WORLD THAT FRIGHTENS THEM. PEOPLE **CRAVE** CERTAINTY AND HOPE!
GB Trudeau
IT'S WHY THERE ARE SO MANY CULT LEADERS AND SCAM ARTISTS AND ASTROLOGISTS AND PSYCHICS...
AND CLERGY.
ENTIRELY DIFFERENT DISCUSSION.

March 24, 2024

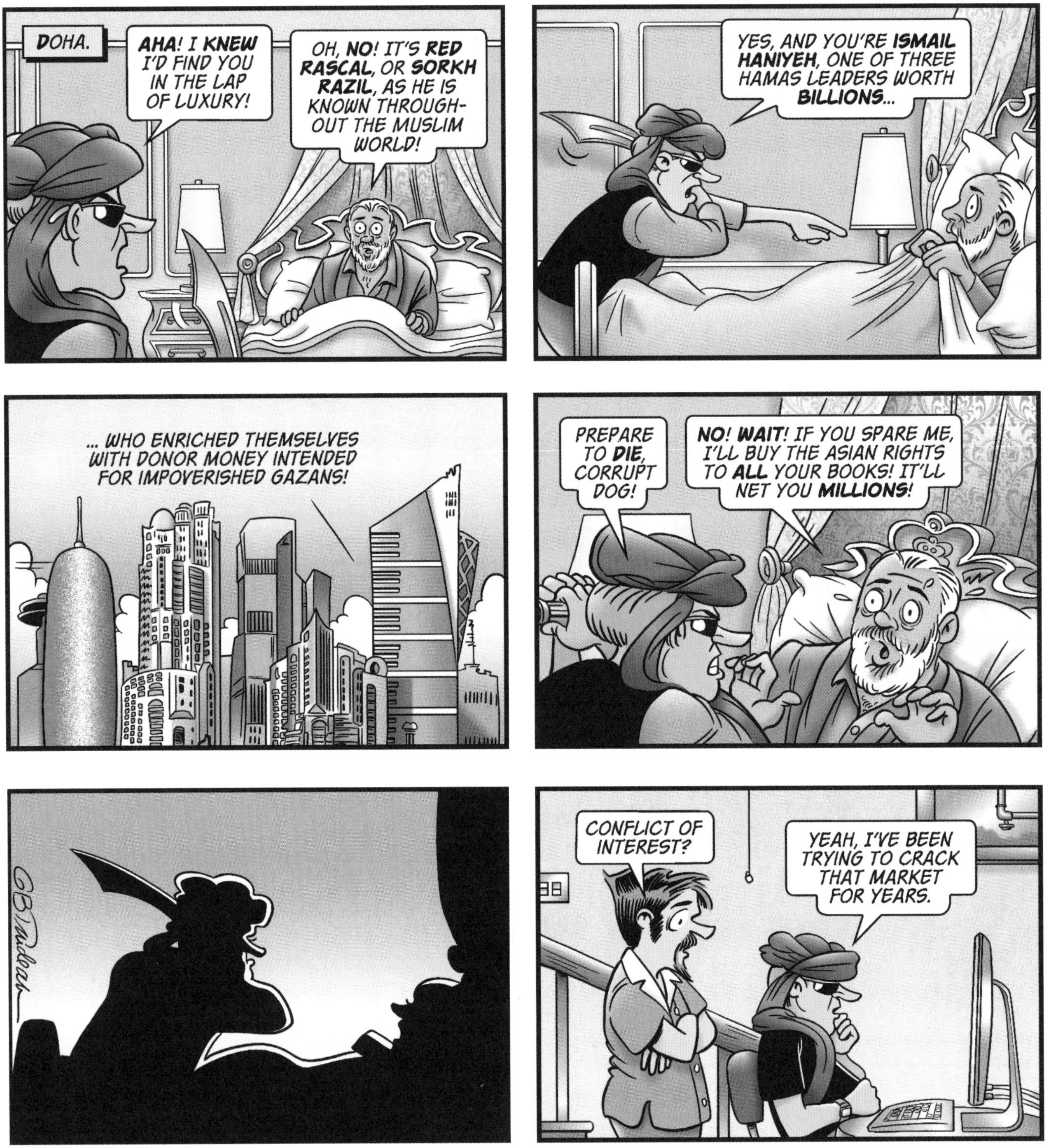
DOHA.
AHA! I KNEW I'D FIND YOU IN THE LAP OF LUXURY!
OH, NO! IT'S RED RASCAL, OR SORKH RAZIL, AS HE IS KNOWN THROUGH-OUT THE MUSLIM WORLD!
YES, AND YOU'RE ISMAIL HANIYEH, ONE OF THREE HAMAS LEADERS WORTH BILLIONS...
... WHO ENRICHED THEMSELVES WITH DONOR MONEY INTENDED FOR IMPOVERISHED GAZANS!
PREPARE TO DIE, CORRUPT DOG!
NO! WAIT! IF YOU SPARE ME, I'LL BUY THE ASIAN RIGHTS TO ALL YOUR BOOKS! IT'LL NET YOU MILLIONS!
GB Trudeau
CONFLICT OF INTEREST?
YEAH, I'VE BEEN TRYING TO CRACK THAT MARKET FOR YEARS.

March 31, 2024

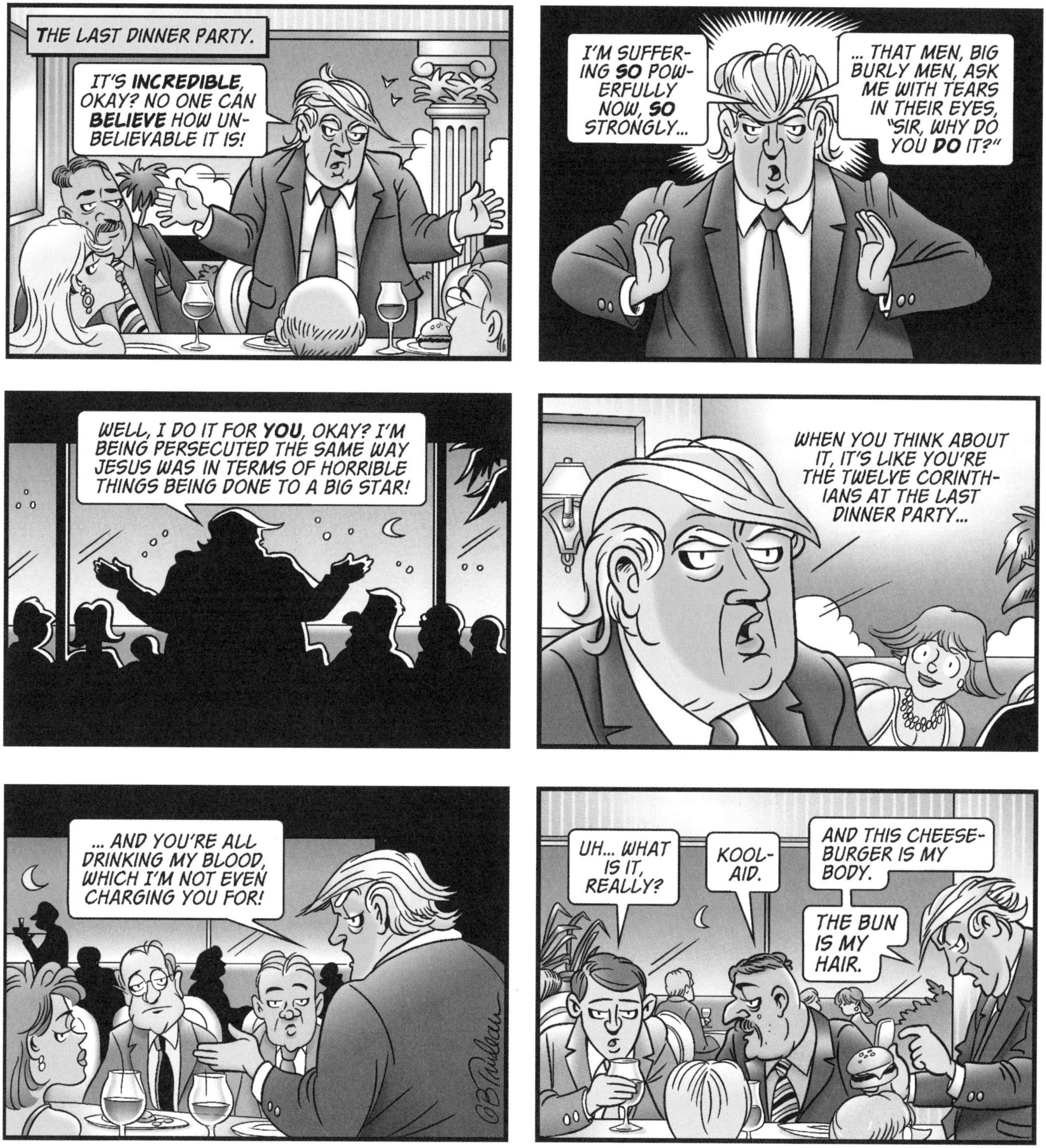
THE LAST DINNER PARTY.
IT'S INCREDIBLE, OKAY? NO ONE CAN BELIEVE HOW UNBELIEVABLE IT IS!
I'M SUFFERING SO POWERFULLY NOW, SO STRONGLY...
... THAT MEN, BIG BURLY MEN, ASK ME WITH TEARS IN THEIR EYES, "SIR, WHY DO YOU DO IT?"
WELL, I DO IT FOR YOU, OKAY? I'M BEING PERSECUTED THE SAME WAY JESUS WAS IN TERMS OF HORRIBLE THINGS BEING DONE TO A BIG STAR!
WHEN YOU THINK ABOUT IT, IT'S LIKE YOU'RE THE TWELVE CORINTHIANS AT THE LAST DINNER PARTY...
... AND YOU'RE ALL DRINKING MY BLOOD, WHICH I'M NOT EVEN CHARGING YOU FOR!
UH... WHAT IS IT, REALLY?
KOOL-AID.
AND THIS CHEESEBURGER IS MY BODY.
THE BUN IS MY HAIR.
GBTrudeau

April 7, 2024

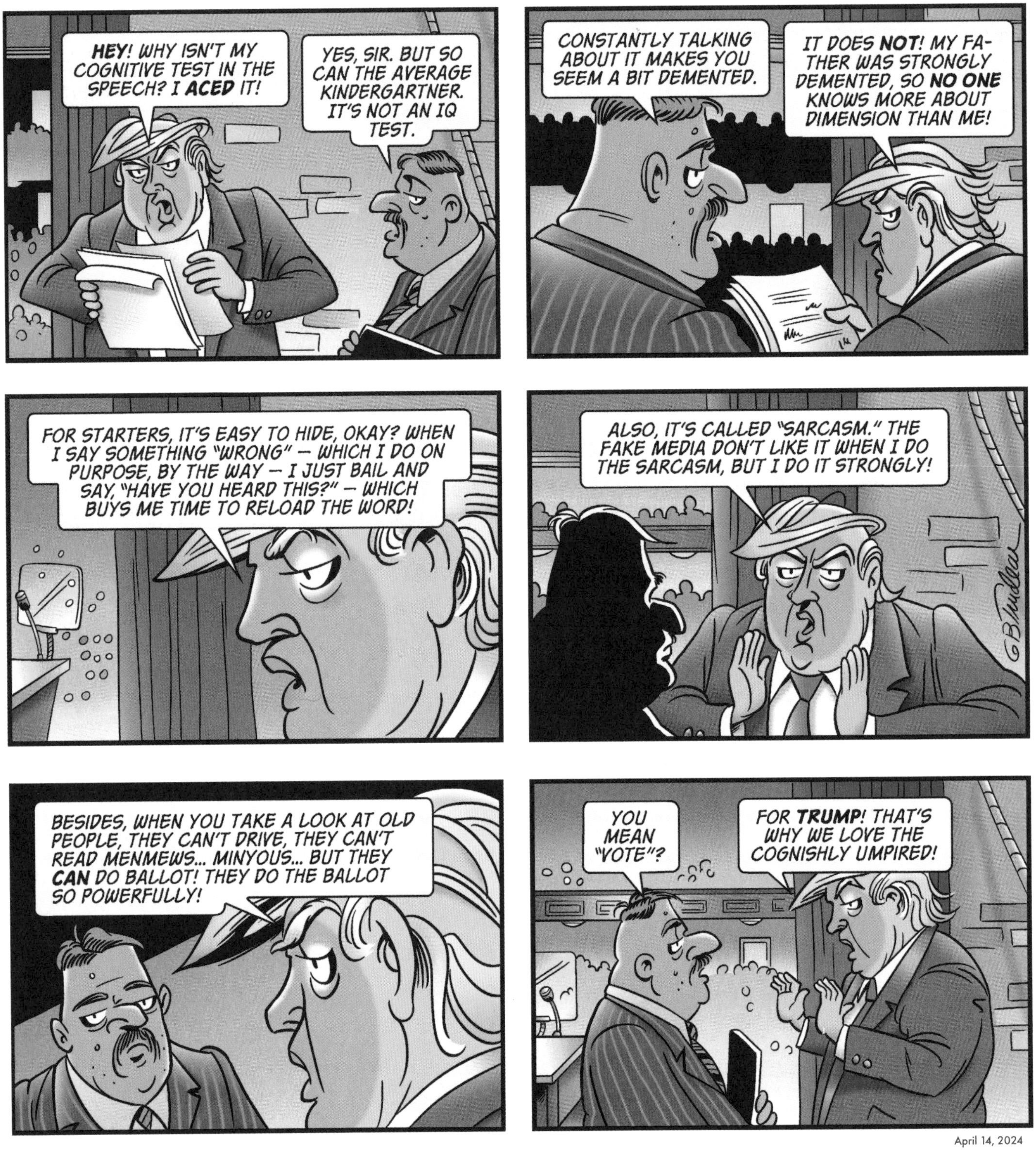
HEY! WHY ISN'T MY COGNITIVE TEST IN THE SPEECH? I ACED IT!
YES, SIR. BUT SO CAN THE AVERAGE KINDERGARTNER. IT'S NOT AN IQ TEST.
CONSTANTLY TALKING ABOUT IT MAKES YOU SEEM A BIT DEMENTED.
IT DOES NOT! MY FATHER WAS STRONGLY DEMENTED, SO NO ONE KNOWS MORE ABOUT DIMENSION THAN ME!
FOR STARTERS, IT'S EASY TO HIDE, OKAY? WHEN I SAY SOMETHING "WRONG" — WHICH I DO ON PURPOSE, BY THE WAY — I JUST BAIL AND SAY, "HAVE YOU HEARD THIS?" — WHICH BUYS ME TIME TO RELOAD THE WORD!
ALSO, IT'S CALLED "SARCASM." THE FAKE MEDIA DON'T LIKE IT WHEN I DO THE SARCASM, BUT I DO IT STRONGLY!
©B. Trudeau
BESIDES, WHEN YOU TAKE A LOOK AT OLD PEOPLE, THEY CAN'T DRIVE, THEY CAN'T READ MENMEWS... MINYOUS... BUT THEY CAN DO BALLOT! THEY DO THE BALLOT SO POWERFULLY!
YOU MEAN "VOTE"?
FOR TRUMP! THAT'S WHY WE LOVE THE COGNISHLY UMPIRED!

April 14, 2024

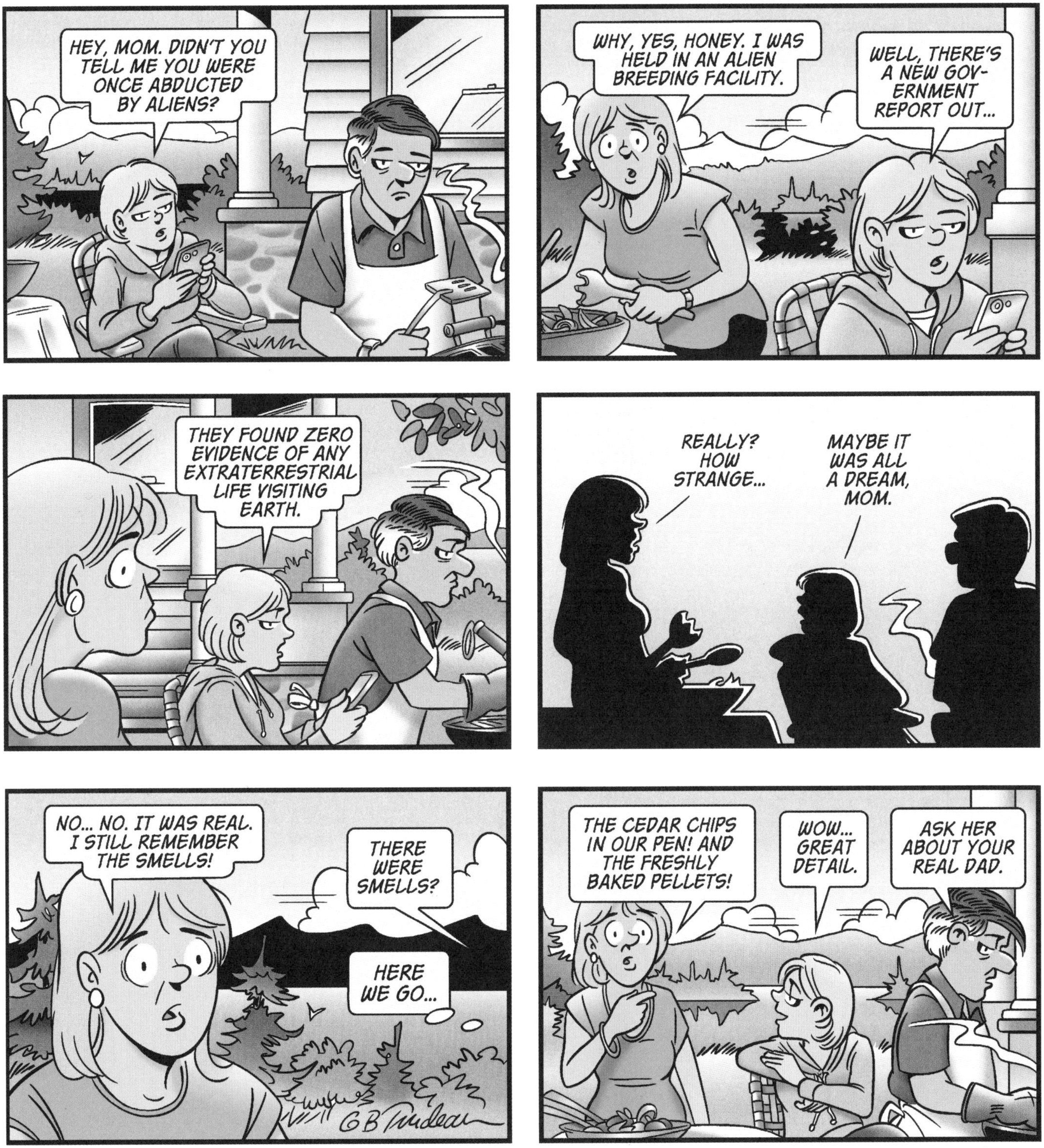
HEY, MOM. DIDN'T YOU TELL ME YOU WERE ONCE ABDUCTED BY ALIENS?
WHY, YES, HONEY. I WAS HELD IN AN ALIEN BREEDING FACILITY.
WELL, THERE'S A NEW GOV-ERNMENT REPORT OUT...
THEY FOUND ZERO EVIDENCE OF ANY EXTRATERRESTRIAL LIFE VISITING EARTH.
REALLY? HOW STRANGE...
MAYBE IT WAS ALL A DREAM, MOM.
NO... NO. IT WAS REAL. I STILL REMEMBER THE SMELLS!
THERE WERE SMELLS?
HERE WE GO...
THE CEDAR CHIPS IN OUR PEN! AND THE FRESHLY BAKED PELLETS!
WOW... GREAT DETAIL.
ASK HER ABOUT YOUR REAL DAD.
GB Trudeau

April 21, 2024

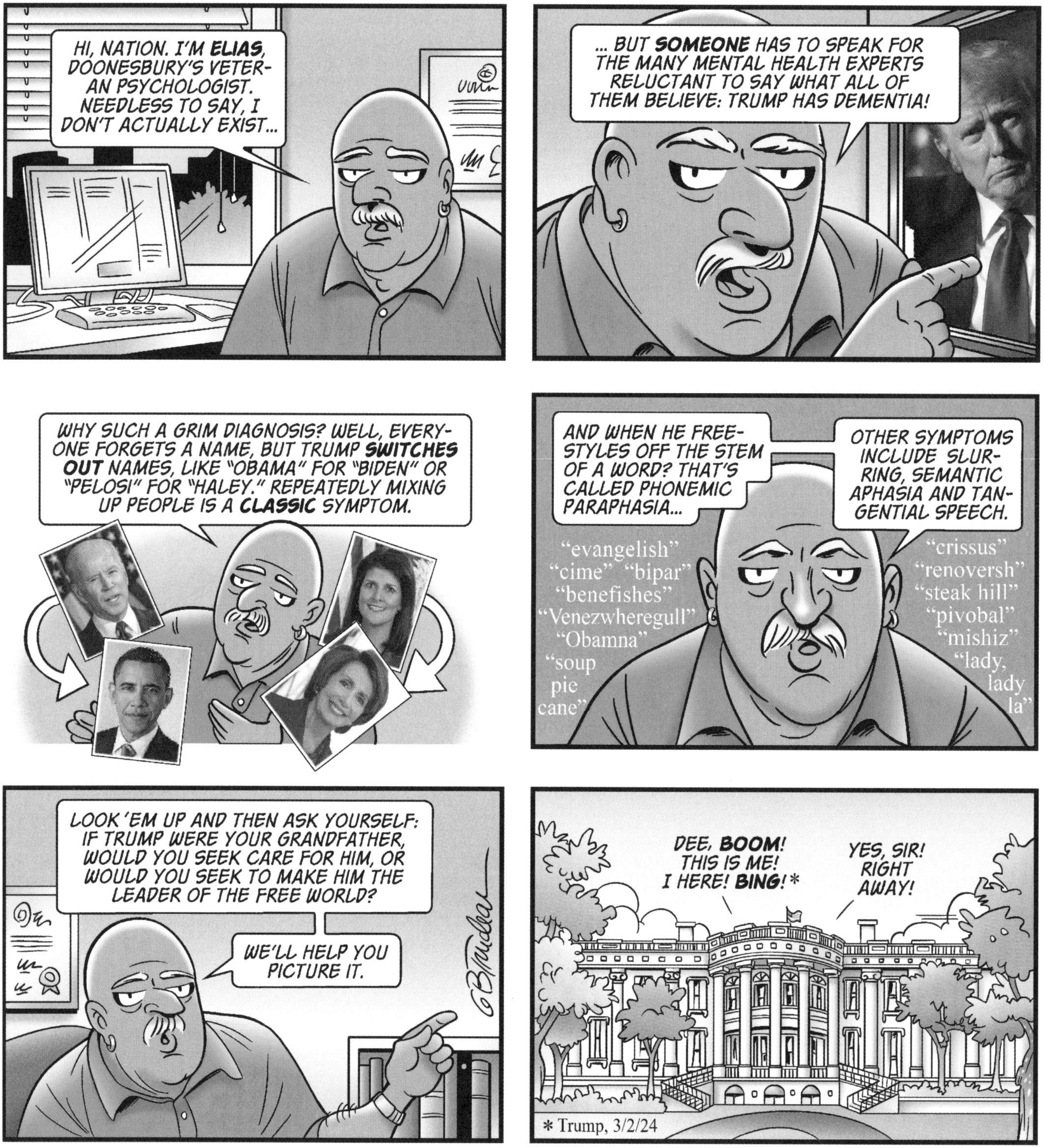
HI, NATION. I'M ELIAS, DOONESBURY'S VETERAN PSYCHOLOGIST. NEEDLESS TO SAY, I DON'T ACTUALLY EXIST...
... BUT SOMEONE HAS TO SPEAK FOR THE MANY MENTAL HEALTH EXPERTS RELUCTANT TO SAY WHAT ALL OF THEM BELIEVE: TRUMP HAS DEMENTIA!
WHY SUCH A GRIM DIAGNOSIS? WELL, EVERYONE FORGETS A NAME, BUT TRUMP SWITCHES OUT NAMES, LIKE "OBAMA" FOR "BIDEN" OR "PELOSI" FOR "HALEY." REPEATEDLY MIXING UP PEOPLE IS A CLASSIC SYMPTOM.
AND WHEN HE FREESTYLES OFF THE STEM OF A WORD? THAT'S CALLED PHONEMIC PARAPHASIA...
OTHER SYMPTOMS INCLUDE SLURRING, SEMANTIC APHASIA AND TANGENTIAL SPEECH.
"evangelish" "cime" "bipar" "benefishes" "Venezwheregull" "Obamna" "soup pie cane"
"crissus" "renoversh" "steak hill" "pivobal" "mishiz" "lady, lady la"
LOOK 'EM UP AND THEN ASK YOURSELF: IF TRUMP WERE YOUR GRANDFATHER, WOULD YOU SEEK CARE FOR HIM, OR WOULD YOU SEEK TO MAKE HIM THE LEADER OF THE FREE WORLD?
WE'LL HELP YOU PICTURE IT.
GBTrudeau
DEE, BOOM! THIS IS ME! I HERE! BING!*
YES, SIR! RIGHT AWAY!
* Trump, 3/2/24

April 28, 2024

ELI WAS... M-M-MESS WHEN I... TUCKED H-HIM IN TONIGHT.

OVER WHAT?

ALL... G-G-GIRLS IN HIS CLASS... ARE NOW TALLER... TH-THAN HE IS.

HE'LL CATCH UP.

I'M JUST GLAD IT'S NOT ANOTHER PROBLEM WE CAN FIX.

WE'RE RAISING SNOWFLAKES, LEO, **NOT** THE RESILIENT, CONFIDENT KIDS WE SHOULD BE.

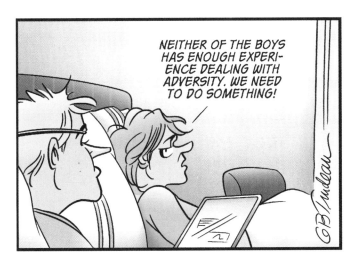

NEITHER OF THE BOYS HAS ENOUGH EXPERIENCE DEALING WITH ADVERSITY. WE NEED TO DO SOMETHING!

LIKE WHAT? H-HIRE A BULLY?

DON'T BE RIDICU...

WAIT. WHAT ABOUT THAT KID ACROSS THE STREET?

May 5, 2024

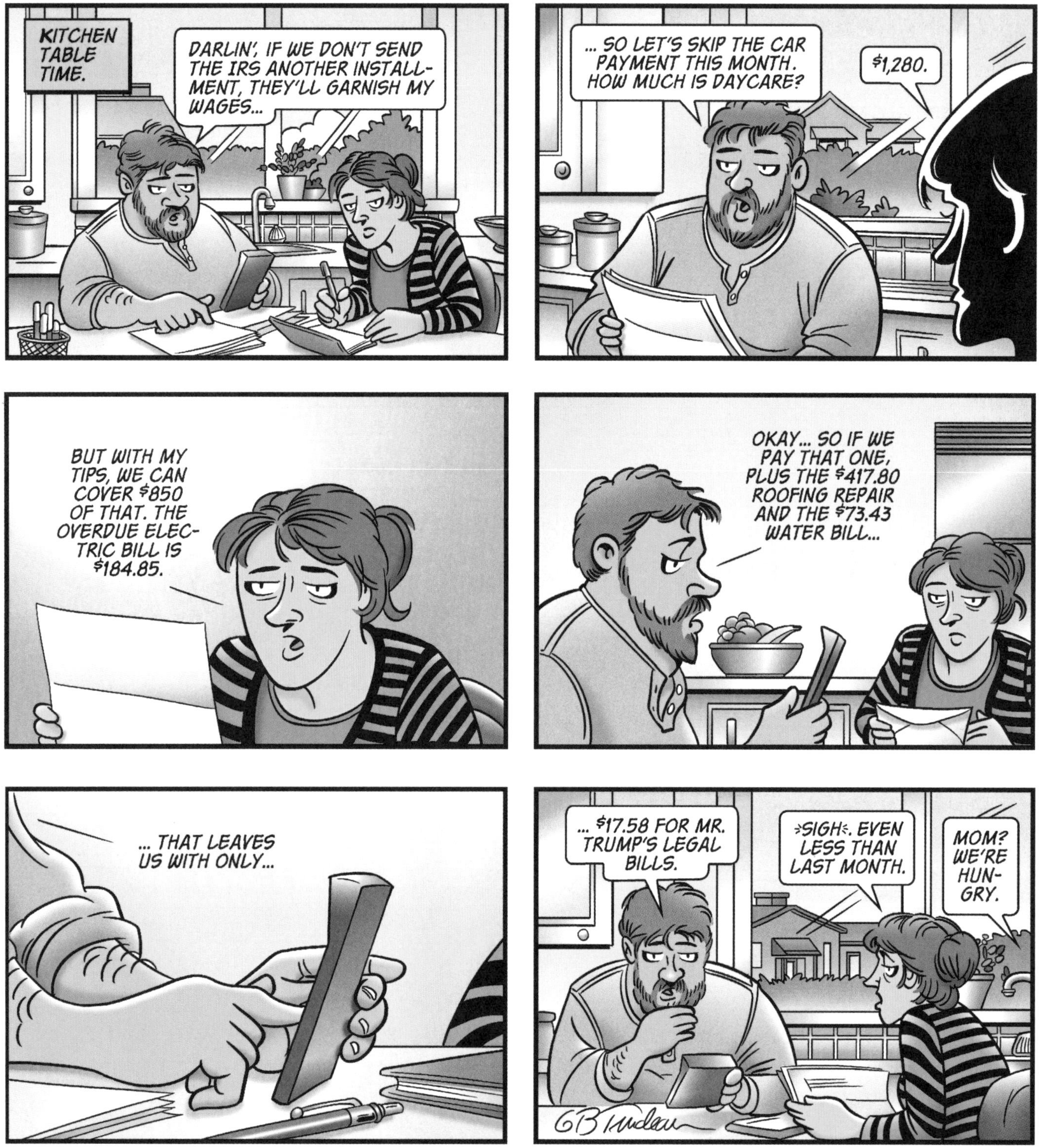
KITCHEN TABLE TIME.
DARLIN', IF WE DON'T SEND THE IRS ANOTHER INSTALL-MENT, THEY'LL GARNISH MY WAGES...
... SO LET'S SKIP THE CAR PAYMENT THIS MONTH. HOW MUCH IS DAYCARE?
$1,280.
BUT WITH MY TIPS, WE CAN COVER $850 OF THAT. THE OVERDUE ELEC-TRIC BILL IS $184.85.
OKAY... SO IF WE PAY THAT ONE, PLUS THE $417.80 ROOFING REPAIR AND THE $73.43 WATER BILL...
... THAT LEAVES US WITH ONLY...
... $17.58 FOR MR. TRUMP'S LEGAL BILLS.
SIGH. EVEN LESS THAN LAST MONTH.
MOM? WE'RE HUN-GRY.
GB Trudeau

May 12, 2024

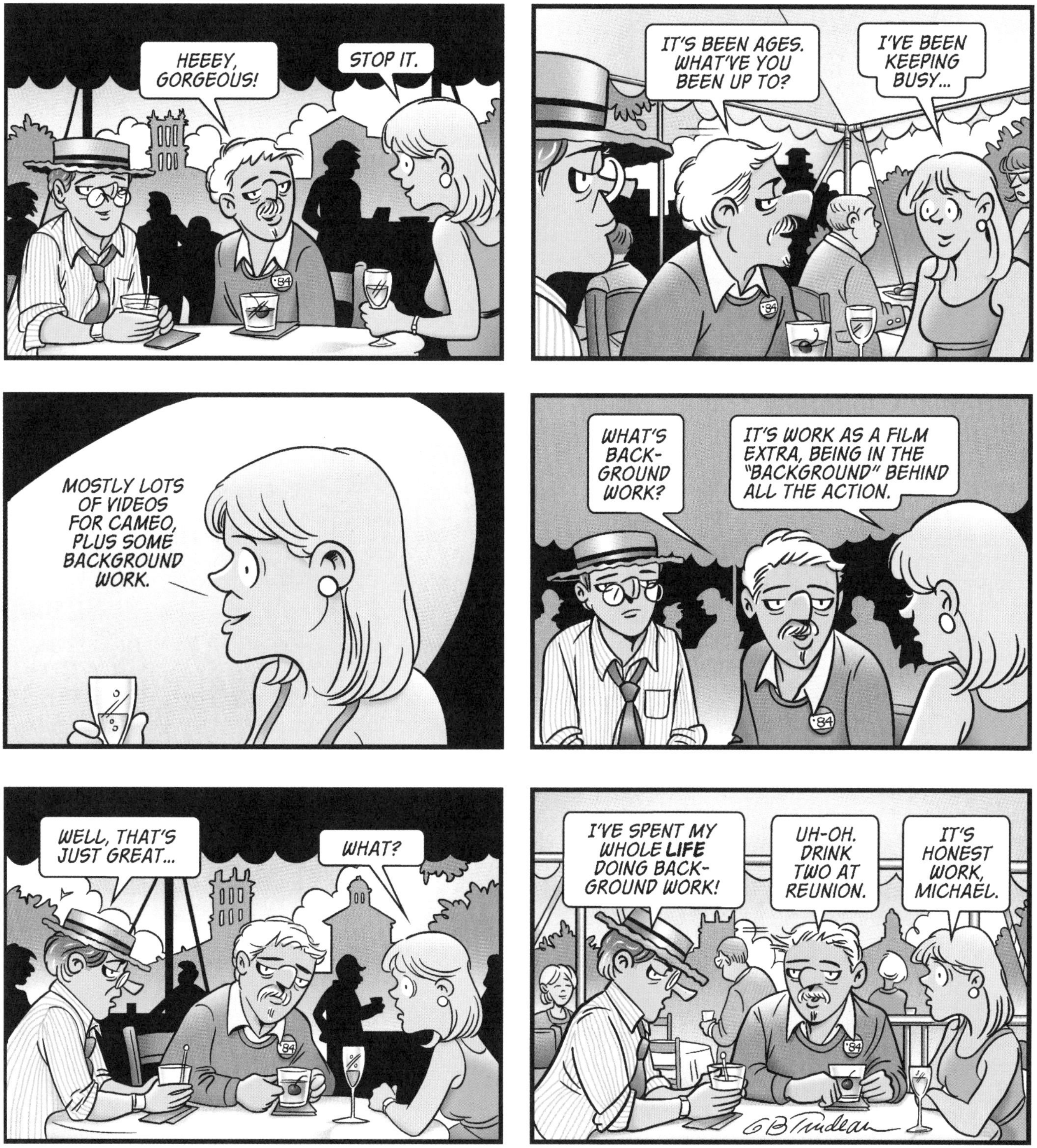
HEEEY, GORGEOUS!
STOP IT.
IT'S BEEN AGES. WHAT'VE YOU BEEN UP TO?
I'VE BEEN KEEPING BUSY...
MOSTLY LOTS OF VIDEOS FOR CAMEO, PLUS SOME BACKGROUND WORK.
WHAT'S BACK-GROUND WORK?
IT'S WORK AS A FILM EXTRA, BEING IN THE "BACKGROUND" BEHIND ALL THE ACTION.
WELL, THAT'S JUST GREAT...
WHAT?
I'VE SPENT MY WHOLE **LIFE** DOING BACK-GROUND WORK!
UH-OH. DRINK TWO AT REUNION.
IT'S HONEST WORK, MICHAEL.
'84
G B Trudeau

May 19, 2024

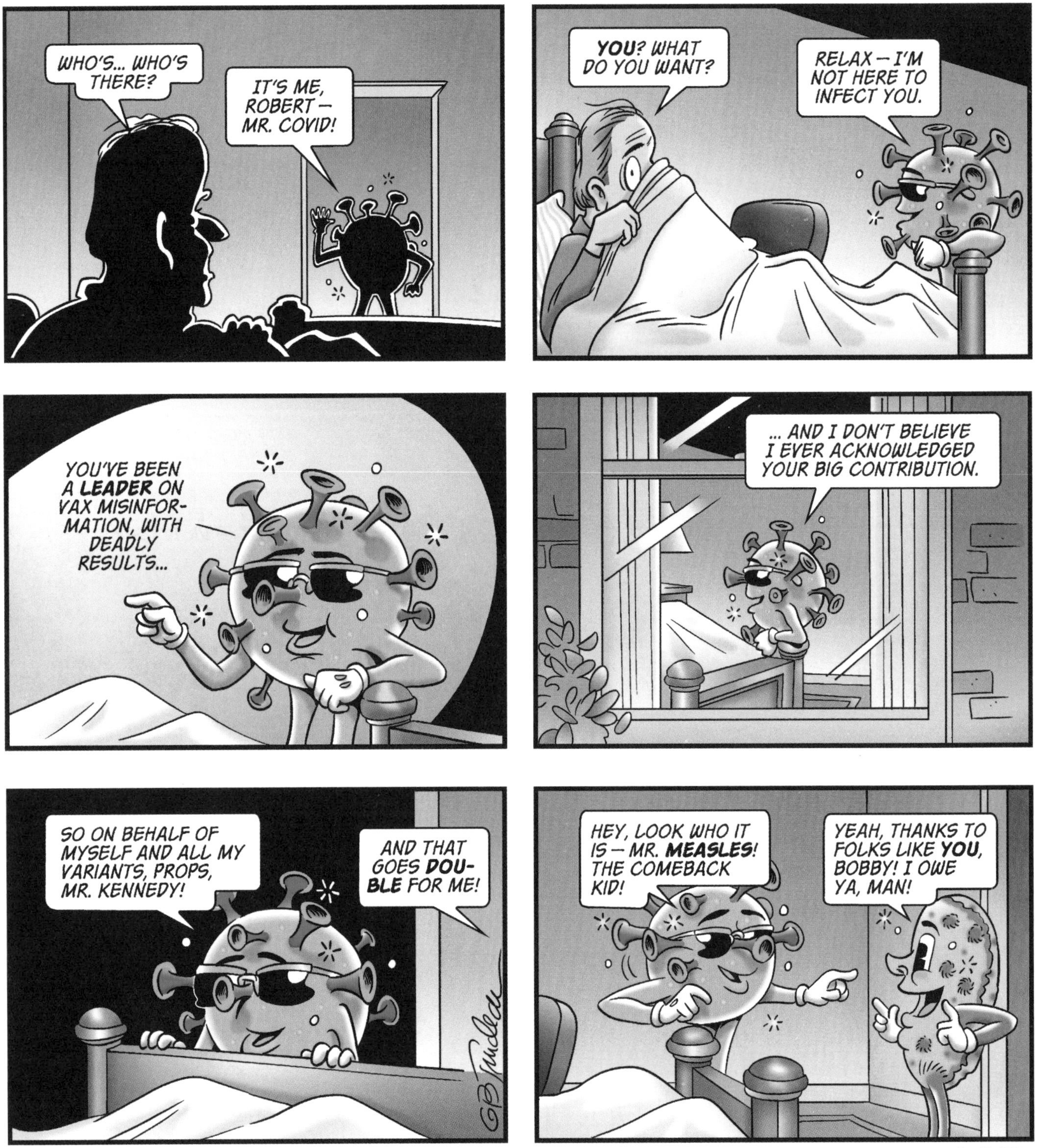
WHO'S... WHO'S THERE?
IT'S ME, ROBERT — MR. COVID!
YOU? WHAT DO YOU WANT?
RELAX — I'M NOT HERE TO INFECT YOU.
YOU'VE BEEN A LEADER ON VAX MISINFORMATION, WITH DEADLY RESULTS...
... AND I DON'T BELIEVE I EVER ACKNOWLEDGED YOUR BIG CONTRIBUTION.
SO ON BEHALF OF MYSELF AND ALL MY VARIANTS, PROPS, MR. KENNEDY!
AND THAT GOES DOUBLE FOR ME!
GBTrudeau
HEY, LOOK WHO IT IS — MR. MEASLES! THE COMEBACK KID!
YEAH, THANKS TO FOLKS LIKE YOU, BOBBY! I OWE YA, MAN!

May 26, 2024

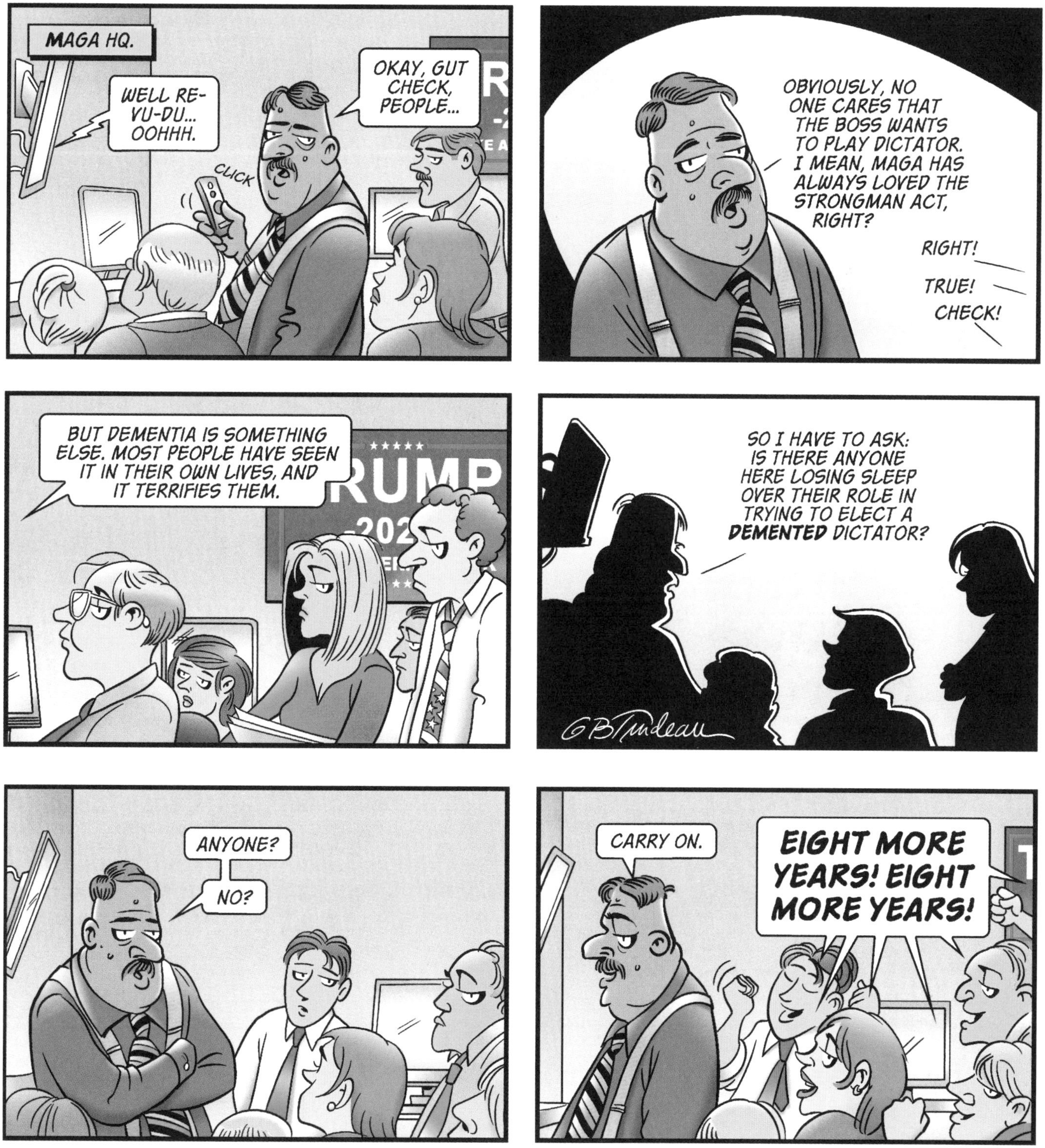
MAGA HQ.
WELL RE-VU-DU... OOHHH.
CLICK
OKAY, GUT CHECK, PEOPLE...
OBVIOUSLY, NO ONE CARES THAT THE BOSS WANTS TO PLAY DICTATOR. I MEAN, MAGA HAS ALWAYS LOVED THE STRONGMAN ACT, RIGHT?
RIGHT!
TRUE!
CHECK!
BUT DEMENTIA IS SOMETHING ELSE. MOST PEOPLE HAVE SEEN IT IN THEIR OWN LIVES, AND IT TERRIFIES THEM.
RUMP
SO I HAVE TO ASK: IS THERE ANYONE HERE LOSING SLEEP OVER THEIR ROLE IN TRYING TO ELECT A **DEMENTED** DICTATOR?
GBTrudeau
ANYONE?
NO?
CARRY ON.
EIGHT MORE YEARS! EIGHT MORE YEARS!

June 2, 2024

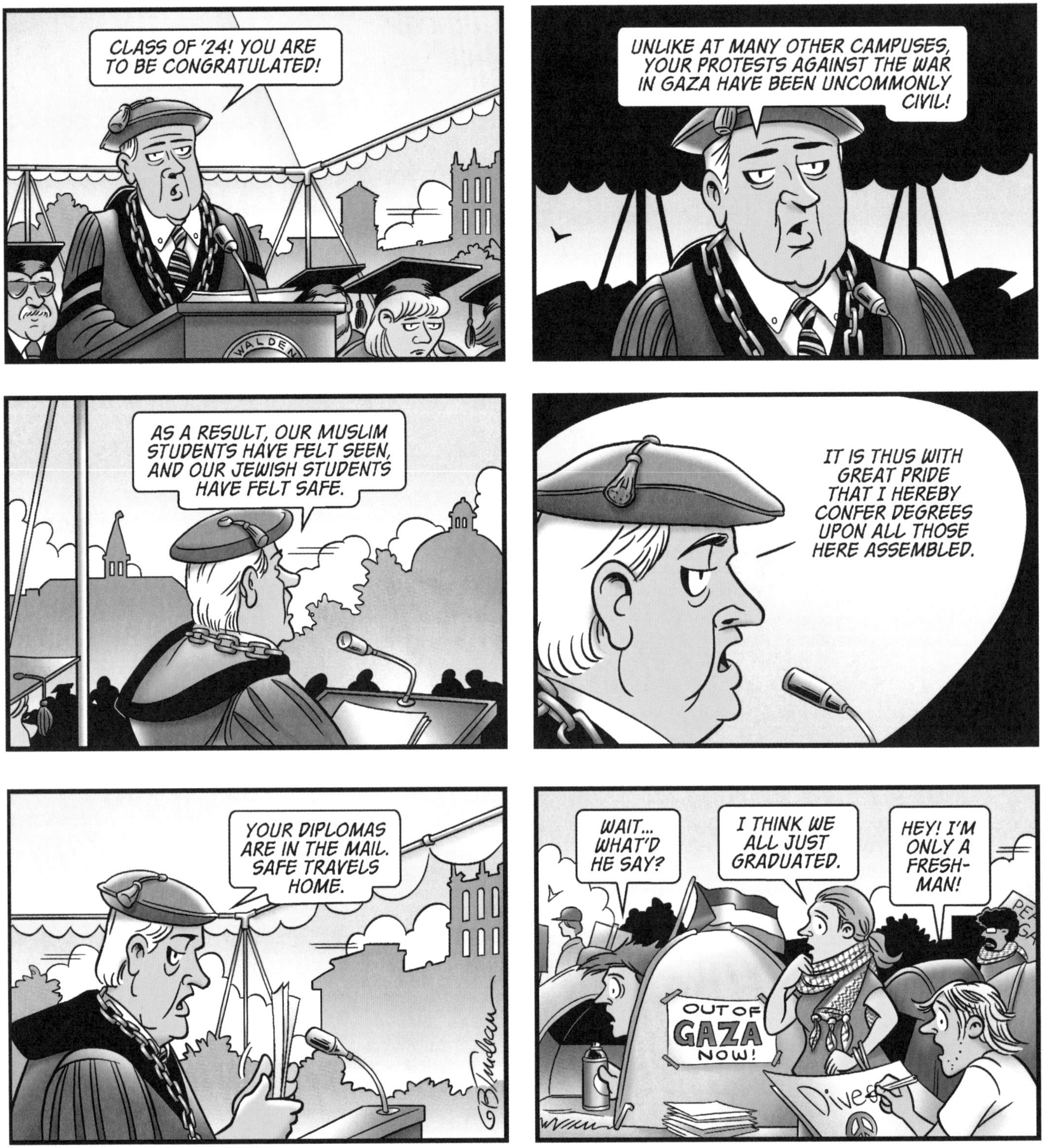
CLASS OF '24! YOU ARE TO BE CONGRATULATED!
WALDEN
UNLIKE AT MANY OTHER CAMPUSES, YOUR PROTESTS AGAINST THE WAR IN GAZA HAVE BEEN UNCOMMONLY CIVIL!
AS A RESULT, OUR MUSLIM STUDENTS HAVE FELT SEEN, AND OUR JEWISH STUDENTS HAVE FELT SAFE.
IT IS THUS WITH GREAT PRIDE THAT I HEREBY CONFER DEGREES UPON ALL THOSE HERE ASSEMBLED.
YOUR DIPLOMAS ARE IN THE MAIL. SAFE TRAVELS HOME.
GBTrudeau
WAIT... WHAT'D HE SAY?
I THINK WE ALL JUST GRADUATED.
HEY! I'M ONLY A FRESH-MAN!
OUT OF GAZA NOW!
Dives

June 9, 2024

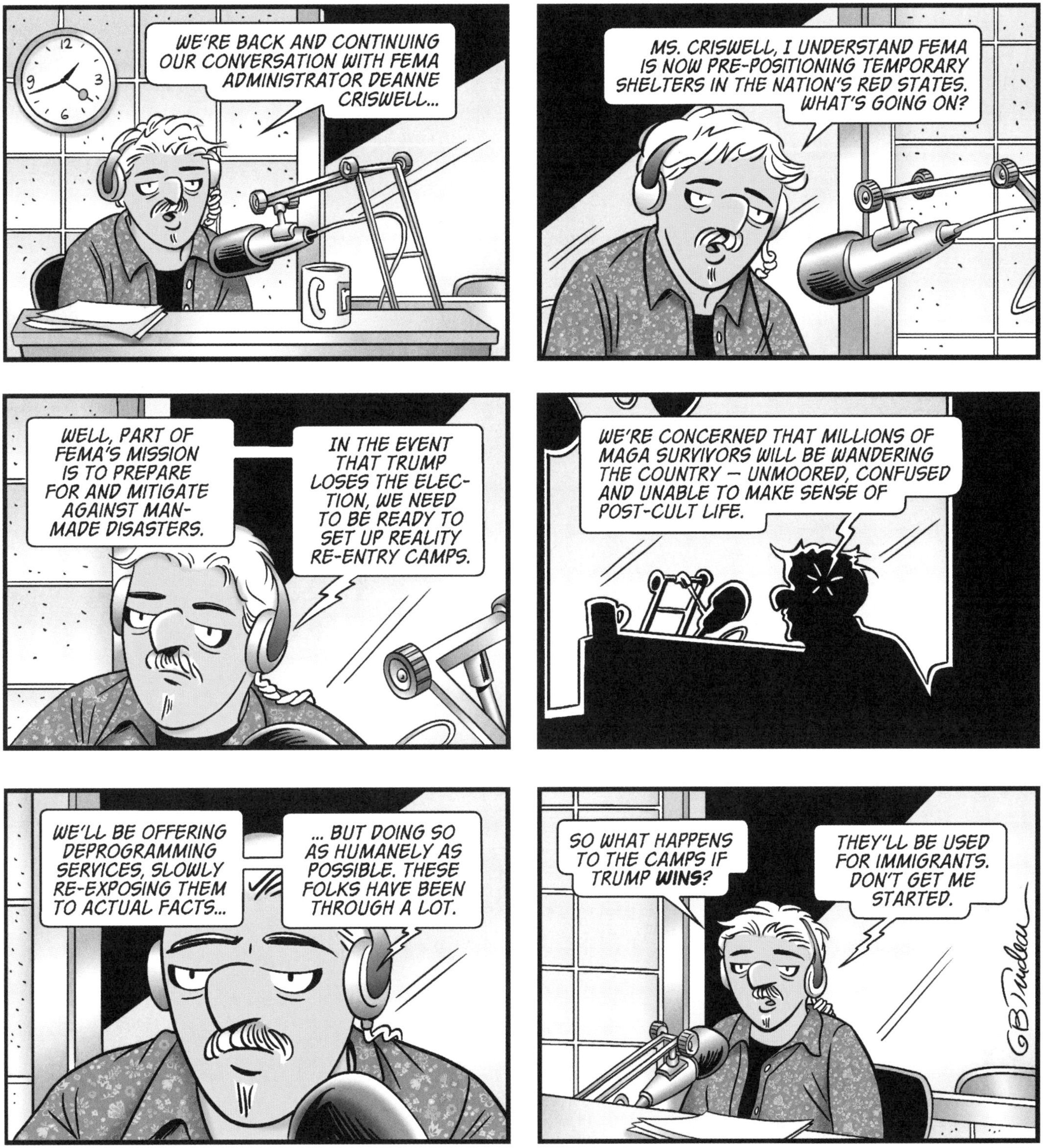
WE'RE BACK AND CONTINUING OUR CONVERSATION WITH FEMA ADMINISTRATOR DEANNE CRISWELL...
MS. CRISWELL, I UNDERSTAND FEMA IS NOW PRE-POSITIONING TEMPORARY SHELTERS IN THE NATION'S RED STATES. WHAT'S GOING ON?
WELL, PART OF FEMA'S MISSION IS TO PREPARE FOR AND MITIGATE AGAINST MAN-MADE DISASTERS.
IN THE EVENT THAT TRUMP LOSES THE ELECTION, WE NEED TO BE READY TO SET UP REALITY RE-ENTRY CAMPS.
WE'RE CONCERNED THAT MILLIONS OF MAGA SURVIVORS WILL BE WANDERING THE COUNTRY — UNMOORED, CONFUSED AND UNABLE TO MAKE SENSE OF POST-CULT LIFE.
WE'LL BE OFFERING DEPROGRAMMING SERVICES, SLOWLY RE-EXPOSING THEM TO ACTUAL FACTS...
... BUT DOING SO AS HUMANELY AS POSSIBLE. THESE FOLKS HAVE BEEN THROUGH A LOT.
SO WHAT HAPPENS TO THE CAMPS IF TRUMP **WINS**?
THEY'LL BE USED FOR IMMIGRANTS. DON'T GET ME STARTED.
GBTrudeau

June 16, 2024

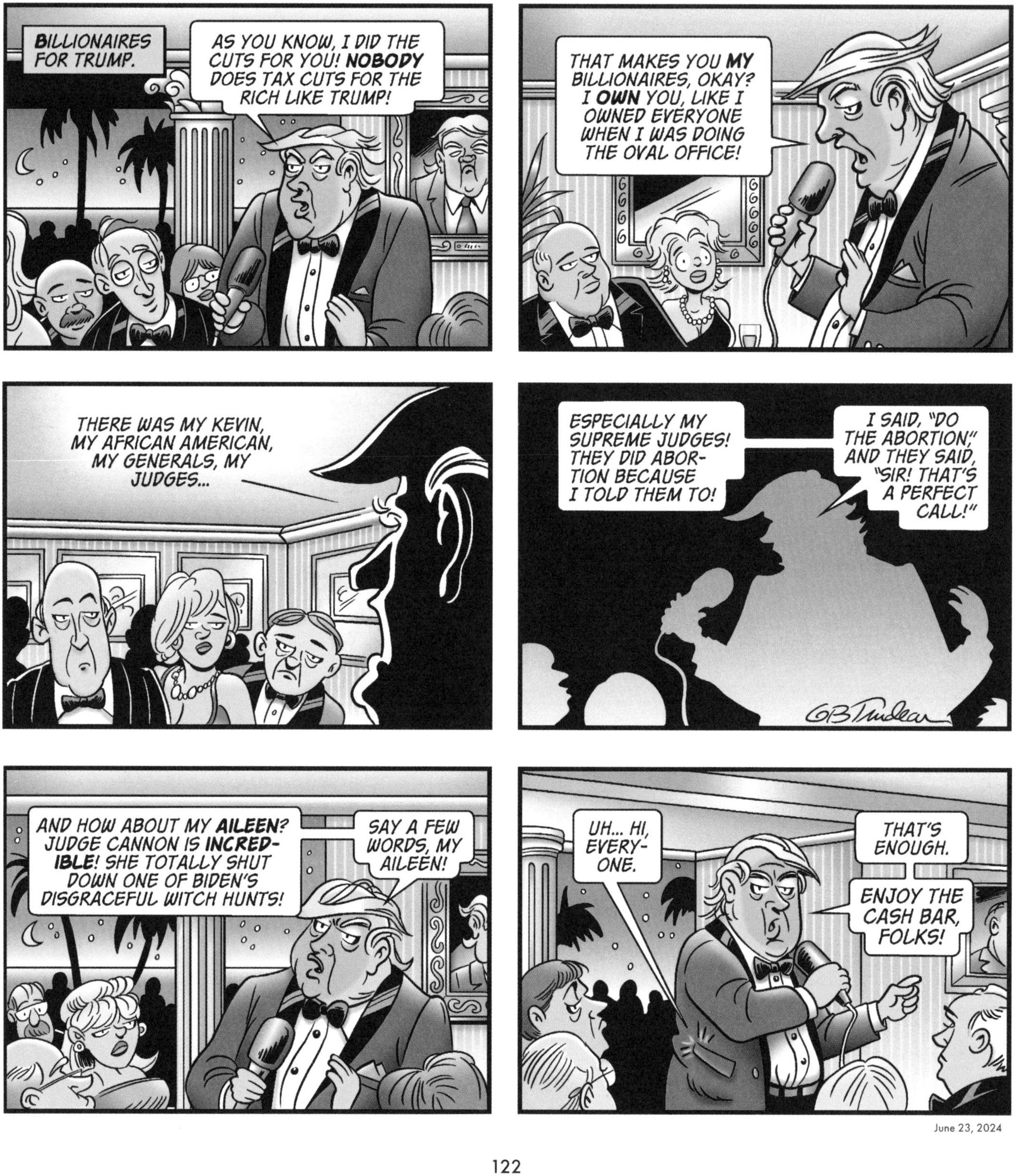
BILLIONAIRES FOR TRUMP.
AS YOU KNOW, I DID THE CUTS FOR YOU! **NOBODY** DOES TAX CUTS FOR THE RICH LIKE TRUMP!
THAT MAKES YOU **MY** BILLIONAIRES, OKAY? I **OWN** YOU, LIKE I OWNED EVERYONE WHEN I WAS DOING THE OVAL OFFICE!
THERE WAS MY KEVIN, MY AFRICAN AMERICAN, MY GENERALS, MY JUDGES...
ESPECIALLY MY SUPREME JUDGES! THEY DID ABOR-TION BECAUSE I TOLD THEM TO!
I SAID, "DO THE ABORTION," AND THEY SAID, "SIR! THAT'S A PERFECT CALL!"
GBTrudeau
AND HOW ABOUT MY **AILEEN**? JUDGE CANNON IS **INCRED-IBLE**! SHE TOTALLY SHUT DOWN ONE OF BIDEN'S DISGRACEFUL WITCH HUNTS!
SAY A FEW WORDS, MY AILEEN!
UH... HI, EVERY-ONE.
THAT'S ENOUGH.
ENJOY THE CASH BAR, FOLKS!

June 23, 2024

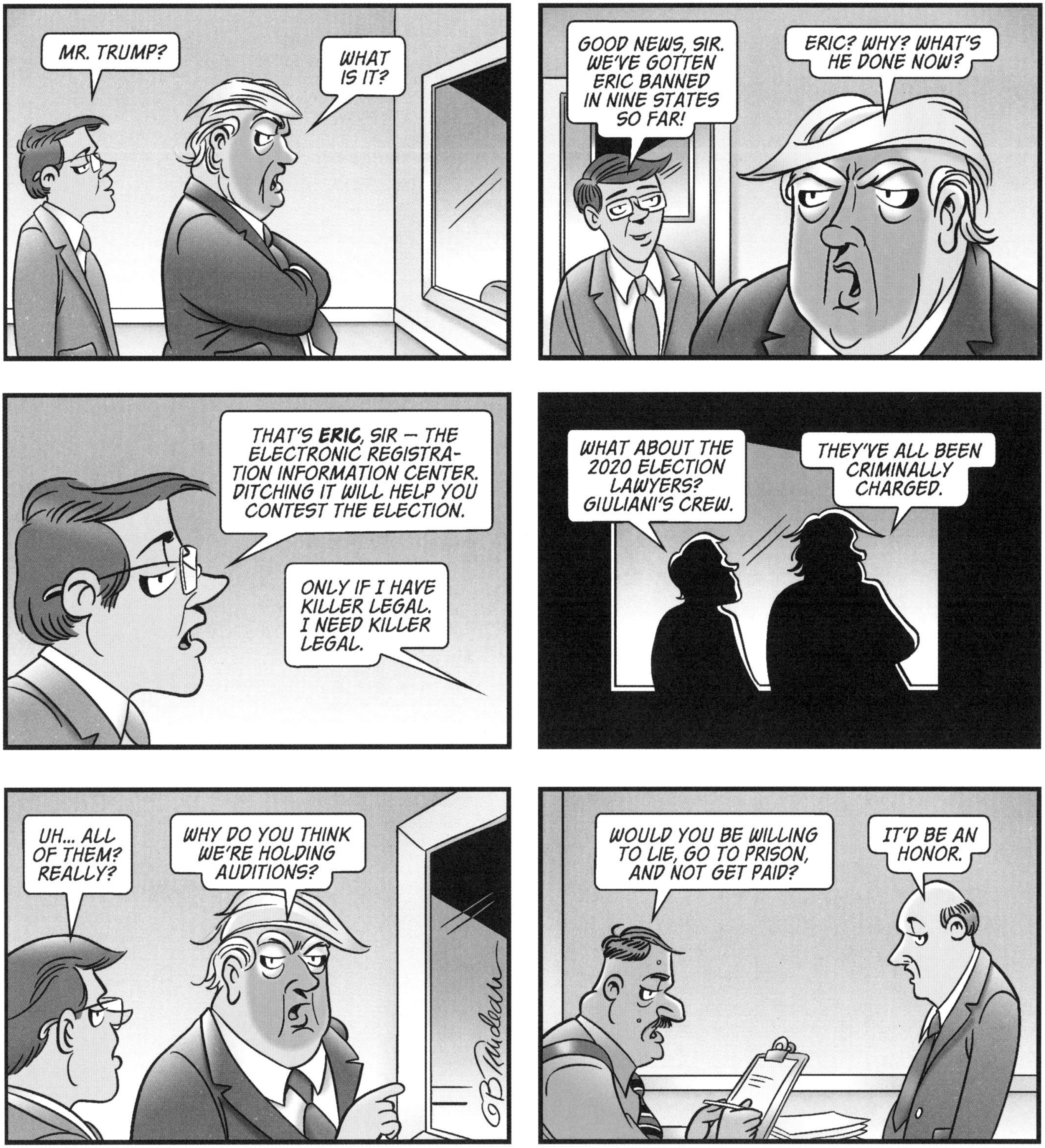
MR. TRUMP?
WHAT IS IT?
GOOD NEWS, SIR. WE'VE GOTTEN ERIC BANNED IN NINE STATES SO FAR!
ERIC? WHY? WHAT'S HE DONE NOW?
THAT'S **ERIC**, SIR — THE ELECTRONIC REGISTRATION INFORMATION CENTER. DITCHING IT WILL HELP YOU CONTEST THE ELECTION.
ONLY IF I HAVE KILLER LEGAL. I NEED KILLER LEGAL.
WHAT ABOUT THE 2020 ELECTION LAWYERS? GIULIANI'S CREW.
THEY'VE ALL BEEN CRIMINALLY CHARGED.
UH... ALL OF THEM? REALLY?
WHY DO YOU THINK WE'RE HOLDING AUDITIONS?
WOULD YOU BE WILLING TO LIE, GO TO PRISON, AND NOT GET PAID?
IT'D BE AN HONOR.

June 30, 2024

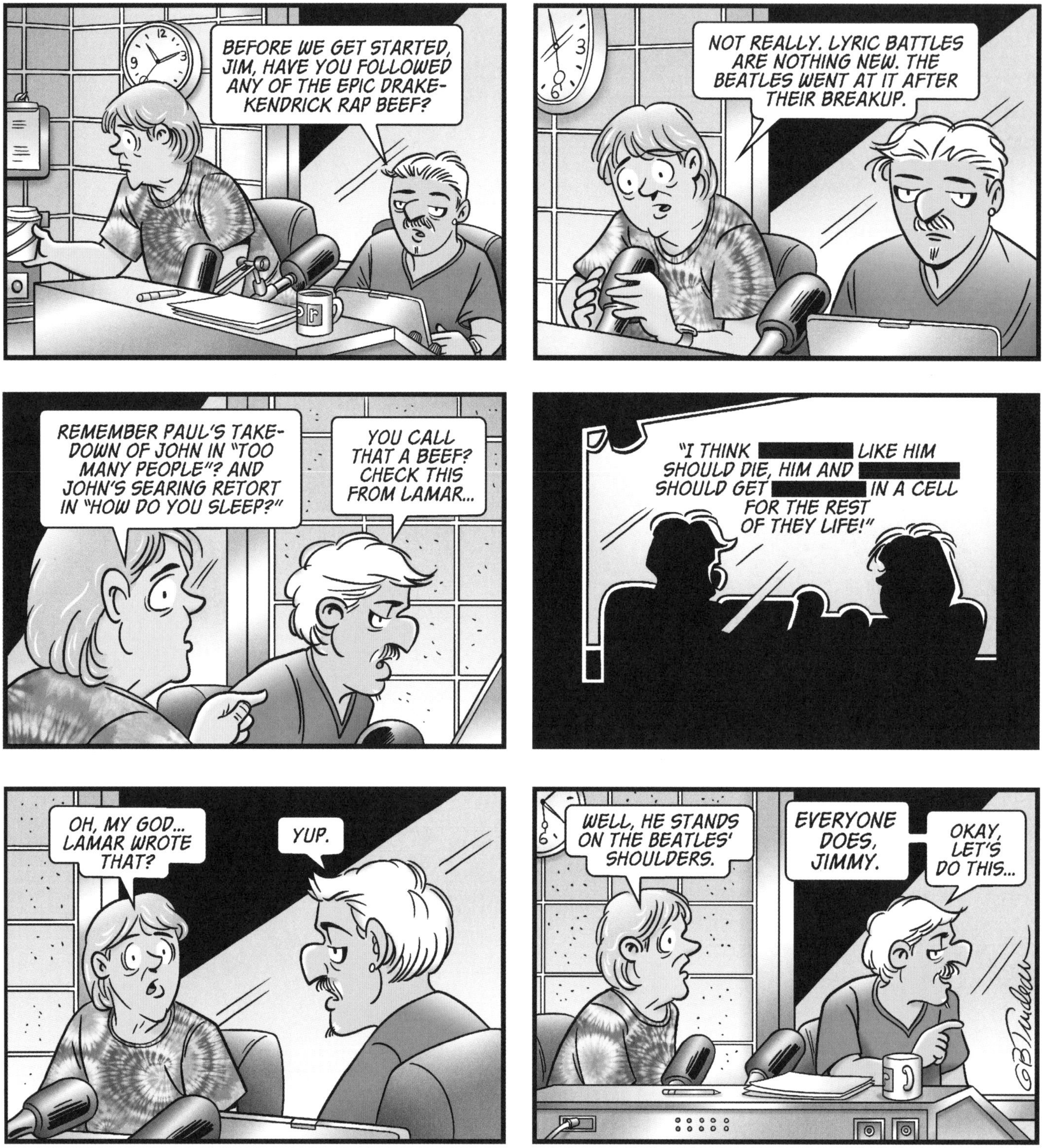
BEFORE WE GET STARTED, JIM, HAVE YOU FOLLOWED ANY OF THE EPIC DRAKE-KENDRICK RAP BEEF?
NOT REALLY. LYRIC BATTLES ARE NOTHING NEW. THE BEATLES WENT AT IT AFTER THEIR BREAKUP.
REMEMBER PAUL'S TAKE-DOWN OF JOHN IN "TOO MANY PEOPLE"? AND JOHN'S SEARING RETORT IN "HOW DO YOU SLEEP?"
YOU CALL THAT A BEEF? CHECK THIS FROM LAMAR...
"I THINK [redacted] LIKE HIM SHOULD DIE, HIM AND [redacted] SHOULD GET [redacted] IN A CELL FOR THE REST OF THEY LIFE!"
OH, MY GOD... LAMAR WROTE THAT?
YUP.
WELL, HE STANDS ON THE BEATLES' SHOULDERS.
EVERYONE DOES, JIMMY.
OKAY, LET'S DO THIS...

July 7, 2024

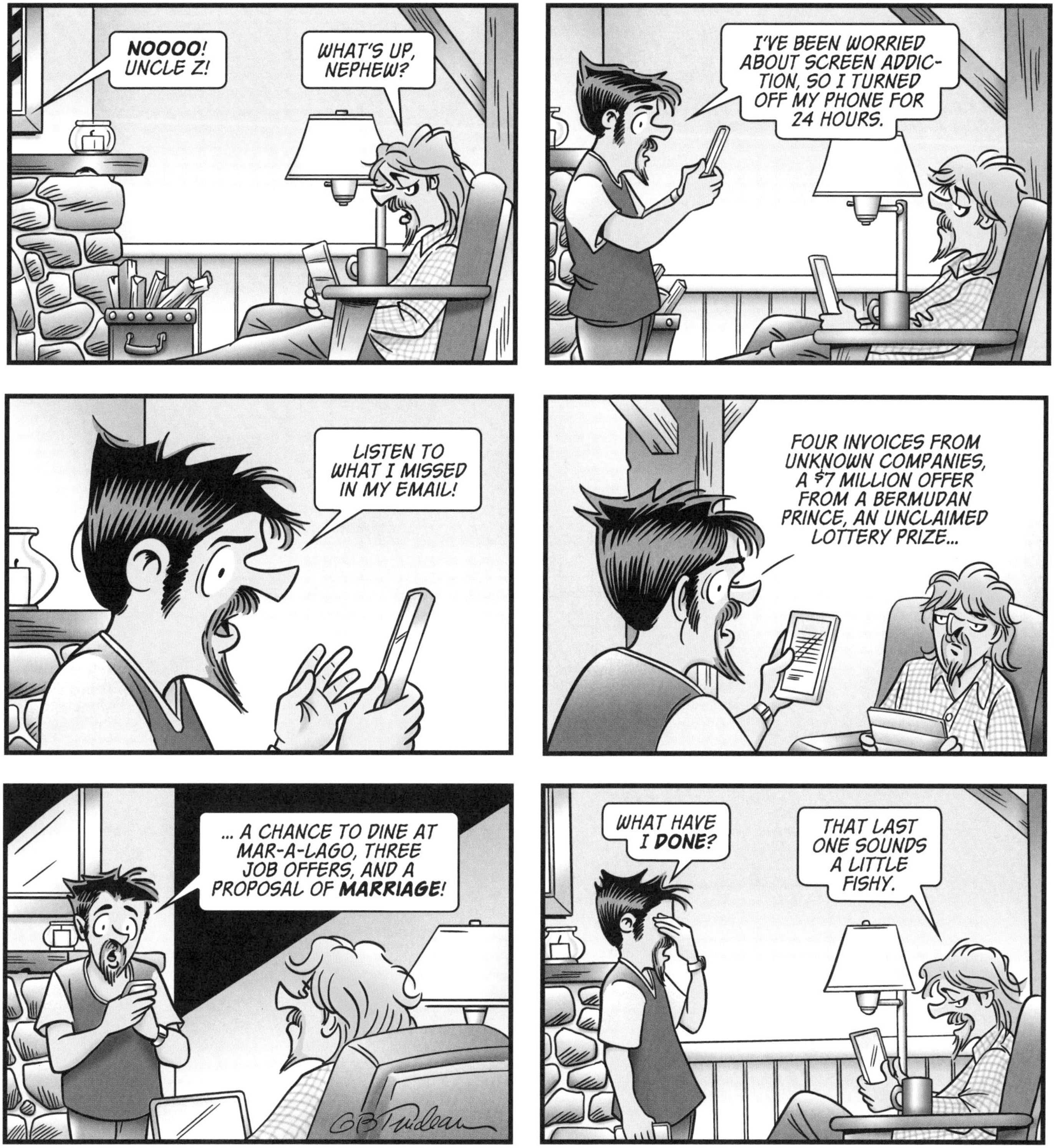
NOOOO! UNCLE Z!
WHAT'S UP, NEPHEW?
I'VE BEEN WORRIED ABOUT SCREEN ADDICTION, SO I TURNED OFF MY PHONE FOR 24 HOURS.
LISTEN TO WHAT I MISSED IN MY EMAIL!
FOUR INVOICES FROM UNKNOWN COMPANIES, A $7 MILLION OFFER FROM A BERMUDAN PRINCE, AN UNCLAIMED LOTTERY PRIZE...
... A CHANCE TO DINE AT MAR-A-LAGO, THREE JOB OFFERS, AND A PROPOSAL OF MARRIAGE!
GBTrudeau
WHAT HAVE I DONE?
THAT LAST ONE SOUNDS A LITTLE FISHY.

July 14, 2024

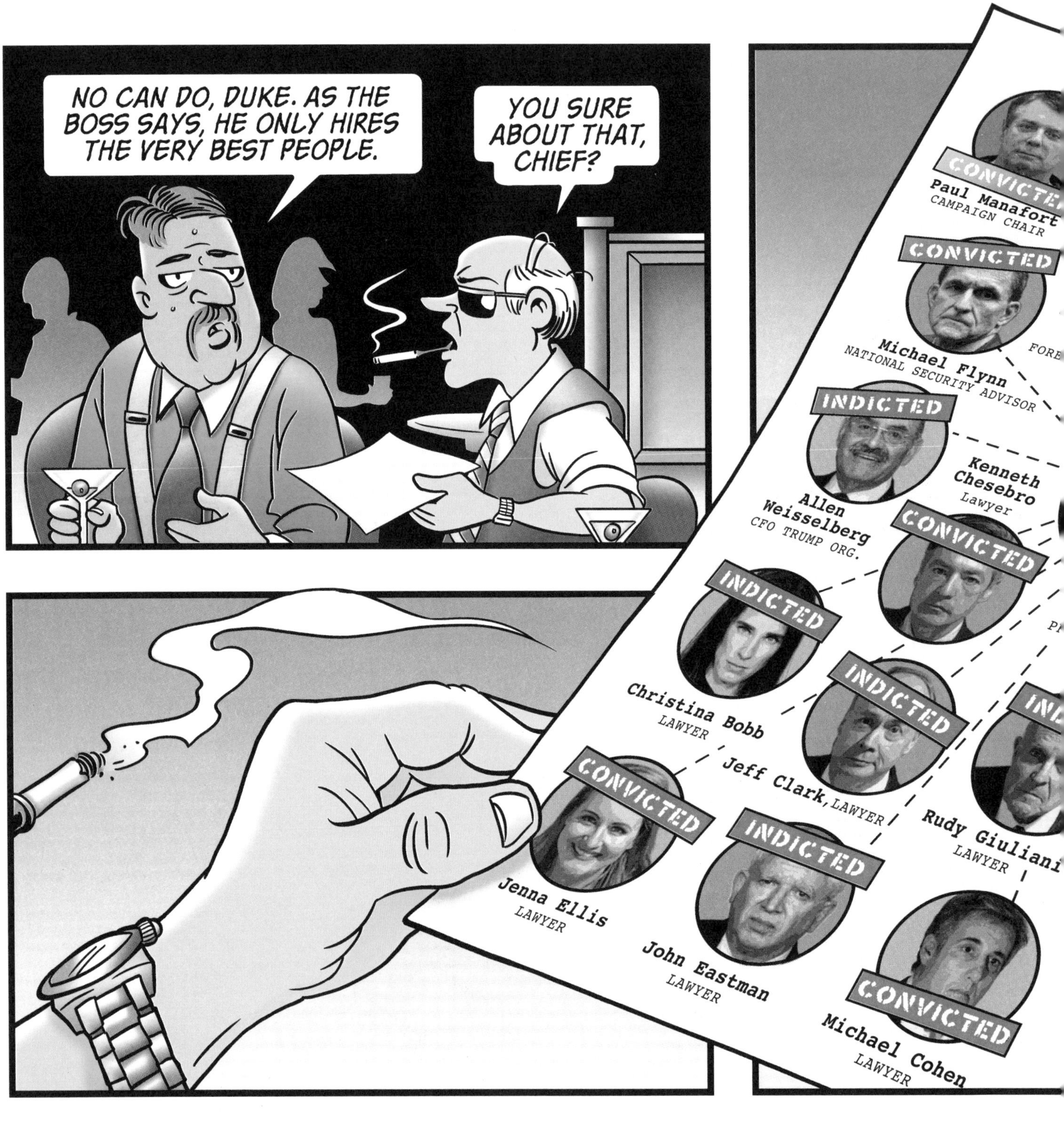
NO CAN DO, DUKE. AS THE BOSS SAYS, HE ONLY HIRES THE VERY BEST PEOPLE.
YOU SURE ABOUT THAT, CHIEF?
Paul Manafort
CAMPAIGN CHAIR
CONVICTED
Michael Flynn
NATIONAL SECURITY ADVISOR
INDICTED
Allen Weisselberg
CFO TRUMP ORG.
Kenneth Chesebro
Lawyer
CONVICTED
INDICTED
Christina Bobb
LAWYER
INDICTED
Jeff Clark, LAWYER
Rudy Giuliani
LAWYER
CONVICTED
Jenna Ellis
LAWYER
INDICTED
John Eastman
LAWYER
CONVICTED
Michael Cohen
LAWYER

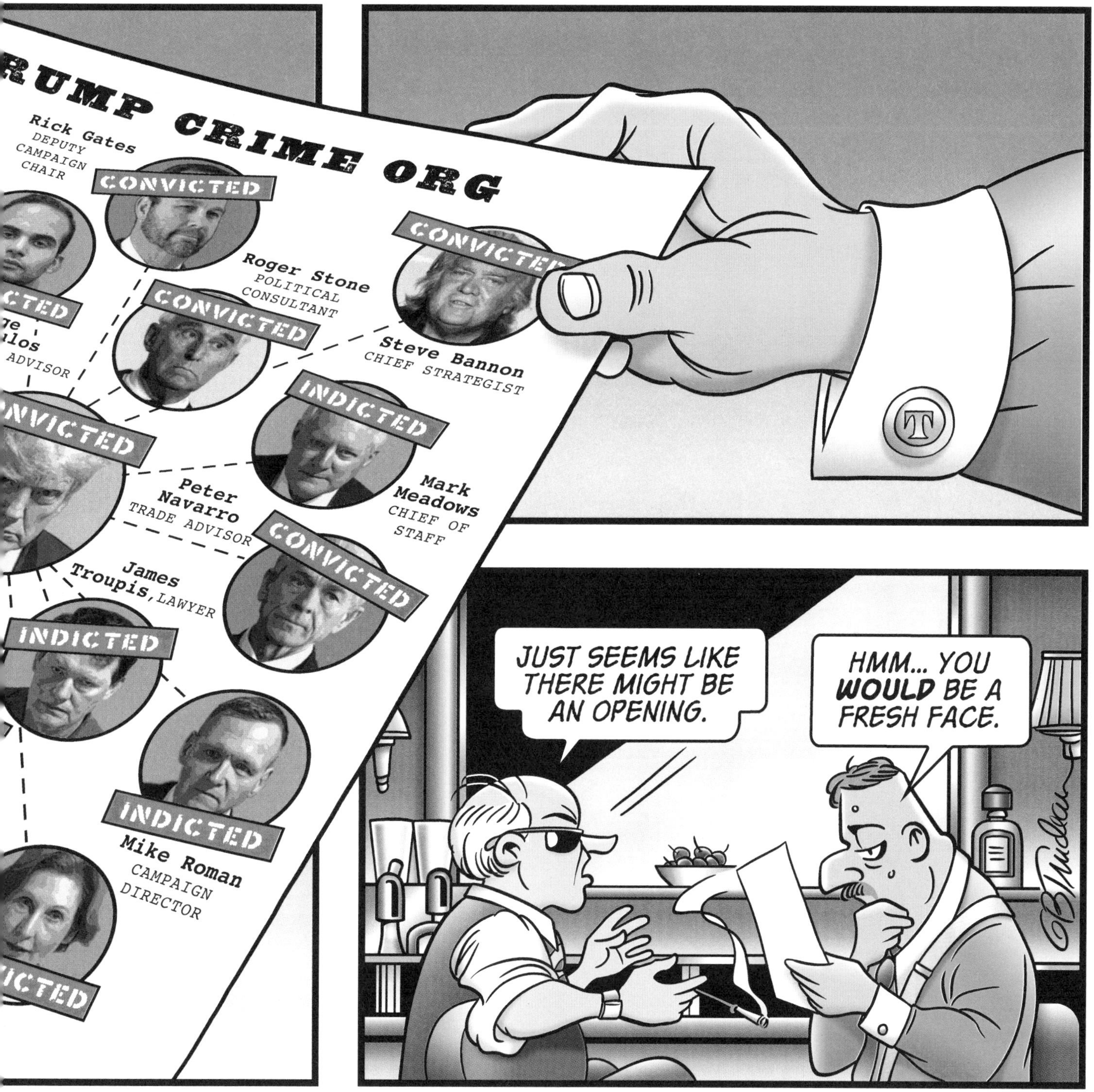
RUMP CRIME ORG
Rick Gates
DEPUTY CAMPAIGN CHAIR
CONVICTED
Roger Stone
POLITICAL CONSULTANT
CONVICTED
Steve Bannon
CHIEF STRATEGIST
CONVICTED
INDICTED
Mark Meadows
CHIEF OF STAFF
Peter Navarro
TRADE ADVISOR
CONVICTED
James Troupis, LAWYER
INDICTED
INDICTED
Mike Roman
CAMPAIGN DIRECTOR
JUST SEEMS LIKE THERE MIGHT BE AN OPENING.
HMM... YOU **WOULD** BE A FRESH FACE.

July 21, 2024

29. Willful Retention of National Defense Information
30. Willful Retention of National Defense Information
31. Willful Retention of National Defense Information
32. Willful Retention of National Defense Information
33. Willful Retention of National Defense Information
34. Willful Retention of National Defense Information
35. Willful Retention of National Defense Information
36. Willful Retention of National Defense Information
37. Willful Retention of National Defense Information
38. Willful Retention of National Defense Information
39. Willful Retention of National Defense Information
40. Willful Retention of National Defense Information

Supreme Court of the State of New York, County of New York

The People of the State of New York v. Donald J. Trump, Defendant

1. Falsifying Business Records in the First Degree
2. Falsifying Business Records in the First Degree
3. Falsifying Business Records in the First Degree
4. Falsifying Business Records in the First Degree
5. Falsifying Business Records in the First Degree
6. Falsifying Business Records in the First Degree
7. Falsifying Business Records in the First Degree
8. Falsifying Business Records in the First Degree
9. Falsifying Business Records in the First Degree
10. Falsifying Business Records in the First Degree
11. Falsifying Business Records in the First Degree
12. Falsifying Business Records in the First Degree
13. Falsifying Business Records in the First Degree
14. Falsifying Business Records in the First Degree
15. Falsifying Business Records in the First Degree
16. Falsifying Business Records in the First Degree
17. Falsifying Business Records in the First Degree
18. Falsifying Business Records in the First Degree
19. Falsifying Business Records in the First Degree
20. Falsifying Business Records in the First Degree
21. Falsifying Business Records in the First Degree
22. Falsifying Business Records in the First Degree
23. Falsifying Business Records in the First Degree
24. Falsifying Business Records in the First Degree
25. Falsifying Business Records in the First Degree
26. Falsifying Business Records in the First Degree
27. Falsifying Business Records in the First Degree
28. Falsifying Business Records in the First Degree
29. Falsifying Business Records in the First Degree
30. Falsifying Business Records in the First Degree
31. Falsifying Business Records in the First Degree
32. Falsifying Business Records in the First Degree
33. Falsifying Business Records in the First Degree
34. Falsifying Business Records in the First Degree